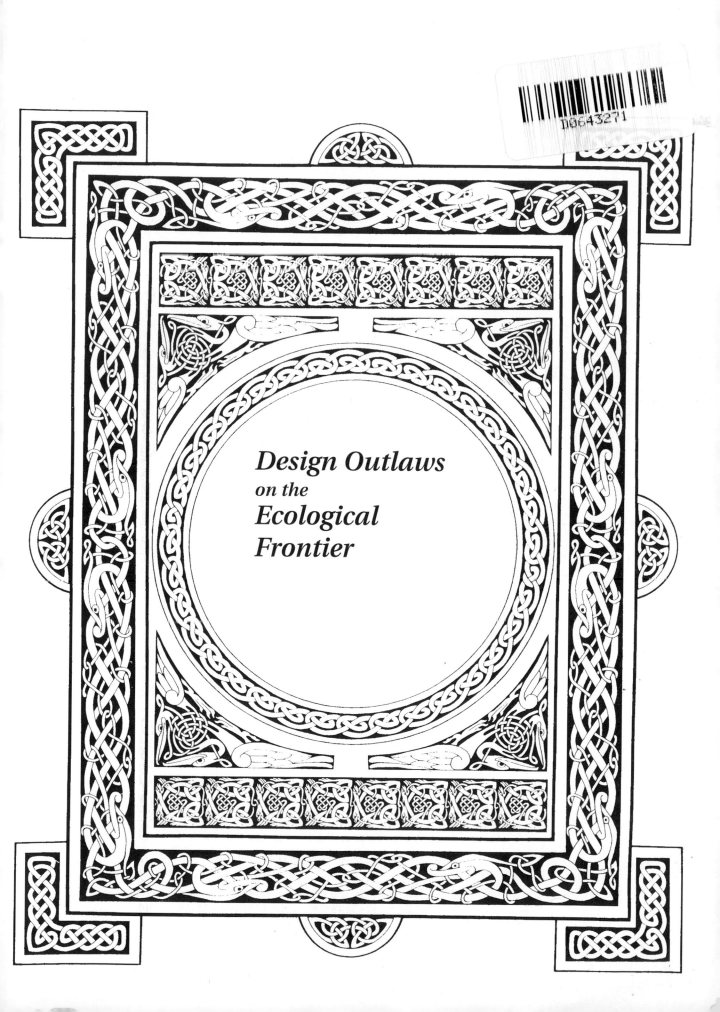

Design Outlaws
on the
Ecological
Frontier

Any student of the rise and fall of cultures
cannot fail to be impressed by the role played
in this historical succession by the image of the future.
The rise and fall of images precedes or accompanies
the rise and fall of cultures.
As long as a society's image is positive and flourishing,
the flower of culture is in full bloom.
Once the image begins to decay and lose vitality, however,
the culture does not long survive.

Fred Polak

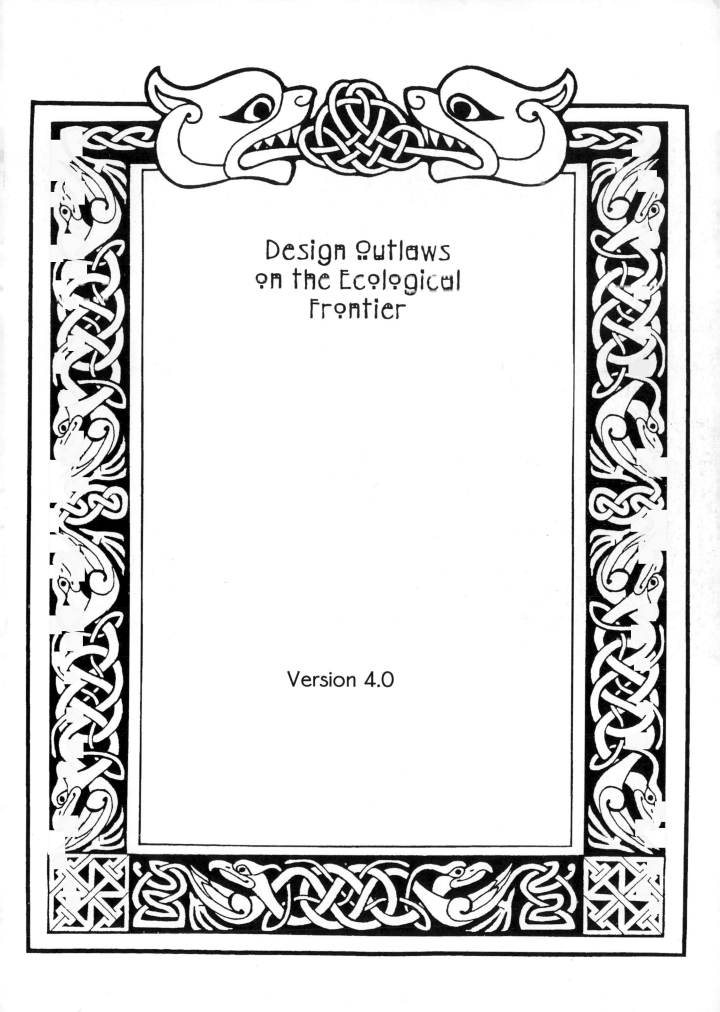

Design Outlaws on the Ecological Frontier

Version 4.0

Knossus Publishing
1259 Northampton Street #340
Easton, PA 18042

Text Copyright © 1997

LIBRARY OF CONGRESS CATALOGING-IN-PUBLICATION DATA
Zelov, Chris
Cousineau, Phil
I. Title

First Impression July, 1997
Second Impression January, 1998
Third Impression September, 1998
Fouth Impression November, 2000
ISBN#0-9650306-2-8

4 5 6 7 8 9 10

Printed in the United States

Graphic Design Consulting: Sean Gannon/Teo Camporeale
Electronic Page Makeup: STELLARViSIONs

Grateful Acknowledgement is made to the following for permission to use their photographs: Martin Crowley, Paolo Soleri, Andropogon Assoc., William McDonough, Pliny
Fisk and Gail Vitorri, Anthony Walmsley, Living Technologies Inc., The Jersey Devils,
Yestermorrow, David Sellers, Dr. John Todd and Ocean Arks International, and the
Buckminster Fuller Institute. Every effort has been made to acknowledge all copyright
holders. If any omissions have occurred, we apologize. Please notify the publisher if this
has occurred.

Cover Art Design Consulting: Fake Art
Cover photoconcept: C. Zelov
On the Road To Austin

This book is dedicated to:

The life and work of
R. Buckminster Fuller
and to the design science explorer
in everybody.

For thousands of years humans have adapted
to their environments through the process
of design. Weaving local materials to meet
their needs and intertwining nature's patterns
with their lives, indigenous communities live
within the limits of their local ecosystem.
Nature, technology, and culture maintain
a dynamic balance.

The designs of the industrialized world have
developed beyond the limits of local
ecosystems. Today our global technologies
are depleting the Earth's resources, darkening
the skies and
waters with waste, and endangering
much of life's diversity.

Can we invent a more comprehensive way of
designing which will integrate the built world
with the natural world?
Can we find a way of life which
will create a harmony between nature,
technology, and humanity?

Contents

Prologue: Chris Zelov
Precessional Navigation
Introduction: Phil Cousineau
"The Outlaw Designers"

Chapter One
Into the Fuller Universe

1

Chapter Two
From a Machine for Living to Living Machines

59

Chapter Three
The Intelligent Use of Energy

100

Chapter Four
The Galactic Explorer Perspective

Chapter Five
The Emergence of an Ecological Design Art

Chapter Six
The New Collective Dream

Chapter Seven
Writing the New Codes

Afterword
Toward a Design Curriculum for the 21st Century

Epilogue
Brian Danitz

Finding Synchronicity's Trail............

BY CHRIS ZELOV

Flashbacking on the year of 1983, I am sitting in a Venetian Cafe, around the corner from the Bridge of Sighs, contemplating a Renaissance horizon. Slipstreaming into a conversation with two fellow-travelers exploring alternatives futures beyond the force-fed American corporate culture we were heavily trained for. At the time, I was carrying Buckminster Fuller's recently published book Critical Path while adventuring on a my own peculiar version of the Grand Tour. My wine soaked elucidation revealed that I had a hitherto hidden desire to make something related to the ecology of ideas contained in this rather strange book.

Rambling through the mazeway of Epicurean European worlds, finds me at a Parisian dinner party with the listeners of a radio show called "Here and Now". Amongst the din of a barely understandable French language, I pulled out a copy of Critical Path to glimpse at while waiting for my first real French meal to arrive. Across the table sits a multi-lingual Frenchman, who later becomes a collaborator in my first post-collegiate project, cross-fertilizing Silicon Valley educational software into the European marketplace. Jean-Paul becomes a mentor in my developing interest with design.

Flashback to the year 1989, I am dreaming of other worlds in a history of alternative film class at New York University. After the much too theoretical class, on the elevator going down, still carrying my copy of Critical Path, I bump into my soon to be filmmaking partner Brian Danitz.

Later that summer I noticed a description for a class at the New York Open Center by Phil Cousineau, who had co-written a documentary on the life and work of mythologist Joseph Campbell,The Hero's Journey. I attended the class and was intrigued enough by his ideas to invite him to dinner that night. Over drinks on Spring Street, Cousineau revealed that Campbell and Fuller taught together several times on cruise ships. For Campbell, Fuller's conception of the Geodesic Dome was a marvelous counterpart to the Hindu image of the "Net of Gems". To the ancient Indians, everything in the Universe was delectably interconnected, and everywhere things connected a gem shone bright as the sun. Furthermore, Campbell thought that Bucky's colorful

X

metaphor of the "critical path" that late 20th Century humans must deal with was equivalent to the "hero's journey".

Once we jointly conceived of making a film dealing with the pattern of ideas Bucky had brought forth, the road of delectable synchronicity unfolded with more velocity. Fortunately, my guiding heuristic during this time in my mid-twenties, came from Goethe: 'Whatever you can do, or dream you can do, begin it. Boldness has genius, power, and magic in it.'

Flashback to 1991, traveling north on route 101, towards the mythic hills of Northern California, through a cow fence, beside a rambling brook, I come upon a short, rather Gnome like man named Jay Baldwin. Once we settled into his California bungalow, he then proceeds to gently guide us through a labyrinthine design science infused Universe of fun and form. After 3 days of receiving enthusiastic wisdom, we left spellbound and blustering forth with new found direction.

Filmmaking as an adventure in the synthesizing imagination. A heuristic approach, where the everyday and the novel are used as artistic props for further inquiry into the truly worthwhile. One thing leads to another. From memes to scenes to the collective dreaming of a mostly unformed vicariously living populace. Soaring through the gates of the known, prying open the crypts of stored knowledge. Bolting past the guard dogs at the castle moat. The magic name "Buckminster" opens the door to many mansions, like a code to a safe of advanced design knowledge.

I am learning to navigate the compelling seas of Comprehensive Anticipatory Design. Inventing the future is another form of the glass bead game, ever strategizing the way to produce delightful form and space. To invent what we truly desire is a way of evolving that unfolds the essential building blocks of a meaningful life, in a place that expresses "Genius, Power and Magic".

This experiment in filmmaking was meant to produce an educational outreach tool to bring the public up to date on where Buckminster Fuller's Idea of Comprehensive Anticipatory Design has meandered through form and content; and taken root in new realization. In deep design exploration, as in fire, musical composition, or the Glass Bead game itself, all the elements of the Universe are synergized and the artificial boundaries between domains begin to vanish.

At it's heart, design is a majestic pursuit of a dynamic harmony between the driving forces of Nature, Humanity and Technology. We humanoid life-forms are uniquely made for this ongoing experiment in movement, thought, and form. Our eyes and hands seem to demand that they be put into creative use.

Unfortunately, rather than reading Viollet-le-Duc's Lectures on Architecture our diminutive political economic system enforcers (see kakistocracy), dressed in brief authority, have been secretly absorbing Jerome Weiner's: The Human Use of Human Beings. We are the last generation of human beings to live with cheap energy (41 years of petroleum reserves remain, according to the CIA), have been duped into an enormously expensive addiction to a non-renewable resource that ultimately damages our economic security. So it goes, the consequences of assumed cheap energy are all around us in this autocentric global economy. Applied Wasteland Inc. is still ravaging the American Landscape. Just look deeply at life in our all too ubiquitous suburbs.

Until, once upon a time, at last we wake-up, like Rip Van Wrinkle, and realize that civilization needs to be re-designed one more time.

Through the power of the principles behind ecological design we can break out of our self-imposed mind forged manacles. As Buckminster Fuller writes in his last book: Cosmography we are powerfully imprisoned in these dark ages simply by the terms in which we have been conditioned to think".

Nothing matters, everything is possible; and there are liberal ideas available to those who seek to access the tools and ideas that unlock the keys to the Realm of the Muses.

In the same way that the musician plays his instrument with delicate precision to produce astounding music, the Architect/Designer organizes materials in such a way that a beautiful and useful form is realized. Ultimately, Ecological Design leads to the clear poetic light of inspiration that shapes a Genius Loci that soothes the soul and allows us to dwell deeply and meaningfully.

The art of *conceiving magnificently is still a lost art in this civilization. It is as if the burst of light that illuminated our metaphors for the built world has gone out. We continue to over utilize inert forms like fossil fuels, concrete, steel, chemicals; rather than the regenerative countenance of Nature: wetlands, forests, oceans, meadows, rivers, beaches, gardens. Can these systems of natural organization be where the fountain head for a more desirable 21st century lies hidden from our television minds?

Where else can we go to learn how to conceive vital possibilities for our life and the community at large? Recall that the Greek concept of *paradise comes forth on this earth as an enclosed garden. This idea was further developed in the Italian concept of the Renaissance Garden. How we children of the 20th century lost touch with this vital ideal is one of the mysterious of our times.

Ultimately, it is the idea of "development" itself that needs to be redefined and expanded. Wolfgang Sachs reveals in his archaeology of the western notion of development that it is based on the following outdated assumptions:

1. Western science is the only true way of understanding the world, which dismisses the accumulated wisdom of most of mankind.

2. That progress and "development" using this science are essentially embodied in the increasing output of market commodities.

3. That the relatively new invention of the nation-state is sovereign within its often artificial borders, which allows "development" to be imposed on its subject populations.

4. The mechanism's that were set up between the North and the South to achieve this end were Debt, Trade, and Aid.

Ecological design is an integrative art form that will allow each of us to get on with the real work connected to our regenerative function in the Universe. Hopefully, in the 21st Century we can finally get beyond the feverish preoccupation with crude money-making gamesmanship. and get into the 3rd person GAIA perspective of facilitating intelligent evolution beyond small definitions of Self. As D.H. Lawrence explains "Not I, Not I, but the wind that bloweth through me".

Transformative Architecture occurs in those rare times when we get glimpses of better worlds, outside of our force-fed economic head. Given the thickness of the rule book now being imposed on us, it is only the fortunate, ever youthful "design outlaws" types who even attempt the treacherous path of self-discovery through creativity in support of the Universe. As Emerson laments "**Too feeble the impressions of Nature on us to make us artists. Every touch should thrill**"

The new world is always waiting for it's poet. I trust that you the reader will find this book to be a source of true inspiration for your own particular Grand Tour of the Universe.
No daring is fatal/Bon Voyage.................

*To Conceive means to:
-impregnate passionately.
-cause to begin.
-something thought of as capable of subsequent growth and development.
-to form an original thought in the mind and then evolve it mentally into something beautiful and useful.
-to bring forth into being.

*Paradise:
1.a place or state in which the souls of the righteous after death enjoy eternal bliss
2. a place of bliss: a region of supreme felicity or delight.
3. an open space in a monastery or next to a church (as in a cloister) or the open court before a basilica.

THE OUTLAW DESIGNER

by Phil Cousineau

The discoverer, adventurer, and visionary are all haunted by the frontier of the unknown. Suspecting that there are great discoveries waiting to be made in unexplored territory, independent thinkers throughout history have been willing to take great risks in their searches for the missing answers to the most pressing issues of their times.

One of the foremost visionaries of the twentieth century was the maverick inventor and futurist philosopher, R. Buckminster Fuller (1895-1983). In the idealistic spirit of the Transcendentalists of his New England heritage, Fuller advocated challenging authority in order to make the world a more liveable place. To him, the independent path was necessary because "all true innovation takes place in the outlaw realm."

Fuller called the innovators who explore beyond the frontier "design outlaws." But he saw the outlaw designer less as a renegade than a pioneer, someone living on the edge of the future, working with little or no support from the establishment, and usually enduring great resistance from the proponents of conventional wisdom. He accepted the notion that Colin Wilson put forth in his study of iconoclastic creativity, that "The visionary is inevitably an Outsider."

As architect Brendan O'Reagan says in one of the following interviews, Fuller had good reason to distinquish the outlaw designer from the traditional one. "That was the only way to go," O'Reagan states, "because he felt the inertia of the system in perpetuating antiquated and outdated ideas. The real hope of the future was the person who was going to exist outside of that system - that any real good would be antithetical to an already existing system."

Neither anarchist nor extremist, outlaw designers from Leonardo da Vinci to Frank Lloyd Wright push back the restricting boundaries of the world with their artifacts and their convictions. In his book **Roots and Branches,** poet Robert Duncan writes, "Foremost we admire the outlaw / who has the strength of his own lawfulness."

As a companion book to the documentary film **Ecological Design: Inventing the Future** (1994), this volume further explores the ideas and innovations of twenty-one trailblazing designers who have been deeply influenced by Fuller and strongly involved in the emergence of ecological design in the twentieth century. Despite their independent paths, there are common themes among these designers. They all express a deep conviction in the need to bring fundamental change to many troubled realms of modern culture - including architecture, transportation, and energy systems - in order to create a sustainable world for future generations. Along with their mentor, they also believe that "the only tolerated authority will be what works." What works is the skeleton key that unlocks this vision of ecological design. As Fuller asserted in **Ideas and Integrities,** the goal is

To make the world work for 100% of
humanity in the shortest possible time through
spontaneous cooperation without
ecological offense or the disadvantage of anyone.

Recently, David Brower, the reigning elder of the ecology movement, has echoed Fuller's concern. "Before we take another step, or force our children to," he warned, "we had better make an environmental U-turn away from the precipice toward a sustainable, peaceful, and just society."

This alertness to the consequences of irresponsible technology and the precariousness of our modern situation arises often in the reflections of the designers included in this compilation. "Everyone I know, from Bucky on down," biochemist John Todd says, "has a... sense of urgency... that everything that has been done could be undone."

Where many of these imaginative designers find hope is in humanity's bittersweet capacity to transform the natural world, a belief that what has been undone can be redone. Afterall, as Fuller said: "We are exquisite entropy." "Exquisite" because there is something profoundly beautiful, as many designers discover, about creations that actually work, and because, as Fuller saw it, it is a human beings proper role to counteract material entropy. The world is constantly breaking down. There is chaos at the heart of creation, and yet the disorder and disintegration may be balanced by creative acts wrought from the human imagination.

The interviews that comprise Design Outlaws were culled from over thirty hours of film footage shot over the four year period from 1990-1994. They range from the comments of architects and city planners to those of biochemists, anthropologists, and energy experts. These are self-reliant thinkers in the Emersonian tradition, intent on forging the development of sustainable architecture and responsible technological change. Theirs is a tocsin call for design with rather than against nature.

However, as businessman Tom Casey points out in this book, there is a vested interest in resisting the kinds of change outlaw designers would bring about. Resistance and even sabotage of his work only strengthened Fuller's resolve. Brendan O'Reagan recalls, "He felt the establishment was always going to protect itself, [so] the really innovative person would have to be prepared to be an outlaw to the system, to get the new idea in. They shouldn't expect establishment support... he never got establishment support and then he always became identified with the outlaw." Inventor J. Baldwin deals with the resistance by regarding his own life as an experiment, believing it's the responsibility of the designer to live in his own designs to prove their efficiency. Developer architect Michael Corbett confronts the thicket of bureaucracy surrounding urban design by breaking many of the very economic rules and planning codes that prevent innovative and sustainable change from occuring.

Another notable distinction between the independent and the institutional designer is the choice of problems they tackle. In the words of social historian Thomas Hughes, "Some inventors feel comfortable improving upon existing situations. These persons I tend to call conservative inventors. Other inventors choose problems that allow them to introduce new systems, not improve upon existing systems. These are the radicals." Because of this, Hughes has written in his book, American Genesis, "Independents [have] invented a disproportionate share of the radical inventions."

Further compressing the issue, architect Ted Nelson says that "The responsibility of the outlaw thinker, certainly, is to try and reach forward beyond the restrictions of today, beyond the stupidities of the current political situation, whatever they may be... the current way of doing things, and ask, "How should we really be doing this?" Popular novelist and futurist Douglas Adams adds that design outlaws are "the people who are driven from within by their own ideas versus the current thinking of the day...they are the ones who give us the fresh insights and fresh ideas and the fresh ways of looking at things."

To anthropologist Mary Catherine Bateson, design outlaws are the pioneers of ecological design, "people who have gone outside the system and found their way of doing things."

In this way, "they prefigure the kind of design process that has to happen in the future." Stewart Brand, one of Fuller's most avid students and founder of the Whole Earth Catalog, says that his teacher believed that society is actually led by design ideas that originate in outlaw territory. In our time, he adds, those ideas have included alternative energy sources, environmental concerns, communication technology, and a growing awareness of the earth as a biosphere, all of which have "expanded its outlaw edge."

Yet the question remains, as Fuller asked himself near the end of his life, "If the success or failure of this planet, and of human beings, depended on how I am and what I do: How would I be? What would I do?"

Does it take a genius to know what will work or can the ordinary individual contribute? Perhaps both. In philosopher William James's classic definition, "genius is nothing more than the faculty of perceiving in an unhabitual way." To this end Bucky Fuller initiated a life long experiment he wittily called "Guinea Pig B." In this playfully serious endeavor he proved again and again that everyday people could accomplish much in the realm of design that could not be achieved by corporations or organizations.

"If man chooses oblivion," he said presciently, "he can go right on leaving his fate to his political leaders. If he chooses Utopia, he must initiate an enormous educational program, immediately, if not sooner."

But where do we begin? What do we teach? Looked at from what many designers now call the galactic perspective, the destiny of the planet is, as John Todd points out, "an exercise in stewardship of a biosphere." Architect Leslie Sauer says that the goal of her Andropogon agency is that "we design every site as if it were the whole planet... which goes to the core of the idea of sustainability." Mary Catherine Bateson suggests to "think in terms of moving toward a society in which every member feels at home, and in which every member feels a participant in creating a home for each other and sustaining the planet as a home for other species."

The ideals of these pioneers of ecological design point to a society in which designing houses, offices, transportation, energy systems that are environmentally safe and harmonious with nature is formost. Their manifesto underscores how the design revolution must be truly global, it must embrace more than just human destiny. In the compassionate words of Mexican poet Ernesto Cardenal:

Not only humans desired liberation. The whole ecology demanded it. The revolution is also of lakes, rivers, trees, animals.

As Bateson eloquently concludes, "We have to have a future that looks like home, to all of us."

Chapter One

Into the Fuller Universe

*The true Romance which the
World exists to realize will be the
transformation of genius into practical power.*

Emerson

— · — · — · — · — · — · — · — · — · — · — · — · — ·

Entering the wilderness
of a civilized landscape,
I set out to find fresh inspiration, leaving the despair of the hand me
down, already described, lawnmowered existing place. The main
headlights were the Quest for a new set of ideas that would open
unique vistas of
topian delight. The path opened ever so slowly.
Engaging the mode of
magical thinking as an navigational tool,
mentors and marauders lit the way. Roads led to freeways,
which led to superhighways out of town. As I tuned into the lower
frequencies, Minds of the Universe appeared like Don Genaro from
behind the canyon wall.

The material of these interviews was engendered out of the search
for where Buckminster Fuller's notion of Comprehensive
Anticipatory Design has meandered through form and content;
and taken root in new
realization. In deep design exploration, as in fire,
musical composition, or the Glass Bead game itself, all the
elements of the Universe are synergized, and the
artificial boundaries between domains begin to vanish.

The heroic participants in this chapter have
reinterpreted the common design language to go beyond the mind
forged manacles that the machine age clamped on our imaginations.
They have opened up a new horizon of ecologically inspired
inventions. From Thomas Hughes' vision of the American genius for
invention to Brendan O'Reagon's ideas about Outlaw creativity;
John Todd's cry for sacred aesthetics and J.Baldwin's affectionate
portrait of Fuller as a radical prophet, the contributors in this
chapter have felt the sense of urgency for change and are doing
something creative about it.

C.Z.

2

Humanity is now maintaining an unstable
collection of local holding patterns,
awaiting a physical or metaphysical
integrity to give structure to
the future and to show
the way out of darkness.

R. Buckminster Fuller

Thomas Hughes

The Frontier Spirit of Invention

This openness, this room, this opportunity for free play of the spirit, was — is — one of the explanations for American achievement.

"In your book *american genesis*, you cover the invention of modern america. what were the key elements that made such a fertile climate for innovation?"

If a historian one hundred years from now looked back on this period from 1870 to 1970, he or she might decide this era in the United States was one of the most creative in Western history in the last thousand years. The period in America from 1870 to 1970 is comparable in many ways to the period of the Renaissance in Italy—one of remarkable creativity.

I believe this country has known, in the modern era, a memorable epoch. By that I mean no other peoples have created the means of production, the means for providing commodities, goods, and services comparable to the production machine that we brought into the world in this period. It's not accidental that this achievement, this producing of material plenty, occurred in a democracy, because we believe that every man and woman, in theory and often in practice, should be well supplied with the goods and with the services. This productive machine provided these goods and services—Ford automobiles, Edison electric lights, the phonograph; we could go on and on.

The Ford plant in the 1920's embodied the American spirit of invention.

This country, by 1920, had become the envy of the world, and the people of this country, at least in the opinion of the rest of the world, had the highest living standard that the world had ever known. Most of what I am saying is in the realm of materialism. We're not talking about art. We're not talking about things of the spirit. Our achievements were material. We have been a remarkable people in making political constitutions, forming a successful way of relating to one another politically. But again, I think when someone looks back centuries from now upon American history, this age—1870 to 1970—will be the most memorable era for its material achievements.

Why should we not be proud of this? Americans lament the fact that we haven't had greater art, greater architecture in the past, and that our music has not been as inspiring. But these other achievements, these material achievements, are fruits of creativity as well. I think Europeans have been envious of these material achievements, these technological achievements. One reason we enthusiastically hurled ourselves into this creative endeavor was because many of us had come from poor backgrounds. In some cases we came from poverty-stricken backgrounds. Material goods meant a great deal to us. To fulfill our material needs was a great achievement. I'm talking about people who have known poverty, people who came from the lower economic levels of society in Europe, Africa, and Asia.

A Model T rolls off the assembly line at the River Rouge plant, Dearborn, Michigan, c. 1920.

Ford and Edison understood that there were no experts about the unknown; no theories, only hypotheses or metaphorical insights, about the uninvented.

Thomas Hughes

OPEN SPACES FOR INVENTION

What I am saying was especially true in the early decades of this modern period when the country was not highly structured. We speak of the American frontier. America in the period of 1870 to 1920 was not only a physical land that was open. We had open spiritual spaces. We had open economic spaces. The country had not yet been fully organized. The rules and regulations of life and business had not been laid down. So there was the opportunity for exploration, the opportunity to bring about changes, the opportunity to make something.

Americans in the 1870s and 1880s dreamed of inventing or creating a new business or building a house, filling up all this space that was American. Whereas the physical frontier may have closed in 1890, according to the census office, the other frontiers were still open. This openness, this room, this opportunity for free play of the spirit, was—is—one of the explanations for American achievement. The notion of openness is abstract, but I think if we dwell on the idea we will see many specific instances. The opportunity, for example, for thousands of people to create Ford agencies and to sell Ford automobiles in small towns. The opportunity to build roads where there had been no roads, to create farms where there was only wilderness. This is what I mean by space, and also the chance to teach in new ways. We were the people who introduced what might be called a very pragmatic, practical way of education. This is an American achievement. American pragmatism. The opportunities were abundant because of space and, again, I'm speaking of spiritual as well as physical space.

THE INVENTIVE WAY OF LOOKING AT THE WORLD

The inventors whom I've known through the letters and the records that they've left—they tend to look at the world as an opportunity for problem solving. This can be a burden to them spiritually. It can also be a deeply rewarding attitude. But they look around them and they see where correction, improvement is needed ... where a new way of doing things is in order. So they see the world as an interacting environment. They look for the components in the interacting environment that are not functioning well or that are falling behind the other components.

This is the reverse salient. It is not a very difficult concept. If you walked into a room in which you expected to have a pleasant party and you looked in one corner of the room and there were two people who were obviously having an argument ... this would be the reverse salient in this system of people. So you would try, if you were taking responsibility for it, to correct that situation.

Buckminster Fuller saw the number of industries that had been "rationalized." Ford had rationalized the production of automobiles. The electrical supply people had rationalized the production and transmission of electricity through large grids and networks. As compared to these high-tech industries, the building industry was lacking. It was not rational. It was not efficient. And so this was a reverse salient. He probably didn't use the term. He saw it as a problem.

Many inventors do this. They walk into a situation looking for an opportunity to use their inventive resources to improve upon the situation. Elmer Sperry, whom I think was a greater inventor than Edison—and I would have to spend a long time defending that statement but I could, I think—would look at situations in which there was a need for a feedback mechanism in order to improve that situation. An example would be an airplane that was

Until 1970 there had always been enough physical resources but not enough metaphysical resources (of experience won know-how) on our planet to render the physical technology capable of taking care of everyone at a sustainable, eminently successful level of physical well being — bloodlessly accomplished and sustainable without the co-existence of either a human slave or working class. Until 1970 it had realistically to be either you or me, not enough for both. Since 1970 it has become realistically you and me — all else is automated acceleration to human-race extinction on planet earth.

R. Buckminster Fuller

7

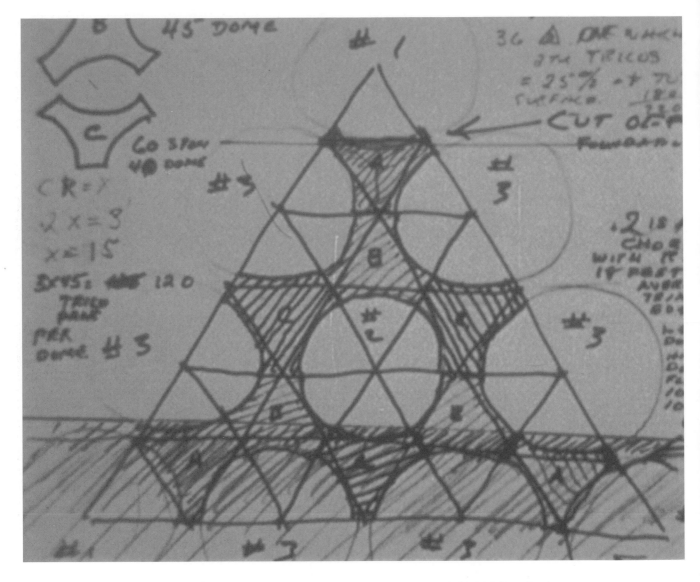

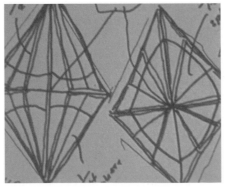
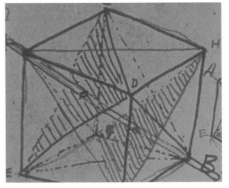

Early sketches of Bucky's Synergetic Geometry.

Bucky holding a model of his Synergistic Geometry.

Only the free-wheeling artist-explorer, non-academic scientist philosopher, mechanic, economist poet who has never waited for patron-startering and accrediting of his coordinate capabilities holds the prime initiative today. If man is to continue as a successful pattern-complex function in universal evolution, it will be because the next decades will have witnessed the artist-scientist's spontaneous seizure of the prime design responsibility and his successful conversion of the total capability of tool-augmented man from killingry to livingry.

R. Buckminster Fuller

 Fuller's assertion was roughly to this effect: the purpose of people on Earth is to counteract the tide of entropy described in the Second Law of Thermodynamics. Physical things are falling apart at a terrific rate; people, on the other hand, put things together. People build bridges and cities and roads; they write music and novels and constitutions; they have ideas. That is why people are here; the Universe as it were needs somebody or something to keep it from falling apart.

Annie Dillard

not stabilized. He saw the possibility of applying a feedback mechanism. He would say: "I can use feedback there to stabilize the airplane." The reverse salient was a lack of stability. He was a solution looking for a problem. Feedback was his solution and he would apply feedback to the stability problem to correct the reverse salient.

Systems are always revealing problems because they are undergoing change. As they change, some component of the system will not come up to the others in performance, and that's where the inventor tends to concentrate, unless she or he is inventing an entirely new system. In that case, the reverse salient is a reverse salient in a larger picture—like the housing industry. You come up with a new way of building houses.

DESIGN OUTLAWS

It is interesting that you use the term outlaw. We've been speaking of frontiers because outlaws felt at home on the frontier, not in the middle of a large city. Outlaw, in a sense, means there is no law, there are no regulations, no rules. There is space. The inventors need to find a space in which there is disorder that they can order, a space which they can make into—I am using space, of course, in a very general sense—which they can order into a useful structure. Inventors do this. But the irony is that once the space has been organized by the inventor, then the freedom to invent no longer exists in that space. So the inventors, the creators of order out of chaos, are making it difficult for us to have an opportunity to invent, because the space that we would use has been structured.

A person like Henry Ford enjoys himself immensely when he's creating the auto. The Ford Motor Company produces automobiles where there had been nothing. But once that's created, he becomes bored by his own creation, because no longer is there the room for invention. These people like Ford are radical in that they are not simply trying to improve upon space, they are not simply trying to modify order that exists and perhaps make it more efficient. They have grand visions of bringing, in the philosophical sense, order out of chaos.

OPPOSITE, ABOVE Bucky with his eye on the future stands in front of his 1934 Dymaxion Car and the Fly's Eye Dome during his 85th Birthday bash in Snowmass, Colorado, 1981.

OPPOSITE, BELOW Bucky sketching out his geometries.

"what is the importance of the design outlaw?"

11

RADICAL VERSUS CONSERVATIVE INVENTION

Some inventors feel comfortable improving upon existing situations. These persons I tend to call conservative inventors. Other inventors choose problems that allow them to introduce new systems, not improve upon existing systems. These are the radicals.

The distinction between radical and conservative is not one of intellectual merit, but is a matter of style and of problem choice. Persons who go to work for large corporations and find their positions, they do their work within industrial laboratories, are almost constrained to work on improvements because the corporation for which they are working has a lot of technology out there in the field that needs improvement. Whereas an independent inventor, one who is not working for a large corporation, is not constrained by a vested interest in existing technology. So you tend to find the radicals—and there is no great mystery about it—the persons who choose the problems that allow for introduction of new systems, rather than the improvement of old systems, you tend to find these people as independents—what Fuller, I guess, called the outlaws.

The Universe is full of magical things patiently waiting for our wits to grow sharper.

Eden Phillpotts

METAPHORIC THINKING

In reading the diaries and the papers of a number of inventors, I have been struck by how often they use metaphors. One person whom I have in mind now is Lee De Forest, inventor of the three-element vacuum tube, the modern vacuum tube. (Of course, they are not modern any more.) Lee De Forest, in his notes, often used vivid physical metaphors. Edison was given to metaphors and Elmer Sperry often referred to machines as animals. Elmer Sperry was especially into control, feedback controls, and he would say "I have to bring that little beast under control." One wonders about the psychological roots of that kind of expression. What was he trying to bring under control besides the little beast that was a machine?

Inventors use metaphors, I think, because a metaphor is a way of moving from the known to the unknown. One uses known expressions and known concepts in an effort to define the unknown. There are many examples; one that comes to mind is "A mighty fortress is my

12

God," which is certainly a metaphor. This is an effort to define God metaphorically by a reference to a mighty fortress. What you see from this example is that a metaphor has to fall on fertile ground. A metaphor has to be used with discretion, because if you have in your mind the vision of a fortress pouring boiling oil down on attackers, that is not exactly what the person using "A mighty fortress is my God" had in mind. One has to have in mind the fortress as a sheltering, protecting place. Then the metaphor works. So you move from a knowledge of what a fortress is—certain qualities of a fortress—into the unknown, trying to define God.

In the case of Sperry, he used the metaphor of control very often. For example, he had used controls on dynamos—electrical generators—and then he would say a street car control is like a dynamo. "Is like," now, that is a simile, which is a form of metaphor—"is like a dynamo." What he was saying was, "I can use some of the inventive notions I had with a dynamo, and use this in bringing about the control of the street car."

So once you find the inventor saying "is like"—in the case of Edison, he would say that a telegraph system is like a system of water pumps—that again is a form of metaphor. Then one is moving from what one knew in the past to what one would like to know in the future.

A metaphor is useful not only in literature, but also in invention. The touch of madness. To see things that other people can't imagine is certainly part of the brilliant radical inventor's storehouse. To see, as a matter of a fact, to bring the absurd into the realm of reality.

Basically, the century began with architects being inspired by an emerging age of industry and technology. I mean everybody wanted a building to somehow function like a combustion engine. As an inspirational force in 1910, one can understand it, but as a continuing inspiration in our post-industrial world of information and ecology, it doesn't make sense anymore.

James Wines

13

AMERICA AND EUROPE

I think America still has a lot to learn from Europe. America in the modern period, from 1870 to 1970, was the most inventive nation. Americans tended to put technological activity, inventiveness, innovation, and so on over here, and they would put literature, music, painting, and architecture over there.

There is a certain reverse snobbery in this attitude. There are the higher things and the lower things. Physical things are lower and spiritual things are higher. Americans feel very uncomfortable, some of them, that they have done the lower physical things and not the higher spiritual things. This was certainly true of past Americans, from 1870 to 1880. Americans, thoughtful Americans, were concerned that whereas they had the greatest inventors (of physical things), they did not have the great musicians; they did not have the outstanding artists.

Europeans take a somewhat different attitude toward low and high culture. Europeans, generally—and this is true today, too—have an anthropological view of culture. Culture includes all aspects of human activity, human institutions, and human social relations and patterns of behavior. Thoughtful Europeans do not tend to separate technology over here as something low.

So in the 1920s, when Europeans were becoming aware of the magnificence of American technology, they began to think of a new culture emerging out of this technology. The technology would shape the new culture; technology would shape the new architecture; technology would shape the new art; technology would influence the new literature. . . .

Some Europeans—especially architects like Le Corbusier, Peter Barrens, and Walter Gropius, the German, the Bauhaus leader—began to speak of a culture of technology, of an industrial culture. They sought for an architecture that expressed the values of the new technology that was coming from America. We didn't see the possibility of a culture based on technology—this sort of reverse snobbery—but they did. It is not accidental (as a matter of a fact, it is logical, in view of the argument I am giving) that the Europeans should have come up with the international style of architecture which drew heavily upon American technological values:

...To be counted off into a heap of mechanism, numbered with its wheels, and weighed with its hammer strokes,—this nature bade not,—God bless not—this humanity for no long time is able to endure.

John Ruskin
The Stones of Venice
1851-53

Fritz Lang's nightmarish vision of a machine age city, as depicted in his classic film, Metropolis, 1929.

Given the trend of our age to eliminate the craftsman more and more, yet greater savings   by means of industrialisation can be foretold, though in our country they may for the time being still appear Utopian.

Walter Gropius, 1910

order, system, control, symmetry. The international style of architecture in Europe drew upon American techniques for construction. As a matter of a fact, Gropius, the head of the Bauhaus, said we must design our houses, must give them form so they can be built by machines efficiently. So there was a fit between the form and the technology of construction.

There were also artists in Europe—the dadaists (in a reverse way) were one group, and the futurists were another group of artists who were all quite interested in what technology meant to the broad culture and tried to express their reactions in their art.

It was in Europe, not in the States—and this is ironic because of technology originating in the States—but it was the Europeans who first articulated a modern culture shaped by the values and the modes of modern technology.

THE GREEN REPUBLIC

Lewis Mumford, the public intellectual, was interested throughout his life in the relationship between technology and society. In his early years, he had high hopes that technology would provide (or bring into being) what he spoke of as the Green Republic, which was a community of people with ample physical goods and services, a people who were democratic in their political relationships, and a people who had used new technology to create a "green" environment. He was an advocate of regionalism.

what role did Lewis mumford play in this cross-cultural fertilization?

Mumford was concerned about the congestion of population and artifacts in the large cities. He thought that with electricity, a means by which one can distribute power and energy, and . . . the automobile, which was (as we used to think) a convenient mode of transportation (sometimes it still is, today), it would be possible to disperse the population, to relieve the congestion in the cities, and to [establish] "green communities"—that is, small cities or large towns that had industries based on local resources. Many of the people in these small cities would not only work in the small factories, but also have gardens, so these communities would be a good mixture of the urban life and the pastoral life. This was his Green Republic. He had high hopes for using modern technology to achieve this vision.

World War II disillusioned him greatly. It created monumental pessimism in his mind about the future of technology, because he saw the technology that he had hoped would bring about the Green Republic being used in destructive ways. He sensed that one reason technology was so horrendously destructive in World War II was because it was organized into large systems, not of production, but systems of destruction. He had in mind the large powers that were brought to bear by organized airpower, by organized mechanized warfare, and so on. He began to speak of the "megasystems" that brought this destruction. He defined these megasystems as the institutions, techniques, and artifacts that brought the destruction. One of his last books was called The Pentagon of Power. The Pentagon was a great megamachine, an institution that brought into play the armies, the air forces, and the weapons. All of this together was the megasystem.

These megasystems, he felt, were so large, so complex that they were virtually out of control. When the megasystem (in this case the military megasystem) used the atom bomb, he anticipated the holocaust that would bring the end of civilization, because once the megasystems were on track, there'd be no way of derailing them, they were so large, so powerful.

Mumford's vision of systems of destruction was expressed powerfully in his books, but there were also other persons—writers, thinkers, social critics—who began to see technology's great overwhelming systems that were deterministic in their effects, that left us little freedom because these systems took on a life of their own. Some of the gurus of the counterculture [saw] these technological systems as the greatest threat that we face, because they constrained our freedom of action, they moved us along routes that would lead ultimately to our destruction. When these people spoke of the "System," they were referring as much to technological systems as to any other organized human institutions.

The System became the target of many members of the counterculture. They were looking for ways of breaking up the large systems. The Whole Earth Catalog, for example, explained the way in which one can supply one's physical needs, and [obtain] the services that are necessary for life without depending on large systems of production, but depending instead on systems of small scale, systems

We must ask the bat-eyed priests of technology what on earth they think they are doing.

Lewis Mumford

17

that were under your control, systems that you directed. There was an effort of the counterculture to decentralize the propellers of production, to break up the large systems. Hence the emphasis upon "small is beautiful," rather than large. There were attacks on large electric light and power systems, there were attacks on large military-industrial systems, on any systems that were large and complex. The counterculture had a vision of another kind of society, in which we'd have more control over our technology and perhaps create the kind of Green Republic that Mumford had in mind.

WE GET THE TECHNOLOGY WE DESERVE

"what are the chances we can transform the military/industrial complex into a benign, livingry oriented system?"

I am inclined not to blame the military megasystems or the military. I think that's simplistic. I think the military systems come out of our values. The values that we hold, they have relations to other nations—what we think are the proper ways of settling disputes, the ways that we think the resources of the earth should be divided among the nations. The values that we have of these international relations tend to become embodied in our military systems because we see force as one of the ways of solving disputes or resolving international problems.

The military is a creature of society's values. I don't see the military as a conspiracy. I would argue that if one wishes to reduce the influence of the military, one would have to become involved in the transformation of values. In order to bring about a change in values, one has to rethink what one values highly, and what one values not-so-highly. Then [there] can be a reorientation of our values that will earn expression in a reconstituted technology. We're now expressing ourselves through our military technology, but we also can express ourselves through our environmental technology. We can express ourselves through the technology that makes communication possible.

Technology is an expression of our values; therefore, I come back to the original proposition: military technology is an expression of values that we hold very strongly. If we wish to rid ourselves of military technology, then we will have to change the values that are embodied in that technology. It is up to us. Now, that it is up to us doesn't make it simple, because to change values is a horrendous problem. I think our reaction to the Gulf War shows that we do value war as a way of solving problems.

TECHNOLOGICAL MOMENTUM

One reason it will be difficult to reduce the role of military systems in our culture is because of the technological momentum of these systems. What I mean by technological momentum is something quite simple but, I think, quite significant.

Hundreds and hundreds of thousands, even millions, of people depend on the military establishment for their livelihood. They are soldiers or they work for the Defense Department. Not only are these people dependent on the military/industrial/university complex, but so are the contractors who supply the weaponry to this complex. The universities who receive research contracts are dependent upon the "Pentagon of Power." We have numerous God-fearing citizens who live by and off the military/industrial system.

This military/industrial/university system has what I call high momentum. That is, it has many, many, many components (institutional components, value components, artifactual components) that bring about immense vested interest in maintaining the System. Look at what happened recently when Congress tried to close a few military bases. The people who depend upon those bases for livelihood were immediately up in arms. Repeat this incident a thousand times and you'll begin to see how deeply we are involved in the military, all of us involved in the university/military/industrial complex. It is ours; it is not a conspiracy imposed upon us. We depend upon it. We use it. We value it.

ABOVE
Solar panels generate electricity alongside a highway in Switzerland.
BELOW
Could this portend the future for mobile homes?
(photos courtesy of American Solar Energy Society/Boulder, Colorado)

THE ROLE OF THE MILITARY IN THE HISTORY OF INVENTION

Americans do not think of themselves as being a people whose history is shot through with military adventure and military commitment. But, the more deeply we go into our history, the more we see of the effect of the military upon our way of life—upon our economic life, our political life, and our social life. Many of our major inventions, for example, many of our outstanding systems in place today, were originally brought into being by the military. Let's examine this proposition for just a moment. We go back to 1900, 1905, 1910—the military was the prime source of funds for those who were developing radio. At that time, the military was the prime source for those who, in this country and abroad, were developing the airplane. The military was also a prime source of funding for those who were developing what we now call automation.

The military was also a supporter of scientific management, a major innovation in management. We could go back to the nineteenth century and I could give you similar examples, interchangeable parts. The so-called American system of production had military origins. The military has been responsible for many of the systems within which we live today: communication systems, transportation systems, and production systems.

That may come as some surprise to some Americans, and you might ask why. Well, one answer is that the military has long been interested in control, order, system, efficiency, and hierarchy. Technology can be used to provide those, to respond to those needs. The airplane being a very good case in point, in this country, of a device that was funded by the military and then spun off into our commercial aircraft.

MOVING "IT" OVER TO LIVINGRY

Back on the military/industrial/university complex which has been so active in the last fifty years, I see a very interesting parallel that can be drawn to earlier history. The period from 1870 to about 1910 was one in which independent inventors flourished. Many of the systems like the telephone and the airplane and the radio had their origins in this early period and resulted from the inventiveness of these independent inventors. That was a remarkable period.

Then we moved to the inter-war period between World War I and World War II. The system builders were remarkable achievers— The Fords, the Insells, who organized the great systems of production that had been invented by the inventors in the earlier period. Now, moving up to the post-World War II period, I hypothesize that we may have gone to another remarkably creative period in the last fifty years.

The creativity has been within the context of the military/industrial/university system. It's hard for some to see this because there's such an ideological barrier for some people to appreciate what might have been done within the confines of the military/industrial/university complex. It's difficult for them to appreciate that this was a very creative context. But, as an historian, as is the case as with other professionals, one must describe it as one sees it.

That life is worth living is the most necessary of assumptions, and were it not assumed, the most impossible of conclusions.

George Santayana

21

If one takes a close look at the last fifty years, one finds remarkably talented scientists and engineers and managers participating wholeheartedly in the development of military systems, and in the belief, with the faith, that this was in the interests of their country. This is surely true of many of them. Perhaps others had reasons less high-minded, but very creative people were involved. I believe that if we closely examine the activities within the realm of the military/industrial/university complex within the last fifty years, we will find some remarkable episodes of creative activity.

Now, I think that the question in many people's minds today, as the Cold War is drawing to a close and the Gulf War was not as horrible as we feared, is, is there a possibility of moving these institutions and these ways of doing science and these modes of achieving technological goals from the military/university/industrial area over into livingry areas? The answer is yes. But technological momentum will make it very difficult, as I explained earlier.

I think the answer's yes because I think the Japanese have used many of the techniques, much of the knowledge, some of the experience that we have developed in these military/industrial/university years. They have already moved it over into science, into technology, into management in Japan. Because the military/university/industrial system builders were remarkably adept at building large systems of production. More adept than Ford at building large systems of production. But this was, in effect, production of destructive devices. While these creative powers created systems of production that, I would assume, could be moved over (and I believe it has been done in Japan; I think the Japanese learned a lot from what we've done in this area), and the products would not be destructive artifacts but constructive artifacts.

One could organize large systems of environment that would respond to environmental problems. I'm of the opinion that this Superfund, which is designed to clear up hazardous waste, could be a very impressive system, a technological system that would solve a very important problem. Some of the talents and some of the organizational abilities and some of the inventive skills that we've seen embodied in military/university/industrial [areas] could be moved over to environmental [areas], and into other areas. One reason that this might generate enthusiasm among Americans ("it" being the military/industrial/university capacity) is because if we moved it over into environmental or into social areas we would have space. It would be a new kind of problem. It would give a new sort of opportunity.

I think the military/industrial/university complex is becoming somewhat boring now. When it was being created in the fifties, I think there was much space for problem solving, for innovation. But now I think it's taken on structure, the kind of structure put on earlier, and I don't think it is attracting as many persons of energy and creative drive as this military/industrial/university complex once attracted. It is becoming routine. It has been systematized. So we've moved over this capacity, this creative potential, in other realms of new challenges and enthusiasm.

When I say "spirit of invention," I am not saying something trivial. What I have in mind is the willingness to go into unexplored territory and know the anxiety of not being surrounded by rules, regulations, and not to know support—that you are guaranteed that there is a resting place, something beneath you to hold you up. There are many opportunities to have this experience of exploring the difficult territory of the unknown or experiencing anxiety in other realms than physical invention. Inventiveness is a very broad concept.

When I am working on a problem, I never think about beauty. I think only how to solve the problem. But when I have finished , if the solution is not beautiful, I know it is wrong.

R. Buckminster Fuller

Harold Cohen

Design As a Way of Making the World Work

We're talking about searching for the core. Functionalism. The ideal. Taking the whole universe together.

"can you talk about your experience with buckminster fuller and the institute of design in chicago?"

Now Bucky was an original. He comes out of a group of crazy ones—transcendentalists, Unitarians, people who challenged everything. He believed and followed the philosophy of transcendentalism - the viewpoint that you don't do anything that is against your nature, you don't get involved in any occupation which would destroy your ability to reason or think, that you have to give your mind the freedom to explore. He took a different approach to looking at nature, he challenged some of the things he heard because he didn't feel they matched a generalized principal of structure in nature and he believed, as the transcendentalists did, that there is a key to nature and he searched for that key. The key is not just a tetrahedron. The key is a way of looking. It's the flight, the search, which is the key. He wanted to create new forms that will help people find their own way. He searched for ways to bring things to the common man by mass production. Searched for the inner core. Functional liberalism. Get rid of the kitsch.

Coming out of the French school of everything being sort of fanciful and going back to the horse and buggy days of the British. That was important. Bucky is an original coming out of that background of the transcendental movement and that great movement that I would call the "turn-of-the-century," here in this country, that was doing things in terms of products. Bucky's major product was thinking. That did not come out of a factory. That is not something you could put a label on.

He led the way, as a machete that cut through some of the red tape and the garbage so that the young people could woosh through. That was his greatness. That was the uniqueness.

What did he contribute to his students? His excitement, his exploration. He taught them how to explore. To have faith in themselves. To learn from mistakes. A good explorer doesn't know what's around the bend. We will always die ignorant, but discovery teaches us how to explore and how to think.

WHAT NEEDS TO BE WORKED ON?

I was in the first class that Bucky taught at the Institute of Design in Chicago where he did say, "Stack up the drafting tables." He spent the morning talking, and in the afternoon we built models of things that he needed to do—"quirks and quints and quacks"—and sections of triangles, etcetera. But we did a lot of talking. What was very special about that talking was that he made me and the others [ask ourselves], "What are the real problems? Do we need another refrigerator? Do we need forty-five pairs of shoes? How do we travel? How many more buildings do we need? If we're going to be designers, what should we be focusing on? What are the real human problems that need work?"

He talked about the products that are for "livingry" or "killingry," and divided them out. Then he talked about two piles—I think it was him but maybe it was Moholy Nagy—a pile of "goodgits" and a pile of gadgets. The world is full of all these gadgetries. you buy things. Look at my desk, look at your house, all full of stuff. A lot of material is being used, raw materials—steels, and woods, and paper, but for what purpose? It doesn't really support the real quality of life. It's a pile of absurdity. Products are coming out that have no real value . . . to maintain quality life. [We just buy] because Miss Jones bought, or Miss Magillicuddy, or Mrs. Cohen, or whatever. There's this kind of consumerism.

Where should we direct our efforts that the earth's energy, and the earth's resources, and our own intellectual energy can be of value? Those were exciting things to think about. My own work, which is in education, is on the development of things when they're needed, or taking away things if they're unneeded. Design doesn't always mean you're building. Sometimes it's better to remove, so it works better. It was wonderful.

The Dymaxion House, which Bucky came up with in 1927, was way ahead of its
time - too far ahead of its time to be successful except in stirring people's minds.
The house was to be mass produced and sold for the price of a Cadillac. It would be
far more luxurious in its own way than any existing house. It wouldn't be large but you
could make it larger by hooking in several modules. The house would clean its own air and
purify its waste water. Clean water would be resupplied sporadically rather than by a
network of piping. The house would greatly reduce the amount of housework expected
of the housewife. This new house cleaned its own air so that it didn't need to be dusted. It
washed the clothes, folded them, and automatically put them away. It would have a telegraph
and short wave radio so you could keep track of world events. All of this in a specific room
with a globe of the earth and a sizeable library, so it would be the information room.
The Dymaxion House was very light. It was air deliverable. It was constructed of stainless
steel and aluminum which would not deteriorate or require any maintenance. Moreover,
the house could be taken apart and reassembled elsewhere if the land use or the zoning
changed or you wanted to upgrade it to the latest model. All of these ideas are right on for
today.. So now is the time to do it. Live in a house that harnesses its own energy, heats and
cools itself, grows most of its own food, recycles its own waste, and is
recyclable itself - in other words, a smart house.

J. Baldwin

OPPOSITE
The Dymaxion House constructed in Wichita, Kansas, 1947.

LEFT
Bucky's original plans for the Dymaxion House.

BELOW LEFT
Newspaper headline announcing the prototype and expected public demand for this revolutionary home.

BELOW, RIGHT
The basic unit, and the container it is shipped in, standing next to it.

For me, the whole Institute of Design experience was that I found a place that was, I guess, what Islam considers Mecca, the place where God lies. But God wasn't the thing or a person. It was a way of looking at life.

Bucky talked about crucial issues. He talked about [what to do with] human feces; he talked about the use of water; he talked about the renewable resources and the nonrenewable resources, things I had not even thought about. He introduced those things, and they became for me a way of looking at my own life.

I thought it was wonderful to be able to take this concept of making the world work, but to remember that you were interested in the human being, and the emotional requirements, and the support of good living and people—whether it came from one -ism or another -ism.

Brendan O'Reagan

Outlaw Creativity

The really innovative person would have to be prepared to be an outlaw to the system to get the new idea in.

"what did you learn from Buckminster Fuller's view on design?"

In thinking about design, Bucky always insisted that we never created anything, that everything was always already there and it was a question of whether we had the ability in terms of pattern recognition to rediscover it, to recreate it. I remember him saying to me on one occasion that he never had new ideas, that whenever he had what seemed to him to be a profoundly important idea, that it seemed to come from far, far away and that it had what he called a "metaphysical mustiness about it, as though I was uncovering something that had been waiting for me to uncover it for a very, very long time."

That was a kind of allusion on his part to the fact that we were, in a sense, always trying to rediscover the Rosetta Stone in nature, and [to find] the basic principle. He was a bit like D'Arcy Thompson and the idea in On Growth and Form, that if you observe nature exquisitely, and intimately, and with great sensitivity, you will be taught everything you need to know, because it is all basically there.

Of course, for him, geodesic architecture was the discovery of nature's way of doing things. In a sense, design was a process of uncovering what nature had already done. It wasn't the case of the human being coming in and inventing great things that wouldn't exist if we weren't there. So, you see, it was kind of a different view than most people have.

There was a streak running through Bucky's ideas that I think came from his experience in the '30s, with the Dymaxion car, in particular, where he ran right into the issue of sabotage. People didn't want designs to happen. They did not want things to be made that should be made. I think he felt, because the establishment is always going to protect itself, that the really innovative person would have to be prepared to be an outlaw to the system to get the new idea in. One shouldn't expect establishment support, and Bucky never got establishment support.

In a sense, he became always identified with the outlaw. That was the only way to go because he felt the inertia of the system in perpetuating antiquated and outdated ideas. The real hope of the future was the person who was going to exist outside of that system—that any really good idea would be antithetical to an already existing system. There was a radical side to him that came through in a more quiet way, but it was there, it was definitely a real part of him.

But, in effect, it worked against him in some ways because when it came down to the issue of the Design Science Institute, and creating an entity that would continue his ideas in his own way, he sabotaged that from ever going anywhere. He would never request money for it. He felt that if God did not provide or nature did not arrive with a check with no strings attached, then he wasn't going to do anything to make it survive. He was very afraid of people capitalizing on his ideas in a way that would imply yet another bureaucracy growing up, and he may have been so good in making sure that that didn't happen that now we don't hear much about his ideas; I think you'll always find there are people that are driven by their own particular ideas rather than by current ideas, rather than the ideas that have sort of settled down to become common currency. The world will often think of them as being completely mad and the world may be right, but we need them like hell, because they are the ones who give us the fresh insights, and the fresh ideas, and the fresh ways of looking at things.

> The concept of a designer as an outlaw is very interesting because really as an individual you have to go the way that you yourself go, from your own experience, your own intuition. A designer is going to be following their own self. They might follow other tracks for a time, but they'll always blend together their own information in a totally original way. So the concept of a designer really is an artist-scientist. They're original but they're using the logic of the world's knowledge welded together. The path they tread is very unknown.
> Tony Gwilliam

Ted Nelson

The Xanadu System is where we will store things and we will not forget the artistic and intellectual work of the past, while at the same time will build on it in a cumulative pleasure-dome of thought and understanding.

In what manner did this image of a hypertext world come to you?

The vision that came to me at that moment could be phrased as having perhaps four parts. That there would be a new genre of writing which we may call hypertext. I didn't call it that then, but that's what it's called now, and I named it in 1965. And, that there would have to be an infrastructure of delivery to our screens for we would all have screens on our desks. There would have to be a worldwide delivery structure. And there would have to be a way of viewing the stuff on screens. And finally, this worldwide delivery system would have to be franchised as the fastest way to raise capital and the fastest way to build something really big. The amusing thing is that I still believe it will happen in exactly that way.

In what ways will xanadu change the written the nature of the written word?

Publishing as we know it is on paper and there will always be paper. People will still carve on stone. People still write on parchment. People still do calligraphy. And having books on your coffee table will presumably always have a certain cache.

For our everyday reading, certainly for our research, assuredly for our documents that have to be done on quick deadlines and for the most pressing matters, screen work will supplant paperwork increasingly as it has of course already, but not in the more serious large quantities of text and graphics that we now get from books and magazines.

I see Xanadu, or Xanadu-like, a xanalogical system, as replacing the printed word, let's say, supplanting the printed word fifty percent by the year 2000.

Now that's a strong statement because wee have only nine more years to go. I could be very wrong. But the year is arbitrary.

There will be a magic moment when suddenly the public gets it. It will be left, roughly, psychologically like the moment when the Berlin Wall came down. It will be like the moment when the Cold War began. It will be a paradigm shift where people say: "Oh, this is how it's going to be."

It will be like that moment when we looked at the photographs taken of earth from space. Suddenly we realized, just, you know, one planet. One fragile ecosphere.

There will be a moment when we realize that paper has now become antique, and that our work on paper, that working on paper becomes so slow compared with the annotations, the manipulative ease that we have on our screens, that there won't be any point in it.

I have always wanted to be a renaissance man. And the old definition of course seems so jolly. To be at once a swordsman, architect, artist, writer, politician, and swordsman of the boudoir. But at the same time the term renaissance man recently has come to me to have another connotation that's far more important.

     I want to start a Renaissance.

The way to do that is to get people thinking again. To get people using words again. To lift the anesthesia that television has poured across the land like marshmallow syrup. We're going to bring this back I think by giving people access to things. Because you see people without hope don't try and don't have a yearning. When hope appears there is yearning. When there's a chance to do things and learn things on your own the explosion of initiative and excitement is staggering.

When you put control of the learning situation in the hands of the learner, everything changes because, at last, they can truly explore.

You have to really do it, you can't give them a choice between vanilla and strawberry. You have to give them a choice between ice cream and sandwich or doing something else entirely.

Putting control in the hands of the student creates incredible, powerful motivation. It just lights people up. Everybody remembers not what they've been taught but what they learned on their own. Those are the things that mean the most to us.

I learned to write on my own and to take pictures and that was the sort of thing that supported me through life. Yet we continue to treat school as a sort of conveyor belt where the students are processed. They go under various slicing and dicing machines. The amazing thing to me is how, well, if factories turned out as many rejects as the schools did we would bulldoze them. Instead, of course, we increase their

> you write in your book literary machines about this potential for a new golden age through a unification of electronic text systems. how will this new paradigm change the way we live?

> why is being in control vital to the student mind?

me is how, well, if factories turned out as many rejects as the schools did we would bulldoze them. Instead, of course, we increase their budgets. The entire thing is governed by the time slot.

Once you have a curriculum in which you've decided you're going to learn this and this and this and this...Then we divide, and this week we're going too learn this and this and this. Then today, class, we have to do that and that. If you're interested you can't spend enough time on it and if you're not interested you spend too much on it. It's a horrible mess. They do this better in Europe and Japan because there is a certain level of dedication on both sides. Whereas, here we're perfunctory. I think, we need a completely, radically different system where students can be put in control and hypertext, hypermedia is going to do this. Not in the present situation because hypermedia right now are sitting on the computer in the corner that only one person can use at a time. Until everybody has got a computer essentially as an item of clothing really, like a pencil and paper, as long as it's a luxury that has to be apportioned to one person at a time, it won't get anywhere. As soon as you can get on a computer all day long, then we don't have a time slot anymore. You don't have a classroom. You don't have a class. You are working at your own speed. Then the class becomes a place where we do something interesting together, it is to be hoped.

does this mean the Role of the teacher will change?

Well I don't know what the role of the teacher is. The role of the teacher is to fulfill the mandated curricular segment. That's the real role of the teacher. In so doing, the teachers go through hell. I used to really have it in for teachers and I've mellowed somewhat since I've become a Californian, but the teachers really have a terrible time because of all the stuff they have to get done: the paperwork, the counseling, and the crowd control, and that has nothing to do with what they got in it for in the first place. They wanted that magical moment of heart to heart contact. They wanted to deliver the ahahs. Instead it's disciplinary, and it's shuffling people in and out. I wouldn't say the teacher has a role now really anyhow. There is the authoritarian role, but that's already been played with so many different shades by different people that to say that there is a single teacher's role I think is erroneous way of looking at the school.

what Responsibility does the design outlaw have to future generations?

What responsibility does the design outlaw have? By definition an outlaw has no responsibility. On the other hand, a conscientious outlaw, like myself, really wants to achieve things that are good for people and do so in ways that, shall we say, bypass, thwart, and occasionally humiliate the establishment, but at the same time with the long term objective of doing well. Doing good by doing well.
So the outlaw should, by t‡hese criteria, try to think of those things which the inlaws would never think of.

Now when I was eleven, I dropped out of school and it was a very tough day for me that day. That was the day I decided most people were fools, and most authority was malignant, and God did not exist and everything was wrong. Those have been my guiding beliefs ever since.

Great truths, indeed, but hard ones for an eleven year old to carry and the corollary of everything being wrong could for some people be that they were just going to go and defy and burn and pillage. But my, the corollary for me was to try to make things right.

In fact it was very much in this frame of mind, that I met, as it were, the work of Bucky Fuller. It was in all things in of all things the Reader's Digest-that bastion of marshmallows and cream and church-on-Sundays as it was then before its present lurid incarnation. The Reader's Digest had of all things an article on Buckminster Fuller and I believe it wàas the June 1949 issue. I reread as a young adult and was astonished at how it had effected me.

Here was a man who had invented his own geometry. Here was a man who talked about the future as something to be dealt with rather than simply met by going about our daily business in the same way we always have. Just the fact that he had invented his own geometry, my God.

Here was a man who was saying that the future was something to be met intelligently, rather than dealt with by default, continuing in our day to day affairs in old habit patterns.

He went out and designed his own car and a very good car it was. He went out and designed buildings in a new way. He went and designed his own geometry which I found thrilling: you're allowed to create your own geometry? This was the model of the kind of person I wanted to be. So he was one of my heroes. Intellectually, the notion that we can design our world rather than taking the things that come out of the factory the way they're being marketed to consumers. This was just such a powerful idea to me. Fuller examined things, not just coming out with individual designs, he had a total philosophy, and this is what gave it the power.

One of the things I got from Bucky Fuller is making up words and I didn't get it just from him, but his wonderful words like Dymaxion and tensegrity. Dymaxion really meant anything he was interested in and dynamic and maximal and ionic and that sounded just great. Others of my heroes had made up words like Edgar Allan Poe and "tintinabulate". Lewis Carroll with "tortle". The notion that one of the ways to leave your mark on the world with a word, I was deep in my fiber and when I realized it was for me to name these new media I thought long and hard before choosing and I chose very carefully. This was no idle technoid's accidental joining of syllables but hypertext and hypermedia which I published in 1965 were fully intended to ring down the decades and I've been amazed. I thought they would catch on like wildfire and they did in fact but not until 20 years later. Transclude is another term I

could you talk about what you mean by transclusion? that's a word I haven't seen in my dictionary.

coined and I happen to believe that any legitimate combination of Latin roots makes a legitimate English word. So far as I'm concerned, all of Latin and all of Greek are part of English. So transclude means what it sounds like, it means you include something from somewhere else across some gap, so Xanadu uniquely has transclusion which means that it, that one object or document as we call it can contain any part of anything else. But, it doesn't copy it. We leave a hole in this document, for that part we're going to take from another document which is filled dynamically at the moment you call it and that solves the problem of copyright, it solves the issues of versioning, it cleans up the entire storage of everything. So transclusion is such a fundamental mechanism it needs a word of its own so that we wouldn't mistake it for anything else.

Interactive design, I may have been the first person to use the term, too, is the, essentially, the design of things that will respond to you. This is a highly abstract system of design. For example, designing a telephone system or a voice-mail system where you dial into, to dial into somebody's office, and the voice says something like "you can leave a message now" or "you can hit 3 and thus blah, blah, blah....This is a form of abstract design but the designer is creating a labyrinth of alternatives and tunnels, as it were, that the user goes through, and yet, we don't, most people don't think of this as design, because they think of design as concerned with physical objects.

> can you further illuminate the differences between your designs and those of negroponte, mit, and xerox parc school of design?

This kind of design of our new worlds is fundamental because everything is now software. A video game, so called, is really a computer game, and it's really software. A VCR, though it may have buttons on the front, is really software. A telephone, with all these buttons, is really software — the program somebody made. Most of these things are god awful. Most people can't get their VCRs to record something a couple of weeks from now because it's too complicated. The engineers who thought it up, it's all obvious to them and absolutely opaque to other people. So we've got to do something about this.

Now, Xerox PARC school is of interactive design and is essentially what we see on the MacIntosh, the notion of pictorial things and icons for one thing and pull-down menus making things very simple visually.

The school of thought represented by the opposite school of thought is Nicholas Negroponte's of MIT at the Media Lab, where essentially he wants to use artificial intelligence as a sort of ketchup to sprinkle over everything so that you don't have to think, you don't have to understand, it'll just sort of do what you want and you'll be very happy. Well, I don't trust that at all. I think he is sincere but at the same time I want direct control over a much broader spread, a panoply of functions that can be selected easily and quickly and in a self revealing fashion. I don't want to use the word intuitive because what's intuitive for one person is not necessarily intuitive for another. So my school of design of computer stuff is essentially video games for the mind, creating conceptual structures that are easy to work with, and that means abstracting the world, in particular, would you want to work or play in and give it those characteristics that are easiest to manipulate, easiest to think about, and I consider this highly artistic design task. My designs tend to be extremely different from other people's, and idiosyncratic, and the computer people like them not at all. On the other hand, this is part of my claim that computer software is really a branch of movie making.

Just as in movies, we are creating and organizing the user's experience, the viewer's experience, we are in software organizing the mental experience of the person who's usiníg it and how it will feel. So the many different touches, aspects, just as a director works: tweaks the music, tweaks the cutting, tweaks the performers, tweaks the composition, all of these contribute to the overall effect. So, too, the software designer should be tweaking all the different parts of the design rather than having a committee design where you do this part, you do that part, which is really the way that stuff comes out now.

My school of software design, as it were, is entirely different. Orson Welles is my mentor in this way— theatrical approach to software design with a great deal of idiosyncratic tweaking.

SOLAR TRACKERS in the Sky

"build it and they will come"

SOLAR TRACKER

0101010101010101
0101010101010101
0101010101010101
0101010101010101
0101010101010101
0101010101010101
0101010101010101

A Solar Futurable/Design Concept: TZelov /Montage by J. Thompson

Tibetan Hillside/Photo by P.Hawes

Douglas Adams

The Mad Ones, The Original Ones

We need them like hell because they are the ones who give us the fresh insights and the fresh ideas and the fresh ways of looking at things.

"buckminster fuller claimed that human advancement occurs in the outlaw realm. what are your thoughts about this notion?"

I always feel we're very much at the mercy of the sort of cry, the war cry of the marketing people—what I tend to get an awful lot of: "You remember that thing you did that everybody loved so much because it was so original, and new, and fresh, and nobody had done anything like it before? Could you do something exactly like that again?" Marketing is the art of being wise after the event, isn't it?

I always remember when, in 1962, all the marketing people were telling the Beatles that guitar groups were out. Nobody was interested in guitar groups anymore. A year later, of course, the Beatles were the biggest thing in the world and the marketing people were telling all the other groups, "You have got to wear your hair like that. That's the secret. That's the trick."

It's actually what you call the design outlaw, though I'm not sure I'm entirely happy with that phrase. You need the people who are the ones who see what is really what and then you've got your marketing people and everybody else sort of running along behind you, trying to explain what it is you've done, and why that was the right thing to do, and how closely it accorded with what they always said.

An example of the
emerging
ecological design
aesthetic
by artist Henry
Dean at
Genius Loci Gallery
in Cape May, NJ,
August 1996

John Todd

The question is: How do you shift from a materialistic-based culture to one in which the highest mode of expression is aesthetic and of the sacred? What you are really asking is, "where are the instructions?"

There is no question that in the last twenty years most of the innovations that are really related to what we are talking about have taken place in what we are calling "outlaw organization."

In agriculture, in energy, in design, in materials, you have all of this using the universities as resources and using their talents as the resources but not trying to consolidate the work within the universities. The reason for this is there has been so much cross-boundary work going on between disciplines. I know for myself I'm a complete omnivore. I'm looking all the time in various disciplines for either news about structure or materials or ideas.

Artificial intelligence work—some of it—is interesting to me for two reasons. One, I know how far behind it is and, two, it allows us to create bridges between living systems and ourselves.

There is a real need to complete something, to create something. The difference between most of what we are talking about is the difference between the scientist and the artist. I think when you use the word "outlaw" you are really referring to the artist, but artists at this point in time are using science as their basis.

I think that the common thread is that most people think of artists as people who are doing paintings or composing, but design is an art form. So much of what is happening is by people whose sensibilities of themselves is art and their basic laboratory is science or their studio is science, the studio of their mind.

Everyone I know, from Bucky on down, who has become an "outlaw" has an extreme sense of urgency that the system that we have created has the potential to undo everything that we would like to see happen. It is that urgency that pushed so many people—the Lovinses,

Dr. Todd gathers material
for the Living Machine

A true partnership between
man and Nature.

Our new friends in waste
treatment.

ABOVE
A Living Machine installation on Rhode Island. This early version of
solar aquatics for sewage treatment cleansed the waste water from over
one hundred households to levels which far exceeded EPA standards.
Current systems are servicing even larger communities and providing
catalyst for broader ecological awareness.

41

A Living Machine addition to a Cape Cod home.

The original Ark.
Falmouth, Mass.

for example. There are God knows how many academic chairs, deanships, or presidencies that would be available to them, but they couldn't get hard at the problems they think will right the wrongs. This kind of ethical dimension, which is a funny dimension, seems to permeate all this.

Thank God the people are nutty enough, so that they enjoy life enough so that it is definitely not sanctimonious. There is a tribe that has formed and, of course, Bucky is one of the inspirers of it. For starters, there has always been this sense among artistic people and, maybe, religiously sensitive people, that there are always moments of connectiveness where the "I" merges with the complete "thou" of other life forms. The question is: How do you shift from a materialistic-based culture to one in which the highest mode of expression is aesthetic and of the sacred? What you are really asking is, "Where are the instructions?"

As far as I am concerned, the instructions come from the natural world itself and from the sense humans have always had of engagement. Once you become "engaged," using the Gary Snyder phrase, then, I think, this all opens up, this kind of sacred journey. I think anybody who has been an explorer of both the inside and the outside at the same time has a strong sense of that.

The bricoleur, a term used by Claude Lévi-Strauss, the anthropologist, is one of my favorite characters. If you were in theater, you would like the joker or the fool. The bricoleur is the technological person who plays that role. That's the genius who is able to reform the world with what's at hand. It's known in some cultures as the enlightened tinkerer, the person who sees what is immediately around her or him and transforms it into a higher or more useful form. We don't have anything in the English language for a person like that, so I guess we will have to stick with the French.

The role of the bricoleur is like this: If you've just come down from an area in Chattanooga that has at least five Superfund sites right in the community, toxic waste sites, how do you move into a community like that and begin to repair the air and the water with the human resources they have and the physical spaces they've got?

The traditionalist or the technologist would say they have the way to solve the problem: to move [everybody] out to a safe place and to bulldoze the area and take the toxic materials probably halfway around the world, which is what they do today, and dispose of it. That would solve the problem.

The bricoleur, in that environment, would basically ask the question, "What is the air like that you breathe in your house? What is the water like that comes out of your tap? Let's start with each individual household and let's slowly put this thing together and let's encase the toxic materials in ways that we have, to prevent these people from dying of leukemia and cancers." He would assume that what is there is the basis of transformation.

Living Machines in a domestic environment.

43

J. Baldwin

Encounters With the Mentor

He said: "I'm going to tell you what's going to happen, and what you have to get ready for, and what you have to start educating yourself for, and the public has to be ready for. Because it's what's coming."

"tell us about the first time you encountered buckminster fuller?"

I was living in a house with a bunch of architects who were mostly older than I was, at the University of Michigan. One of the graduate students, Tunny Lee, said: "You should come hear this guy." So I went to an evening lecture at the University of Michigan's architecture department. When Fuller came out on stage I had no idea who he was, though I had played with one of his maps [from Life magazine] when I was a kid in the forties didn't put the name together with the map at all. When this man came out on the stage, I thought he looked like one of cartoonist Al Capp's "Shmooes," because, at the time, Fuller was pretty overweight.

He was working that year on the Rotunda dome at the Ford Motor Company [in Dearborn, Michigan]. That dome isn't there anymore, but it was the [biggest] dome since the building of Saint Peter's in Rome. Of course, it was drastically lighter, and was going up much faster. It was fascinating, the theories that he was talking about, like no part of the dome was too heavy to lift with one hand so a workman could install it with the other hand. That kind of thing. So they didn't need big cranes. The idea of making a large structure out of a whole bunch of very lightweight parts was intriguing. I had never thought of that.

Anyway, he came out on the stage and he started talking. Right away, the first thing he talked about was that you could come over with a zeppelin and drop a bomb, and then plant a building in the crater. I thought that was outrageous. Some of the people in the audience actually snickered because it was so outrageous. They thought it was silly. But, he said it was possible to do this, and he went on to outline how he would actually do it. That required a lightweight building that you could sling under a zeppelin. Of course, they didn't have any zeppelins in the fifties; the zeppelins were long gone. But you could certainly make zeppelins even now. So the idea wasn't that crazy.

He was also talking about autonomous housing that didn't need the umbilical system of sewage, and electronic wires, fresh water, and roads (which are part of the umbilical)—it's the umbilicals that make property so expensive. He thought that one way to bring down the cost of housing, and to house everybody who needed a house in the world was to make houses that didn't need an umbilical system. He thought of that in 1927—houses should be energy efficient, make their own electricity, make their own power, distill and purify their own water, and recycle their own water, and process their own sewage. He did not, at the time, however, discuss houses raising their own food, which was something that came much later.

As he talked, he stood out on the edge of this stage with his toes out in the air, looking very unsteady, with part of the slide being projected onto his body so he made this big silhouette behind him on the screen. In those days they didn't have remote controls for slide projectors, so he would, growl, "Next slide," as was his custom, and he went on and on. He had a lot of slides, hundreds of slides.

As the evening went on, the professors there were clearly uneasy because if what he was saying made sense (and it seemed to me that it did), they were getting their toes stepped on. He referred to the construction industry as the craft and graft industry. He said it was the only major business in modern Western society that was still anachronistic, and was, in fact, downright medieval. Its technology was still at a medieval level, despite little glimmers here and there of modernity.

He showed that the way a furnace is chosen is that you design the building and then say, "how big a furnace does it need?" Instead of from the beginning, saying, "Let's make the building in a way that doesn't need a furnace, or needs the smallest possible furnace." In other words, built-in wastrel philosophy was being done as a matter of course, and was indeed being taught at University of Michigan. He also referred to architects as exterior decorators, which caused a noticeable ripple in the audience (which was 99 percent architects) and quite a bit of displeasure.

Then he went too far: he made a prediction. He said that within

The great man is the play-actor of his ideal.

Friedrich Nietzsche

45

Bucky passionately discussing the World Game at a New York design studio. 1969

just a few years, we would be going coast to coast in five hours in jet airliners. An outright guffaw went through the audience. People looked at their watches, and said, "our babysitter is waiting," and so on. Most of the audience got up and left.

After they left, Fuller was polite. He had people move down front, and he went on and on, and when it got to be about midnight, people began getting uneasy. It was mostly students by then. Most of them left. [Of an] audience of maybe three hundred people originally, there were only about twenty of us left, and he said, "Okay. Now we've determined who the people in this audience are who are interested. Now, I'll tell you something." He said, "I'm going to tell you what's going to happen, and what you have to get ready for. What you have to start educating yourself for, and the public has to be ready for. Because it's what's coming." He showed all these graphs that he'd worked out; the way trends go. The way that people move faster and faster, and that there are cycles of obsolescence, going faster and faster. The faster the medium that you're discussing, the faster the cycle of obsolescence. So cars go obsolete much more slowly than aircraft do and aircraft go obsolete much more slowly than electronic stuff.

In fact, before electronic things get into production they're already obsolete, and manufacturers know what the successor's going to be before they've even produced the ones that are going to be the next lot. Fuller turned out to be right on about that. Some of his ideas and predictions have turned out not to be very accurate. There were things he couldn't know.

He had plenty of hubris. Too much, some people thought. But I have found that [those who] I call high-voltage people make mistakes. Bucky was not afraid to make mistakes. I say "Bucky." That is not a sign of disrespect. Everybody called him Bucky, except for his wife (who called him Richard). Whether you were Mahatma Gandhi or you were a street bum, he was Bucky. There was just no question of calling him anything else. He was a really loving man. You could tell that.

I had heard a lot of lecturers over the years as a kid because my Dad was an engineer, and he took me to hear things. Fuller seemed to be very unpretentious. He might have had a big ego, but he was not pretentious. His basic schtick was that he claimed he was not an extraordinary man, that anybody could do what he did, if they just had the discipline to work the kind of hours that he worked, and to pay attention at the level that he paid attention to. I have found this to be true.

EPHEMERALIZATION: DOING MORE WITH LESS

The most stunning thing he said from the stage was that we did not have to earn a living. That if there was a God, God did not put us on this earth in order to be driven out of the Garden of Eden and have to live in squalor and filth, and struggle or die. All religions were based on the idea that there wasn't enough to go around; and that this earth was awful. The next earth, where we go after we die would be better. That was all based on the idea that there wasn't enough to go around—Thomas Malthus's theory. Fuller said there's plenty to go around, if we just use it wisely, and that we had to do more with less. He used the term ephemeralization, which, even though I was only eighteen at the time, hit me right between the eyes, because it was a dematerialization—it was a metaphysical idea. If you carry that more-with-less to the extreme, instead of more with less, you do everything with nothing. He showed that the moon is spinning around the earth as if it was on the end of a cable; being centrifugally flung around like you tie a string around a rock and spin it around your head. But the "cable" was infinitely small. It was invisible. It was a force and the cable wasn't actually there.

He went on and on with his usual things that he went on about over the years: That you don't go up and down, you go in and out, the sun doesn't rise and set, the earth turns towards the sun. So he continued into the early morning hours. We took him to breakfast (which it turned out we had to pay for). We politely said, "Let us pick up your tab." But it turned out we had to—he didn't have any money. He put all of his money into his research.

If you would learn the secrets of nature, you must practice more humanity than others.

Thoreau

47

When I invented and developed my first clear-span, all-weather geodesic dome, the two largest domes in the world were both in Rome and were each about 50 metres in diameter. They are St. Peter's, built around A.D. 1500, and the Pantheon, built around A.D. 1. Each weighs approximately 15,000 tonnes. In contrast, my first 50 metre diameter geodesic all-weather dome installed in Hawaii weighs only 15 tonnes - one-thousandth the weight of its masonry counterpart. An earthquake would tumble both the Roman domes, but would leave the geodesic dome unharmed.

R. Buckminster Fuller, 1983.

Fuller was a very moral man, I thought. He had some of the highest morals I've ever found. But they weren't based on an "-ism" or an arbitrary set of beliefs. He didn't like beliefs because beliefs may or may not have any basis in fact. He insisted that we do not have beliefs, but that we have knowledge, which is a big difference, and that if you go forward on the basis of beliefs you're likely to do something silly or possibly even dangerous.

Most belief systems are built on oversimplifying something that is in fact very complex. One thing I learned from Fuller is that whenever something is simple or whenever anybody harks back to when times were simpler, whenever the term simple is used, usually something very important is being left out. People say, "I really liked cars when they were simple enough to work on." What was left out was the pollution and the safety. That's why they were simple. If they had been safe and pollution free, they wouldn't have been simple at all.

48

Ian McHarg

Fuller's Contribution

He was entirely unpredictable. He was likely to sail off in unexpected directions.

"how did working with buckminster fuller affect you?"

First of all, he was an incredible man. He was, certainly, the most original man I've ever met in my entire life. He was entirely unpredictable. He was likely to sail off in unexpected directions. He was, without a doubt, one of the great monologists. I mean, any man who could talk for four hours, as his audience disappears—he'll probably stop at nothing! He had an unusual capability. His contributions were absolutely enormous. I will make no criticism of the man, because the man's contribution to the world is so large. It really would be unkind to ask him to be more. Unkind.

I would have wished for some other things. For instance, I would have loved dearly if Fuller had been in contact with a good biologist. Because there's no question about it, he really saw the world from the point of view of somebody who is engaged in the physical aspects of the world, and he did fascinating things with these insights. But he never used biological analogs. And there's a big difference, you know, between silicon, which is inert stuff, and life, carbon. There's a big, big difference. He lived in a silicon world all of his life. He never really was able to "get" carbon. This is not a criticism of the man, simply a regret. Because the kind of insights he had could've been vastly expanded had he had a partner, a colleague, somebody, who could've introduced him to the miracle of life.

For me, I am intensely grateful. I had him many, many times as a consultant. He wrote love letters to the Empress of Iran, on my behalf, to follow up on an environmental park in Teheran I was designing. The man was a genius beyond description. I think everything he touched was a gem. It's hard to think that in the late 1930s he designed that little Dymaxion car. It had an engine that was equivalent to a lawn mower, and an incredible efficiency. During which time Detroit was producing these great turgid behemoths. He continued to do this, obdurately, while the British took over, and then the Germans took over, and then the Japanese took over. Of course, all they had to do was listen to Buckminster Fuller, right? They could have learned the lesson right there and then. Lightness and efficiency, that's the clue.

Of course, the fact that he used the sailing ship as the great exemplar for conservation, is another great model. Conservation of energy is only now becoming fashionable. But Fuller's commitment to this idea is fifty years old. You know, in terms of conservation of energy, a combination of inspired hull design and windpower that is absolutely magic.

The Dymaxion house—that one I never liked. Domes or hemispheres seem to me a slight aberration. Now again you see it would have been wonderful if he had been a biologist, because when he was off in his tetrahedrons and his bloody hemispheres, a biologist would've said, "Okay, look. Why don't we forget about this physical analog? Why don't we think about bee hives? Now hexagons are a much better idea. You can't deal with circles. You can't nest circles. There's always an interstitial space. But bee hives are great because you can nest hexagons, right?" What this man could've done with hexagons! They don't produce these terrible spaces—[in domes] you don't know what to do with this area below head level, and you don't know how to do a window in the damned thing.

Again, this is only a small regret. He was a wonderful man. I love his math, his commitment to tensile structures, his addiction to lightness and efficiency, his wonderful idea about an electric grid which goes from Russia all the way down to Alaska, down the Western Seaboard of the United States. Absolutely inspiring. Somebody someday will do it, once we have these low-temperature conductors which virtually don't lose any energy. Maybe then it's going to become possible, and it'll be quite wonderful.

Bucky running circles around the NYPD traffic police in his Dymaxion car.

Paul MacCready

The Inventive Process

In a new area, where you can't do everything by prediction, it's just so important to get out there and make mistakes: have things break, not work, and learn about it early. Then you're able to improve.

"discuss the creative process that led to your inventions."

People in aviation began with nature as a role model. Watching birds, and then trying to duplicate them, with things that even looked like birds. It was the impetus and the idea for getting airplanes going. Once engines arrived, and humans began achieving all sorts of wonderful goals with airplanes, spanning continents and so on, they forgot about birds. Every now and then, after some big aeronautical development, they realize that birds have been doing this for a couple of hundred million years. At the very end, you do realize that nature is one fantastic designer. Not designed by intention, but designed by evolutionary selection.

In a new area, where you can't do everything by prediction, it's just so important to get out there and make mistakes: have things break, not work, and learn about it early. Then you're able to improve them. If your first test in some new area is a success, it is rarely the quickest way to get a [lasting] success, because something will be wrong. It's much better to get quickly to that point where you're doing testing.

You must tailor the technique to the job. Breaking and having something seem like it's going wrong in a development program is not bad. It's just one of the best ways to get information and speed the program along. If you've had nothing but success in a development program, it means that you shot too low, and were too cautious, and that you could've done it in half the time. Pursuing excellence is not often a worthy goal. You should pursue good enough, which, in many cases, requires excellence, but in other cases is quick and dirty. This pursuit of excellence has infected our society. Excellence is not a goal; good enough is a goal. Nature just worries about what is good enough. What succeeds enough to pass the genes down and have progeny.

Paul MaCready flying into
the future on the wings of
his Gossamer aircraft.

Final preparations before the historic launching of the Gossamer Albatross.

Notice the long wing span of this incredibly light aircraft and the proportion to its body which carries one pedaling passenger.

The Gossamer Albatross flies across the English Channel powered solely by human energy—with much help from the ingenuity of its design.

CREATIVE THINKING: GETTING BEYOND OUR MENTAL BLINDERS

One of the most common questions was, why did you guys win the Kramer Prize with this very small team in such a short time, when all these other teams, mostly in England, who were much larger (more people, more resources, more competence, and so on) didn't come close to winning? That question caused me to think a lot. There are several answers that I think are important.

Some of the groups in Germany that were making the world's best sail planes at the time, and obviously had all the technical talent to do it, [didn't win because] the most prestigious professor of aeronautics in Germany would give talks there about why the Kramer

Angels fly because they take themselves lightly.

Anonymous

56

Prize could not be won. I guess they respect their professors there, so nobody tried. In the United States, a professor making a statement like that would have his students probably starting to glue sticks together that very night. That's a much healthier state of affairs. But seriously, that kind of following ideas of authority is important in stifling some creativity. Shouldn't have too much respect for authority.

The biggest reason [that we won], I realized, was that all those teams in England had a very good professional for every aspect of the work. The wing structure was designed by a wing structure designer from the aviation industry. It was done conventionally with spars and ribs, albeit tailored to the needs of human-powered flight. It still was much too heavy, much too complicated, very difficult to repair. The secret weapon I had was an aerodynamics background, but no background in aircraft wing structure. It was easy for me to start out with some old ideas of indoor model airplanes, hang gliders, and end up with the gossamer aircraft. Very quick and lightweight. It was easy for me, but the people in England tended to have blinders. They had so much professional capability in the line, they really didn't see this easy way to do it.

Paul showing the joy of the inventive spirit. Notice the similarity between the cab of the model and the form of the Solar Challenger car.

Now, thank goodness, the airplanes in which I fly are designed by them, and not designed by me, because it takes somebody with a good professional capability in wing design to handle the design requirements for airliners. But this naivete of mine (with a little fundamental engineering background behind it) permitted me to make connections to a very different approach. That realization got me turned on to the whole subject of mental blinders. I began realizing how much I have them, you have them, everybody has them: they're just a characteristic of the human mind.

This whole area was greatly augmented, in my mind, by getting acquainted with Dr. Edward de Bono in England, who has developed a lot of rather ingenious and extremely simple techniques for fostering thinking skills in people. They are based on an understanding of how the human mind has as one of its fundamental characteristics this sort of narrowing, doing things the way you've done them in the past. The way to describe this most succinctly is to think of the mind as a smooth, sandy beach. Just a nice, long, straight beach. An idea, an observation, a thought comes in like a little local rain shower and lands locally, right here, and runs off to the ocean and leaves behind a bunch of ruts in the ground. Then the next observation or thought on that same topic comes in and lands just about the same place or very nearby, but it doesn't start a new erosion pattern because there's already one existing there a little bit lower. There are gullies for the water to run in, so the water runs down those and wears them even deeper. Each new idea just keeps building up on the pattern that was there before, builds up the prejudice, strengthens the filter by which you're going to interpret new information on that same subject. It really is the way the human mind works. That has to do with information coming into the mind, but also it is the same the way we process information. If we walk along the beach, we keep falling in those same ruts. We think we're looking at things broadly, but we're not. We're looking at them on the basis of all our prior thoughts and experiences. Nobody interprets things the same way you do because nobody has had the same background experiences in the same order. So it's a very simple concept of huge importance. When you understand it, it gets to where you understand why, if you were a teenager in the '30s in Germany, you'd have been a good Hitler Youth like all the people there were. If they were over here, they'd be good patriotic Americans. It's not genetic, it's the way our minds work.

Only an inventor knows how to borrow, and every man is or should be an inventor.

Ralph Waldo Emerson

Chapter Two

From
Machines for Living
to Living Machines

*Architecture has devolved into an
exercise which is in supreme
competition with millinery and confectionery.*

Ian McHarg

The rapidly emerging shift
from an emphasis on the fields of
physics and engineering providing the
inspiration for the built world, to the worlds of biology
and ecology as the form generators, eventually will
profoundly alter what gets developed. In addition, it ought to
enhance our capability to design more bountifully with nature. At
least, that is the prospect of ecological design.

In this vein, the trees of planet earth
are a hushed and enduring
witness to the incessant process of human civilization. With the
perspective of ecology, we can begin to see how trees and
civilization are inextricably intertwined. Trees nurture the life of
the soil and offer us multiple building materials for the City. What
do humans do for the trees in exchange?

The current reality is such that, forests
once covered 75% of the planets land area.
The figure is now less than 30%. Tropical forests alone covered
14% of the land, today less than 7%. If man feels that he has the
right to wrought this level of resource plundering, then he at least
ought to be made to think about the consequences of
such actions. For better or worse, it is left
to the designer to find ways of turning
this havoc into delectation. Clearly, we need new metaphors to guide
us into enchanted worlds where Nature, Technology, and Humanity
are in synergetic alignment.

Living Machines represent a pioneering innovation that will create a
major shift in the way the built environment is thought about, forged
and maintained. Rather than constructing dead structures that are
energy sink-holes, we can build living structures that are energy
harvesters. Instead of continuing the cycle of retrogression by
consuming non-renewable energy supplies, buildings can actually
enhance natural evolution and become net exporters of energy,
food, beauty, and intelligence. Of course, these understandings can
and must be applied at the city level as well.

C.Z.

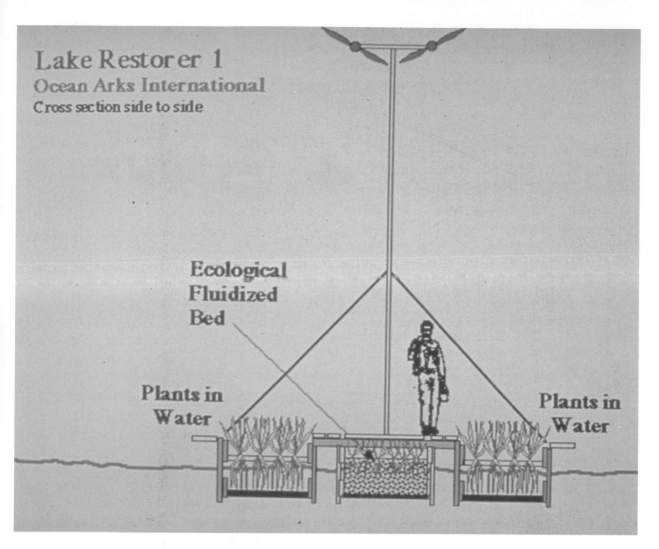

Lake Restorer 1
Ocean Arks International
Cross section side to side

Ecological Fluidized Bed

Plants in Water

Plants in Water

John Todd's Living Machine technology was employed to bio-remediate a "dead" pond in Hartwich, Connecticut. Today people are swimming in a body of water once considered beyond repair.

Ian McHarg

Why Is Architecture Oblivious to the Environment?

Modern architecture is not even remotely modern. It doesn't partake of any significant body of knowledge which has been developed in modern times.

"you wrote the book, design with nature. what does this title mean?"

I'm very pleased with the title [of my book Design with Nature because it really has so many shades of meaning. The first important one is the preposition "with." By and large, almost all architecture since the industrial revolution has been designed without reference to nature. As if the environment, either natural or social, was not consequential. The egos of the artists were the crucial thing, and the signature of the artist was really the most important thing. Reference to the environment as a basis for finding form was not ever involved. It was absolutely categorically rejected in the International Style, where the assumption was that there was a generic architectural solution which was appropriate to all people, in all places, at all times, which of course, has been demonstrated to be inappropriate for all places, and all people, and all times! Design with Nature is our protestation. If you're going to design, design with nature. Nature's been designing so much longer than man. The idea that we can invent it is a kind of maniacal delusion.

"what are your thoughts on the state of architecture today?"

I suppose we've got to consider the subject of architecture. I've been teaching at this university for thirty-seven years. I am a—what's the word—well, I speak loudly, and with a good deal of conviction! I will say, of all my failures, my greatest failure has been at the University of Pennsylvania where, after thirty-seven years of very noisy and assertive teaching, I have had absolutely no effect on architecture whatsoever. I've spoken at most architecture schools in the United States with, I would say, virtually no effect. Moreover, my book, which was described by the American Collegiate Schools of Architecture as one of the most widely read textbooks in architecture, has, to the best of my knowledge, had no effect whatsoever. So there's a sadness about this.

Now why is architecture so oblivious to the environment? Why do no architecture schools require any students, ever, to learn anything about the environment, either natural or social? I think that an architect, really, fundamentally, is a prima donna, and that intelligence is not really thought to be an important attribute in the process of creating buildings and places. This is thought to occur by drawing interminably, preferably late at night, in an advanced state of exhaustion, on yellow paper. It's believed that this will produce some creative experience. I've often said that perhaps, architecture could be most effective by a frontal lobotomy. If the brain is not really used, then it should be removed as an impediment.

Formal intelligence about the natural environment, the social environment, is not a part of the curriculum of architecture. Of course it's not a part of the practice of architecture. Architecture has devolved into an exercise which is in supreme competition with millinery and confectionery. At best it's simply, obviously, a cosmetic addition. A sort of wallpaper on the surface which is subject only to style. But at worst, I think it's probably more properly described as fixing a smile on a cadaver. Anyway, it's certainly not serious. The word "modern," which is used for modern physics, modern chemistry, modern biology, is erroneously used in modern architecture. Modern architecture is not even remotely modern. It doesn't partake of any significant body of knowledge which has been developed in modern times.

THE QUEST FOR MODERN ARCHITECTURE

I think the remedy is very, very simple. People should be required to know what they're doing before they do it. They should know the implications of their contemplated acts. If you go into work in the physical world, you should well know about physical processes, in terms of the environment, geology, hydrology, meteorology, and so on. You're living in the biological world, so somebody's got to know about the plants, and the animals, and the microorganisms, because they're a very, very complex interacting system, and you can disturb them to a great detriment (not only to them, but to yourself).

I'd require students to be able to understand something about

how do we correct this obliviousness?

63

physics, physical processes, physical environment. Along with biological processes, the biological environment. Something about social processes, the social environment. Then the next step is far and away the most difficult one. It's not enough simply to know what the environment says. It's more important to understand what the implications are of building in some environments. Some environments are very tolerant. Some environments are incredibly intolerant. One should be able to distinguish this. Some environments are suitable for one purpose, but not suitable for other purposes. The discrimination to know which, that's an important skill.

By far and away, the most important task is to have an appropriate expression of adaptations. We mentioned this before. I mean, if you go to a pueblo you know perfectly well you're in an arid environment. You know something about the culture, too. The building expresses this. It would seem to me there should be an expression which is appropriate to the place, both in terms of materials and in terms of forms.

The quest for modern architecture, it seems to me, should have two parts. People have been engaged in architecture for thousands and thousands of years, and a very large number of very intelligent and very passionate people have engaged in this thing, so there must be a lesson to be learned. When I went to Harvard, Walter Gropius insisted that modern architects do not study historic architecture until their last year, lest they become corrupted. Can you believe this? In every other science you observe all the insights of previous years, right? Of generations, of centuries, which are continuously corrected and so on. That body of knowledge—if there's something learned and time passes and if it still holds true today—by all means, learn it today.

I must study politics and war that my sons may have the liberty to study mathematics and philosophy. My sons ought to study mathematics and philosophy, geography, natural history, naval architecture, navigation, commerce, and agriculture, in order to give their children a right to study painting, poetry, music, architecture, statuary, tapestry, and porcelain.

John Adams in a letter to Abigal Adams

That's not true in architecture. It would seem to me there are two great realms, or three, perhaps. One is to understand physical and biological systems. The other is to identify the appropriateness of adaptations which have been accomplished in historic times, and so on. Then the third is to identify from these historic times that there were many problems not solved and many technologies which were not available, and there should be a possibility of our improving on all of these.

The beginning of a modern architecture, and appropriate architecture, and landscape architecture, and planning, I think, should have to engage people who know about the land: how it came to be, how it works, what the implications upon that land are of making any adaptation, being able to discriminate about where are appropriate places, and most of all, being able to find appropriate locations and appropriate form.

The next one, of course, is the invocation of a grand design: God's Grand Design, which evolution represents. Of course, the final part of it is an imperative: Design with nature. I am a censorious Presbyterian. I like this imperative thing: You bastards! Design with nature, or else I'll grind you up for dog food!

RESPONDING TO THE ENVIRONMENT

The question is, did man historically design with nature? Of course the answer is yes! They had to understand nature for their survival. Ethnographers who study primitive societies today realize they've got to understand the environment to understand the culture, its language, its religion, its ethics, its art. All the stuff that ethnographers and anthropologists have done around the world is very, very clear testimony these peoples are, in fact, specific adaptations of specific environments. Which is visible, again, in their religions, and their art, and their economy, and their language, and their foodstuff. The

The long road from the Amazon to urban jungle.

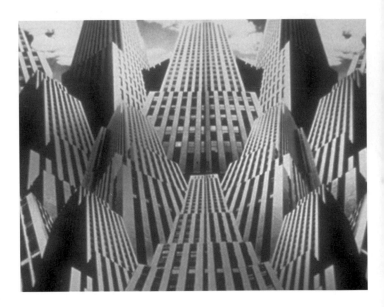

The German Expressionist inspired vision of a city devoid of human scale or meaning is presented in this still from Fritz Lang's Metropolis. In many of our urban centers we can see the truth in this prediction of an architecture without soul or genius of place.

whole damned thing. This immediacy of the environment and the person has been lost in the Western culture. It's been lost not only physically, it's also been lost intellectually. Yet if one wants to be serious about it, the problem has not changed. The problem of design really does require that we do understand the environment. What it is. What it can permit. Which areas are suitable for what. Which areas are unsuitable.

There should be a response of adaptation, a response of design. Of course this was true in the whole world until the advent of the Industrial Revolution. People didn't know any other way of doing it. A simple little boy like me, with a book called The Book of the British Empire, which I got on my fourteenth birthday, could turn the pages, and I didn't have to look at the captions to realize I was in China, or Malaysia, or seeing Australian Aboriginals, or Eskimos. It was not only people. It was a conjunction of the people, the buildings, the forms of plants, and the animals, the whole. All of these things spoke about adaptation to specific environment. The environments were characteristic, and they were absolutely different.

Then along comes the bloody International Style and says the same stupid stencil is coequally suitable for everyone, everywhere. So that everywhere, whether Reykjavík, or Glasgow, or Hong Kong, or Singapore, or New York, they have the same stupid, bloody buildings made, obviously, for termites or lobotomized human beings. Why? Because of their abstractions. They've got nothing to do with human physiology, human psychology, and certainly nothing to do with geology, hydrology, rocks, salts, plants, or animals!

Taos Pueblo, New Mexico.

How can a tradition which has lasted for the whole history of man be so quickly abandoned? Well, it has been! The question is, can we retrieve it? I don't know whether we can or cannot. Should we retrieve it? Of course.

All the plants and all the animals are specific to their environment, so when you invoke an environment, the plants and animals spring to mind. I say prairie. You see the short and the long grasses—that's right—and you see the buffalo, and so on. I say desert, right? And I suddenly see all the sand, and you see the scrubby thing, and you see the nocturnal animals. I say tundra, and we've got reindeer, and we've got mosses, and lichen, and so on. In every single case, you identify arctic, tundra, taiga, burrow, forest, savannah, short grass prairie, long grass prairie, tropical rain forest, every single one of these. When you make a statement about the environment, you already see, in your mind's eye, the plants, the animals that comprise it, right? They're exquisitely fit. They're appropriate.

So should the works of man be. Why shouldn't the work of men be as appropriate? If I were dropped from a plane by night (and I was a parachutist, once upon a time) then, as the dawn lifted and I had to find out where the hell I was and identify it, there's only one place in the United States where I could do it infallibly. That's the pueblo. If I found myself somewhere in New Mexico, in Zuni [pueblo], or Acoma, and saw these thick walls, and small apertures, and flat roofs, I would know that I'm in a desert environment.

The oldest continually inhabited building in America.
Nine hundred years being the Taos Pueblo.

All work passes out
of the hands of the
architect into the hands
of nature to be perfected.

Henry David Thoreau

James Wines

A concern for the earth, is certainly the iconography of the future.

"can you illuminate for us the nature of the shift taking place in the architecture world?"

Well, basically the century began with architects being inspired by an emerging age of industry and technology. I mean, everybody wanted a building to somehow function like a combustion engine. As an inspirational force in 1910 one can understand it, but as a continuing inspiration in our post industrial world of information and ecology it doesn't make sense anymore. That's basically one of the problems. I think most people are relatively unmoved by architecture. The most common complaint from just about everybody is, you know, I never noticed a building or I never noticed architecture.

In that sense it's the least charismatic of the arts. You know within its own circle of professionalism there's obviously a dialogue and there's obviously a lot going on that seems very important, but it hasn't spread out into the rest of the world. I think the reason for that is the imagery. The dominant imagery is pretty irrelevant. I think you know the average person senses when something's had it and you know without really knowing. You don't have to be particularly knowledgeable about architecture to understand that something is incredibly irrelevant about buildings that still look like they were designed in 1910 or 1930. You know you have dominant influences, modernism for one, constructivism for another, cubism; these were all dynamic movements ninety years ago or eighty years ago, but they certainly are not anymore.

For some reason architecture has remained the most regressive of all the arts. So my feeling is that it's time for a change. Basically its got to change from the bottom up.

It just means throwing out all the old baggage. You know you go to an

AIA conference, like Chicago's recently, and you realize how much baggage is still around, that probably eighty to ninety percent of the architects who are practicing are still drawing on sources from early modernism or early constructivism. This is all very well, I mean everybody has traditions that they draw on. Every artist looks at some other epoch, some other decade.

But the difference is whether you're enslaved by it or whether you are in fact expanding towards the future. So I think that's the basic issue that involves me is: how do you go on to the next step?

If machines influenced the first half of the century, then clearly a concern for the earth and a response to this incredible global network of information is certainly the iconography of the future.

I have ascertained by full enquiry that Utopia lies outside the bounds of the known world.

Kaspar

Ed Bacon

Nature As Design Paradigm

Everything I work at in the city I see not only in terms of its own shape, which is organic (and not artificial geometry), but also as the setting into motion of a force, a directional force which will extend indefinitely outward on its own initiative and which really has no termination.

"what is the role of the designer?"

Bucky was very conscious, as I am, of the role of the designer in the deepest sense of the word. I find it very sad that this idea is almost gone from the face of the earth. A true designer, even though he or she is asked to work with a tiny spot of earth, sees it as part of the total system and sees it as part of all history. By working to make it alive and vital, he or she contributes to the strengthening of the larger environment. There is so much of education that is based on analysis. Actually, no idea ever came out of analysis at all, and I find it quite tragic. I think that a true designer, who has the faculty and the ability to make a beautiful structure, or a beautiful garden, or a beautiful section of the city, becomes able to leverage this energy, to set up a force which radiates outward.

I think that Bucky understood that. My great teacher Eero Saarinen at Cranbrook Academy also understood this very well. As this happens in different parts of the world, you really can get a force with geographical roots in different countries, different cultures, different economic and social systems. Together they can begin to extend outward, in a series of forces which may look quite modest to begin with, but will really be a very significant new direction in the way we treat our universe and ourselves.

All thought is done by paradigms and Bucky and I agree deeply that nature is the source of the best paradigms. Then come two questions: What aspects of nature do you use as a paradigm? Secondly, what are the consequences of choosing that particular aspect? I spoke about Bucky's preoccupation with the pure geometrical relationships of tetrahedrons, and spheres, and pyramids, and so forth. It doesn't work to try to transfer these as forms for living objects because no living objects, at all, are shaped in accordance with cubes, or spheres, or tetrahedrons, or any other artificial geometrical construct you can speak of.

There's another issue beyond just the question of the shape, and that's the question of the forces which the object unleashes. A cube, a tetrahedron, a pyramid, and particularly a sphere—[each] is a completely self-contained object unto itself. It's complete, total, and resolved, and it has no outward thrust. My teacher, Eero Saarinen, talked about a tree. He says the form of the tree is determined by the inner action of two forces. There is the impulse in the seed to expand, and expand, and expand, and if this were unchecked, a single seed for a tree would produce an object that would expand and fill the whole universe. But there is another force, which is the necessity of correlating the nutrients for the tree from the outermost roots in the earth up through the trunk and to the outermost branches. The form of the tree is the point of equilibrium between these two forces, the urge to expand and the requirement of correlation. This is an entirely different view of a tree, [different] than thinking of a tree as a cylindrical trunk and a sphere, or a cone. It's the thing that's influenced my life the most. Everything I work at in the city I see not only in terms of its own shape, which is organic (and not artificial geometry), but also as the setting into motion of a force, a directional force which will extend indefinitely outward on its own initiative and which really has no termination. It is capable of extending itself on and on and on to the indefinite future and producing a spin-off and consequences which are really unforeseen at the beginning.

This gives a whole different approach to what a designer does. I think it is very well illustrated in the work [Post Petroleum City], In which my thought is not to tell the cities how they should plan to work without petroleum, but rather to set in motion the force [to bring that about] by raising the question in a way that motivates their participation. Then the force is a real projection into the future, from the series of geometrical points that will move outward, to consequences, which, I think, will be very constructive and which cannot be foreseen at the present moment.

I come from a long line of Quakers. I am perhaps the 8th or 9th

Always design a thing by considering it in its largest context, a chair in a room, a room in a house, a house in an environment, an environment in a city plan.

Eero Saarinen
1958

"The quaker's have a particular understanding of man's relationship to the universe. how has this affected your role as a city planner?"

generation in Philadelphia. My ancestor, Henry Comley, came over in 1862 and bought five hundred acres for a farm in Bucks County. The Quakers believe in the direct connection between the individual and God without the need for a priesthood or other form of intermediary. We each have in us what the Quakers refer to as the still, small voice. This is God speaking directly to us. Many Quakers use this concept as a very convenient device for keeping their children in line by making them feel guilty for not following the parent's opinions of right and wrong. But for myself, I probably acquired a sense of my own entity to an extraordinary degree.

At present, I have no allegiance to any institution. Also, the fact that I haven't any money is fine because I don't have to bother with it. This provides me with a freedom of movement and freedom of thought which is a luxury many people don't have.

I think, in this regard, I was very close to Bucky Fuller. Out of it came the idea that when I planned Philadelphia, which was my preoccupation for the greatest part of my career, it was my job to create internally formulated images, or visions, of what I thought the city ought to be, and to communicate these to the community at large. I did find as I worked with it that, in fact, I did have hold of a very important way to get things done, which was the power of the idea. Really, most of my career in Philadelphia was the systematic transmission to the community at large—the collective unconscious of the community— images of the way the city could be that had never existed before. This, of course, is exactly contrary to much of the education now, which is that you must do research about what people already want as a basis for your design. I reject that completely and say that's simply a system for assuring that nothing good or worthwhile happens.

I found that this concept of the power of the idea worked very well in Philadelphia. However, it required extremely intensive effort over about a forty-year period, and it worked only because I made the commitment in 1939 that, come hell or high water, I would devote every energy I had in my own life's blood to try and make this tiny piece of geography as fine as I could manage. Now, in my eightieth year, I find it interesting that I am indeed moving into a kind of a global village viewpoint and that my work on the post-petroleum city is extending out to cover nations throughout the world. It will be, really, I think, a sudden jump from this extreme concentration on a tiny, defined piece of geography to seeing the network of cities throughout the world working together through their own concern—which I'm bringing to their attention—of how they will operate when we no longer can use petroleum for transportation.

©Thomas Slagle

Civilization is the process of reducing the infinite to the finite.

Oliver Wendell Holmes

Stewart Brand

Sitting at the Counterculture

The main connection—and you see this in the whole skein of the Whole Earth Catalogs—is there between Buckminster Fuller and Gregory Bateson.

"what can you tell us about the driving forces behind the creation of the whole earth catalog?"

The Whole Earth Catalog was, I suppose, three things. It was an antidote to college, it was an antidote to the counterculture, and it was set up partly as a tool for the intentional communities that were cranking up at that time, both within the counterculture and against college. So it sort of blended in with what fairly young creative people were doing at the time to try to fill in the gaps. In my case it meant that I could work on the communes without actually having to live on one.

It's certainly the case that the original Whole Earth Catalog was very much the intellectual child of Buckminster Fuller, and many people who were attracted to him were attracted to what we were up to. Having people like J. Baldwin around—who was in many ways Fuller's closest disciple—made [the catalog] grow. And we participated in Steve Bears's conference in New Mexico, called [Alloy], which was completely a gathering of outlaw designers.

The Whole Earth Catalog took a definitely countercountercultural relationship to technology. Right from the beginning, technology was seen as the enemy by a lot of the counterculture, and so the underground went out of their way to remain ignorant about it. We went directly against that and went not only out of our way to become smart about technology but to take over the control of it and invent our own. In a sense, the group of the counterculture period of the '60s that was most consistent with what we were doing—we didn't even know about them at the time—were the hackers at MIT and places like that, were inventing what became personal computers. They were absolutely invisible in that decade. Later, we connected with them and have [stayed connected] ever since. So we just partly came with the notion of access to tools. Technology was just seen as a tool, not as a threat.

The main connection—and you see this in the whole skein of Whole Earth Catalogs—is there between Buckminster Fuller and Gregory Bateson. Both of them talked about understanding whole systems. Bucky's approach was a very material approach and gained a lot from being rigorous that way, and Bateson's approach was equally rigorous but much more philosophical, cognitive, aesthetic, a number of things that Fuller would probably deny the significance of. The combination was, I think, pretty strong. Over time, I find I keep learning new things from Gregory Bateson, even though he's been dead for a while. Bucky Fuller I got a great deal from, but I don't keep getting new things from him, for whatever that's worth.

One of Gregory Bateson's great stories was about the oak beams of New College, Oxford. He suggests that the beams, when they were replaced in the 1980s, were from trees that had been planted many hundreds of years before with the expectation that those beams would have to be replaced one day. So one carefully took care of the trees that would serve that function centuries later. He says that's the way to run a culture.

And that's very much what my book [How Buildings Learn] is about: moving design, especially building design, away from ignoring time to employing time as a tool. That's, in a sense, what I'm going at now, I suppose—redesigning the field of building design, because I think the whole set of professions that serve buildings are in a very bad fit with the way the world actually works right now. Especially the way it can work responsibly at buildings really being useful, and getting better and better from decade to decade and century to century.

People keep telling me I should be embarrassed about [having said] "We are as gods and might as well get good at it. so far, power and glory via government, big business, formal education, and the church have succeeded to the point where gross defects obscure actual gains. In response to this dilemma and to these gains, a realm of intimate personal power is developing, the power of indi-

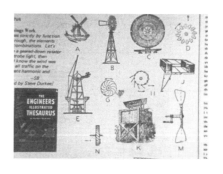

Cover and pages from the Whole Earth Catalogue.

viduals to conduct their own education, find their own inspiration, shape their own environment, and share the adventure with whoever is interested. Tools that aid this process are sought and promoted by the Whole Earth Catalog.

Whole Systems

Buckminster Fuller

The insights of Buckminster Fuller initiated this Catalog.

Among his books listed here, his most recent is probably the best introduction—it's a succint summary of what's been on his mind for many a year and what's on his mind now: how mankind may hatch and survive the hatching. An Operating Manual for Spaceship Earth.

Of the other, larger, books, Nine Chains to the Moon *is his earliest and most openly metaphysical,* The Unfinished Epic of Industrialization *the most beautiful,* Ideas and Integrities *his most personal,* No More Secondhand God *the most generalized,* World Design Science Decade *(co-authored with John McHale) the most programmatic.*

J. Baldwin

Into the Design Revolution

Here was a pattern that made some sense, that had some structural integrity. The time was right.

"In what ways did buckminster fuller influence the 1960's?"

In the '60s, Bucky clearly thought—and said right straight out without any metaphors or fooling around—that the young people who were aware of social injustice, who were aware of the needs of humanity, and who were aware of environmental degradation, and so forth, in a way that their parents had not been, were the hope of the world. He deplored drugs pretty much because he thought that they would deflect people from doing the homework that they should do and that the weak ones would get sucked into [drugs] and drown. But that's Darwin's law, and the '60s were not a time for weak kids. A lot of people got hurt. But a lot of people didn't get hurt and Fuller rightly thought that the young people were going to be what made the difference and in the future make things better, and he said so.

In one of his best addresses, on what got to be known as Hippie

An exuberant J. Baldwin bursting thru the roof of a geodesic creation into the design revolution.

Hill in Golden Gate Park, he gave an address extemporaneously to a couple of thousand long-haired boys and girls, telling them what their responsibilities were and that the ball was theirs to carry. He was very popular at that time. I've heard it said the Beatle's song "Fool on the Hill" was referring to him, and that was the lecture it was referring to. I've heard that from enough places now that I think it's probably true.

Anyway, one of the effects that he had on the kids was that he got them interested in building geodesic stuff. It was one way to answer the problem that you had when you heard Fuller, when you picked up on what he was saying, but didn't know what to do the next day. Well, in the '60s you could build a geodesic dome, and this appealed to people who were going back to the land, who were living on beaches, who were living in state parks and on BLM [Bureau of Land Management] land, and all the places it was illegal to live. I was teaching at San Francisco State at the time, and I had kids building geodesic domes there. It went with the interest in Eastern mysticism and so forth: there were patterns that had significance other than the mere whim of the architect-as-artist.

Here was a pattern that made some sense, that had some structural integrity. The time was right. People heard that. What they didn't hear, and Fuller didn't bring it up because he really didn't know what to do about it, was that it is very difficult to build a geodesic dome that does not leak, unless you really think it out. Fuller said the way you should think about it is as if you were

J. Baldwin's protoype for the Pillow Dome.

81

building a boat, only the other side up. You wouldn't build a boat deliberately full of leaks, so don't build a dome deliberately full of leaks. Easier said than done. This led, eventually, to a lot of frustration. A lot of geodesic domes got built, and most of them are gone now because they were awful and they leaked like sieves and you couldn't live in them. Nobody can tolerate a wet bed more than a couple of nights. To get around that, I and a couple of other people tried to make domes that wouldn't leak. Some were successful, and some weren't. But it was determined in the '60s how to make domes that didn't leak, out of a variety of materials (including plywood, which I don't happen to like very much).

THE DUTY OF INVENTORS

After you discover what sort of human is being tried by your genetic make-up, you should drive that human just as far as you can to see what it's good for. I think that is our responsibility. Also, I think it is the responsibility of people acting as designers to carry out their ideas all the way to the point of living in them. You don't go home at Five O'clock. You live in what you are doing which is a kind of ultimate proof.... you don't hire someone else to do your living for you. It is not a simulation. You are actually doing the deed yourself. So, you become the world's expert on whatever it is you are doing. You look around you and can say there is nobody you can ask for advice - and then you know you are doing O.K.

R. Buckminster Fuller opening the door to the first Pillow Dome. This prototype shelter provides for the inhabitants energy, waste treatment, and food production.

Fuller was very duty driven. He said humankind, up until now, was like the nestling that had just pecked its way out of the egg and had turned around and had eaten the remnants of the yoke. After that, the mother brought it food. Then it was on its own. He said the fossil fuel reserves of the earth which are being rapidly depleted are our mother feeding us and pretty soon we're going to be on our own and we're going to have to live by our wits. He considered burning coal, and oil, and so forth the same thing, as if Ford made cars by tearing the factory apart and melting it down to make the fenders. You can't keep doing that very long. He was against nuclear energy, too. He said that's also using part of the earth. Using the earth's income and the natural cycles, the ebb and flow of energy (which would include gravity), the earth's rotation, weather systems, sunlight, that sort of thing is the smart way to do it—and Fuller felt that if we didn't smarten up, we were doomed.

He rarely used the term God directly. He said Universe—with a capital U. Universe is trying to see if the way of balancing entropy is through human beings' intellect. To be good human beings, we have to do our best. To not do your best—when you know you're not doing your best is the definition of sin. He said that right straight out: "This is what sin is: doing badly when you know how to do better." He made quite a point of that. When he saw people doing badly, he got pretty upset. When you were a student around him, the one thing he couldn't stand was laziness. He just really wouldn't tolerate it. You didn't have to be physically in action, whizzing around making it look like you were working, but, as he said: "Good hardware is one of the few irrefutable

Freedom of will is the ability to do gladly that which I must do.
Carl Jung

J. B. directing the building of the Pillow Dome.

> *Initiative springs only from the individual. Initiative can neither be created nor delegated. It can only be vacated. Initiative can only be taken by the individual on his own self-conviction of the necessity to overcome his conditioned reflexing which has accustomed him theretofore to always yield authority to the wisdom of others. Initiative is only innate and highly perishable.*
> R. Buckminster Fuller

"how does this viewpoint affect the way one should go about designing?"

proofs of clear thinking."

Bucky thought there were several ways you could spend your life. One way he referred to as plugging leaks and leak pluggers. An example of leak plugging is what I call the drunk-in-the-gutter syndrome. This is where you pick up a drunk, bring him home, clean him up, dry him out, dress him, get him a job and they say, "Golly, thanks, all I needed was a good boost. Then you go out and and there's another drunk. There's an endless supply of drunks... you'll never run out of them. Fuller tended to go for what is causing the drunks; the way society was being run. Was society being run in that way because it was being run from the standpoint that there wasn't enough to go around and somebody was going to lose and not get their share because there wasn't enough for everybody to have a share. He thought there was nothing wrong with leak plugging. It requires some innovation, but the problem is usually very well defined locally; there is this person lying in the gutter that we have to deal with or he will freeze to death tonight.

Fuller was more interested in looking at the big picture. One of the great pieces of luck was the occurrence of the computer in his lifetime. It enables you to look at the big picture in a way that no other means allows. He came to many of his conclusions before there were computers. He did it intuitively which is one mark of what I call his genius. He tended to look at the macro pictures. When he said shelter, he meant that approximately thirty percent of humanity on any given night does not have the shelter they need just for health purposes, let alone luxury. That's a lot of people.

Inside the gardenscape of the Pillow-Dome.

The Pillow-Dome in its full glory, Falmouth, Mass.

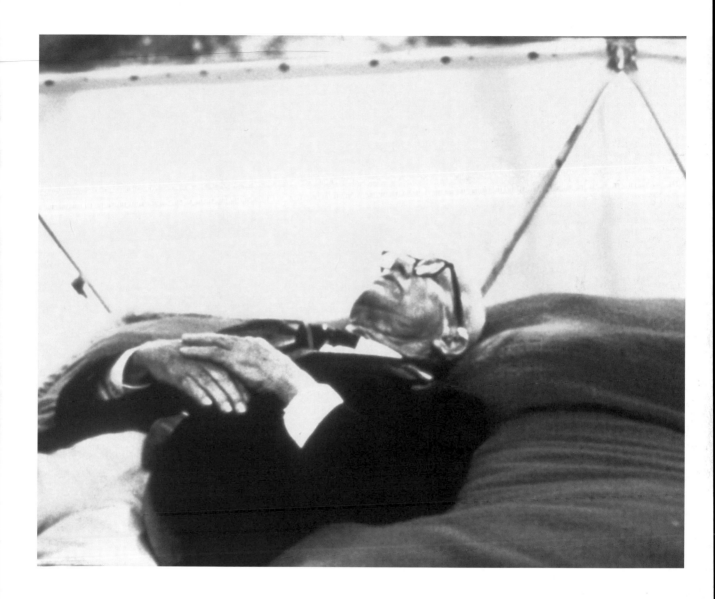

We live not only our lives but, whether
we know it or not, also
the life of our time.

Laurens Van der Post

Tony Gwilliam

Organic Building

We're very enamored of buildings that have all this history built into them . . . they put us in connection with ourselves in the past and other people in the past and tell us about our continuity.

A building is like an organism because it has a life and changes over its life. It has real life. It's created, to start with, from nonmolecular elements and energetic repatterning of components. We can either build very simply from the earth itself, or from cutting down trees, or from cutting up rocks, or we can build with a very high degree of technology, by having very, very thin skins with one-layer-thick membranes to reflect or deflect energy.

> "how is a building similar to a living organism?"

Basically, buildings are an extension of ourselves and will change according to our needs. This is the same with any tool that we make—[it] is an extension of ourselves, and should be, and should evolve according to our needs. If you look at a historic building, you can see that it changes over many, many centuries, so we're very enamored of buildings that have all this history built into them so they've got a sort of memory, and consciousness, and skeleton from different times, and so they put us in connection with ourselves in the past, and other people in the past, and tell us about our continuity.

Within our time, at the moment, when we're living very fast in a time of very fast transformation, the building itself has to change and transform. Even the plans of buildings—I mean kitchens, and bathrooms, and dining rooms—the plans of buildings are changing today. The whole concept of co-housing is coming in, where we've got old folks and young folks [living together]. Who looks after the children? What is our work? Is our work coming back into the home, and what is our education? Is our education going to come back into the home, or is it going out? Are we going to push it into boxes called schools?

A lot of this stuff is changing very rapidly, so any of the buildings we do today have to be very capable of modification, of self-

Organic Architecture in the Amazon

monitoring to change themselves. So I've been looking a lot at the "DNA" of a building or a city, so the thing is considered live, so the building has this capacity to be live, the same as we now consider the earth as a live organism, [as in] the Gaian hypothesis by Lovelock. Why shouldn't we also consider the industry and the systems that we have created life systems? This gets very exciting, because it's really getting back into bioengineering. Because we can actually create living systems, can mankind become a god in a way and create living systems? That's what I've been studying more about, more about the total system: where we come from, the big bang, the universe as a whole. One of Fuller's things was that we are monitors for the universe, so we need to understand about system. We now are starting to understand globally, interplanetarily, about the whole system of interactions, and we can't isolate out. We can't just look at little bits and say that by understanding a bit that we're going to resolve the whole, so we're being forced by the problems we've created to look at the whole, the whole thing, again.

So if we're looking at the case of a city, we can't have architects designing the architecture, the planners deciding this, the industry people coming in and zoning for this. It's an integrated thing, the same as the human body. Every system is interrelated with every other system, so we have to plan and look at how things are integrated. So the way the water that comes into the house is collected and used and purified, and [the way it] goes out of the house again and is reused is part of our living system. We can't just take stuff and dump it back onto the land, the planet: there's nowhere to dump it. It's still part of that continuity, a continuing cycle. So we have to be in balance all the way through. Designing anything, we have to, consider all those systems.

Lovelock calls this imaginative perception of planetary dynamics "Gaia," and what Gaia is, is certainly not simply an object, a mere chunk of rock in the void of black Newtonian space; Gaia is the phase-space of our planet, and a phase-portrait of the geometry of its behavior would not produce the familiar billiard ball, but a complex topology of permeable membranes between the solar wind and the Van Allen belts. In the words of Lewis Thomas, what the Earth would look like in this new imagination would be a living cell.

William Irwin Thompson

©Thomas Slagle

Mary Catherine Bateson

Understanding Natural Systems

We're coming out of a period when the subtext of design was design against nature, design that was creating environments that were different from nature.

> "how can the tools and language of ecology provide better metaphors for re-shaping the world?"

We're not going to solve our ecological problems today unless we really bear in mind that human beings have been designing and redesigning their patterns of adaptation throughout all human history. That's why they're so different from place to place. We're the species that invents new ways of living in new environments. Now we're coming out of a period when the subtext of design was design against nature, design that was creating environments that were different from nature. I believe that with the shift from an emphasis on physics and engineering providing our metaphors to a period when biology is the area that's really popping scientifically, we're moving into an area where we will be learning to design with nature. But all human patterns of adaptation are designed not so much by individuals as by communities that refine and adapt their patterns over long periods of time. But now we do it faster.

When we think about design, we tend to think about material things: machines, automobiles, houses, highway systems. But you can apply the concept of design to social arrangements, social institutions, educational systems, economic systems. We're going to have to design new patterns at all of those levels, and they have to fit together. Our machines, our value systems, our educational systems will all have to be informed by this switch, from the machine age when we tried to design schools to be like factories, to an ecological age, when we want to design schools, and families, and social institutions in terms of maintaining the quality of life not just for our species, but for the whole planet.

There's a saying that any plant that's growing where you don't want it is a weed. Where you want it, it represents wealth. Where you don't want it, it not only doesn't represent wealth, it's a weed, it's a pest. What that really says is that the shift from something you can use and value to something you regard as valueless or as an impediment is, above all, a cognitive shift. You have to learn to value this plant, you have to learn to use it. You have to understand how it fits in, in an interdependent ecological system, offering a benefit. So the critical step in creating wealth is a shift in understanding, and we have to make that shift in our understanding of natural systems. This is a larger application of some of the very specific things that are being said today about the wealth that will be lost if the rainforests are cut down, about the loss of species, about the loss of wetlands. The more we understand the integration of the natural world, the more we're able to look around us and feel rich.

If, however, humanity prepares for this marriage of heaven
and Earth not through systems of technological domination,
but through forms of cooperation in what John Todd calls
"living machines,"—by reuniting itself with the elemental (bacterial)
and angelic (mathematical) domains—then civilized religion
with its priesthood and priestcraft will no longer
be needed, and life will become the spirituality of
the ordinary and everyday cosmic life.

William Irwin Thompson

William McDonough

Not a Machine for Living In—A Living Machine!

What we really need to be doing is saying not that a house is a machine for living in, but [that] it is a living machine, and that it has distant effects as well as local ones.

"In what manner is the design profession enduring?"

I think design, as a fundamental indication of human intention, is adjusting itself to our understanding of real intention. When we look at the objects of design we can see, for example, the notion of Emerson leaving for Europe on a sailboat and returning on a steamship. When you abstract that concept, you realize that he went over on a solar-powered vehicle made of recyclable materials operated by craftspeople practicing ancient arts in the open air, and he returned on a steel rustbucket putting oil slicks on the water and smoke into the sky operated by people working in the dark shoving fossil fuels into the face of a boiler. So as a fundamental issue, we're looking at designed objects and if design is the indication of human intention, what does that steamship imply as our intention?

Since these are designed objects, what is the future of design if it is to recognize the distant effects that are now being recognized, in terms of environment, in terms of ecology, in terms of natural resources?

So we have a strange new problem, which is actually an ancient problem: How do we work efficiently and effectively in a place without destroying it in the very process of living there? I like the model of a boat for Thoreau. It begs all sorts of interesting questions, because Thoreau didn't like to travel that much, didn't feel that he needed to, and when asked why he didn't travel, responded that he'd traveled much in Concord. The notion of working very closely with your place and recognizing distant effects is fundamental to a new design paradigm.

If we look at how we got here, in terms of architecture, for example, we recognize that the ancient art of architecture had the modeling of, essentially, the putty of the earth, the clay, and the fabric, the bedouin tent, the mud hut. When you add, at the beginning of this century, the large sheet of glass and cheap energy, you find people like Le Corbusier saying things like "a house is a machine for living in," and glorifying this new age of technology with the steamship, the airplane, the grain elevator, and saying these are the models.

What we've now discovered is that if we glorify the object itself, before we understand real human need and real natural need, we could find ourselves running off in a direction that is not propitious on the larger scale. What we really need to be doing is saying not that a house is a machine for living in, but it is a living machine, and that it has distant effects as well as local ones. So that shift is the fundamental shift that has to occur, and it involves understanding very simple principles, such as the notion that waste must equal food. This shift must model itself on natural systems, where there is no such thing as waste, except species waste. We have to protect biodiversity. . . and we have to utilize natural energy flows.

The early modernists were still attuned to some of these issues, but, unfortunately, things got simplified and engineering methodology maintained, essentially, a linear system, one very simple in ecological terms, for example, or evolutionary terms. . . . Now we're going to be shifting over to much more complex systems and understanding their reactions, and then pulling together design methodologies that deal with making things based on these fundamental kinds of principles.

The process of thought that occurs after you have a revelation—such as the one that a building should be a living machine—is essentially a large shift in the process of design, away from a linear 1-2-3 kind of system into one that's highly complex and that recognizes complexity. At the same time, it understands distant and local effects. So, for example, in the largest context it means that you broaden your reach from, say chemistry and physics, with its implied mechanics, to biology. That is a major difference.

Early models of the Gap Corporate Campus, San Bruno, California

No more petroleum based products on our roofs.

Chapter Three

The Intelligent use of Energy

*We confuse ourselves into thinking that we are
producing oil, when what we are really doing is digging it up and
burning it.*

Amory Lovins

❋ ❋ ❋ ❋ ❋ ❋ ❋ ❋ ❋ ❋ ❋ ❋ ❋ ❋ ❋ ❋ ❋ ❋ ❋ ❋

According to the March 1998 Scientific American, within the next decade, the supply of conventional oil will be unable to keep up with demand. Consequently, the era of design driven by cheap energy is officially over. We can no longer design structures that further our dependence on foreign sources of energy. Given the current reality that the built environment is responsible for fully two-thirds of our energy demand; this metaphorical shift from a physics and engineering driven conception of a building as a Machine for Living in—- to a biological and ecological conception of a building as a Living Machine is one the keys to the realm of the muses, as mythologist Joseph Campbell called acts of the imagination, that will assist in the building of a compassionate Architecture for the 21st Century.

In contrast, making money with money independent of producing goods and services that provide actual life support has become a bizarre aspect of our current economic system. In the global currency markets, $800 billion to $21 trillion changes hands each day, unrelated to productive investment or trade in actual goods and services. Bureaucrats policing bureaucrats. What is worth doing with our brief time aboard this spinning planet? As Buckminster Fuller said in many different ways we live in a regenerative scenario Universe where real wealth is knowing what to do with our intellectual and physical energy. This highly discriminating form of knowledge has its metaphorical root in the art of gardening that knows a weed from a flower, and product design that knows a finely crafted product from a mass produced toxic avenger.

Getting off the "hard path" of energy production and finding our way to the "soft path" is a heroic quest of re-perceiving our relationship to the earth. Can we value having a healthy relationship with the planet, as much as enjoying the fruits of material wealth?

As Amory Lovins articulates "soft energy technologies are renewable. They provide energy of the right kind, and at the right scale, to do the task in the cheapest way. They're diverse. You don't have to have specialized institutions to buy billion-dollar, very large, complex machines with brass knobs to meet your own needs. Hard energies are the opposite. They're not diverse. It is largely Stalinistic. It's top-down central planning. "We will decide what to build. We will build it. You will use it. You will pay for it".

It is truly amazing to realize how we in industrial society have become dependent on centralized control systems using non-local resources to provide services that can be homespun. How did we let this process of disempowerment occur?

Amory Lovins sets the tone for this chapter by distinguishing between the "hard path" of energy production and the "soft path" of re-perceiving our relationship with mother earth. Peter Calthorpe then offers a vision of whole systems design and Hazel Henderson passionately describes the imperative of redefining wealth in our times. William McDonough closes with a vision of sustainable prosperity.

C.Z.

Amory Lovins

The Road Least Taken

Now, fortunately, even when the thing to beat is apparently cheap oil, energy efficiency turns out to be much cheaper still.

"how is it true that petroleum has been kept artificially inexpensive?"

The world has been awash in cheap oil for decades and has gone on the sort of binge you would expect when gasoline, for example, in the United States costs less than bottled water or less than soft drinks.

When the great Russian chemist, Mendeleyev, first analyzed oil and found out all those wonderful molecules that are were in it, he said this stuff is too valuable to burn, and he was, of course, correct. But we have been burning it ever since. The main reason we have been treating it as an almost free good is that it is not priced at anywhere near long-run replacement cost, which is near infinite. It's pretty hard to make molecules like that from scratch; it took a very long time to do it. Of course, we confuse ourselves into thinking that we are producing oil when what we are really doing is digging it up and burning it.

The use of the economic term "production" confuses us, because, in English, what we are really doing is "consumption." But the economists call it production. I think also our economists have gotten into a very bad habit of treating depletion of resources as if it were income, as if you could develop your bank account by withdrawing money from it. I sure wish I knew how to do that! The economic process tends to get treated as this endless disembodied circular flow between production and consumption, as if there were not also a flow from depletion to pollution, as Herman Daley says. This is as if we tried to understand an animal only on the basis of its circulatory system, without noticing that it also has a digestive tract that ties it firmly to its environment at both ends. If we go back to Hick's definition of income, we find that it is the maximum amount that you can consume over a given period without being worse off than when you started, though Hick meant this definition to apply expressly to consumption of capital. If we really did our bookkeeping right, we would find that what we think of as the wealth created by burning all this oil has actually made us a lot poorer in many respects.

I remember once briefing many of the managing directors of an extremely large oil company about why they should put more effort into selling "nega-barrels"—efficient use of oil—because they would make more money and have less risk that way. After we got through, there was a pause, and then one of the directors said, "Well you know the trouble with these nega-barrels is once you've sold it to a chap, he's got it, and you can't sell to him again." To which my wife and colleague, Hunter, replied, "Y'all, the trouble with these barrels is that once you've sold it, you haven't got it, and you can't sell it to him again."

I think they got the point that their business is based on a wasting asset. They need an acorn farm for its renewal. The consequence of the cheap oil that we have been floating on all these decades is that we have an extremely unsustainable system in industrial production, in transportation, in where we live. We need to run around so much in the kinds of buildings we live and work in. They are all on the order of five or ten times more wasteful than they would be if we used energy in a way that saved money.

Now, fortunately, even when the thing to beat is apparently cheap oil, energy efficiency turns out to be much cheaper still. We can save about four-fifths of the

The choice is before us. We can continue to burn fossil fuels and compromise the health of our communities or we can begin to access the eternal abundance of nature through soft energy technologies.

Compare the aesthetic of our current form of refining energy with Solar Shingles integrated into the architecture of our homes.

oil used in the United States, at an average cost of about three dollars a barrel. That is cheaper than drilling for more, let alone doing something with it if you find it. Those efficiency improvements are starting to come in so rapidly that the savings Americans have made since 1973, mainly in oil and gas, now amount to a whole new energy source for the nation—two-fifths bigger than the entire domestic oil industry, which took a century to build. Oil has dwindling reserves, rising costs, and falling output, at least in the United States; whereas efficiency has expanding reserves, falling costs , and rising output. Which one sounds like the better buy? Yet it is not the one favored in the national energy strategy.

So we absolutely have all the classic symptoms of addictive behavior, including denial. I think there are much better alternatives to oil addiction, than, say, methadone is to heroin addiction. It will be much easier to kick the habit than it is with drugs. The main reason for that is that the efficiency alternative works better, costs less, provides better services, and puts money in your pocket. The United States has already cut about a hundred and fifty billion dollars a year off its energy bill, but we are still wasting twice that much [in] energy than we could save by substituting cheaper, more effective efficiency measures on the market. That wasted energy is costing us about three hundred billion dollars a year—slightly more than the entire military budget, which is ten thousand million dollars a second. So we have quite a long way to go

SOFT VERSUS HARD ENERGY TECHNOLOGIES

"will you draw the distinction between hard energy and soft energy for us?"

There are, broadly, two ways our energy system could evolve over the next half-century or so. One is to get more energy of any kind, of any source, at any price. If you think that is the problem, then the answer you get tends to be burning up depletable fuels faster and faster. Converting them in ever larger, more complex, more centralized, more costly plans into premium forms, especially electricity. There are a lot of reasons that did not happen and will not happen, even though it is what all the official projections showed. It is That approach just died of an incurable attack of market forces.

What has been happening instead is that we started to remember people do not just want sticky barrels of black goo, or raw kilowatt-hours. What they're after is hot showers, cold beer, light comfort, mobility: the services energy gives us. So it makes sense to start at that end of the problem by asking, "How much energy do we need?" What quality, at what scale, from what source will do the job in the cheapest way? Because if we ask that question, we will understand better how people behave in a competitive energy service market, where electricity, say, to heat your house, has to compete not just with natural gas, but also with windows and weather stripping. People tend to pick the cheapest way to do the job. That means that we will be spending most of our money on efficiency, and what is left are the next-best buys in appropriate renewable sources, which I call soft technology.

This is what has actually happened since 1979. The United States got four and one-half times more energy from saving as from all net increases in supply. A third of the new supply was renewable. In fact, up through 1986, when our attention wandered, those numbers were seven times as much from efficiency as from supply. And the majority of the new supply was renewable. [Editors' note: See Soft Energy Technologies by Amory Lovins.]

There are some even more remarkable individual examples. The state of Maine, for example, has gone from about 2 percent to about a 35 or 37 percent private, almost all-renewable power supply in the past seven years. California has cut its electric intensity by a fifth. The biggest investor-owned utility in the United States now says it's going to get at least three-quarters of its power needs in the '90s from efficiency and the rest from renewables, which it says are now the next-best buy. The advanced gas technologies are the third best, so they get pushed off the table. So in this rapidly growing area Northern California, this for-profit utility, for the first time in forty years, is neither building nor planning any conventional power plants, and probably never will again, because it's taking economics seriously.

Speak to the Earth, and it shall teach thee.

JOB, 12:8

Soft energy technologies are renewable. They provide energy of the right kind, and at the right scale, to do the taskn the cheapest way. They're diverse. You don't try to do everything with just one kind. You use each one to do what it does best. They tend to be, in some sense, vernacular, or accessible. You can actually go get them yourself, then use them, or do so in small groups on a local scale. You don't have to have specialized institutions to buy billion-dollar, very large, complex machines with brass knobs to meet your own needs.

Sundown on the petroleum age.

Hard energy technologies are the opposite. They tend to be of a very few kinds. They're not diverse. They work on depletable energy or also on some renewables. For example, if you were to build a big hydro dam to heat lots of houses, that would be pretty silly. It would be a mismatch in both the quality and the scale of the energy you need for the task, and it would be, correspondingly, very expensive. Also, hard technologies require very centralized and rather unaccountable institutions to do them, so they incur a lot of political costs because they're so centralized. The energy and the side effects go to different people at opposite ends of the distribution system. So there's a lot of inequity and conflict as well, whereas with technologies of the right size, you give the energy and the side effects to the same people at the same time, so that they candecide how much is enough.

Our dyspeptic skyline.

You could get to a soft energy path, in technical terms, with a kind of top-down central planning approach. That's not my own preference, and I don't think it would work very well. In fact, politically, what distinguishes the soft path is that it's the perestroika model of energy development, rather than the Stalinist model. What we've had in energy, so far, is largely very Stalinistic. It's top-down central planning. "We" will decide what to build—by we, I mean a very small group of technocrats: "We will build it. You will use it. You will pay for it. "

POSITIVE FORCES FOR CHANGE

Meanwhile, perestroika's been bubbling up through the cracks, and something like forty-three of the United States (and many other places) now require that utilities do the cheapest things first. So if it's cheaper to save electricity than to make it, then they should save it instead of building plants or even running existing plants. This approach really gives primacy to individual choice in a relatively free market. In fact, many utility regulators are now changing the rules, so that utilities will no longer be rewarded for selling you more electricity nor penalized for selling you less, but if they do something smart to cut your bills, they'll get a special reward—for example, they'll be allowed to keep part of the savings as extra profit, so that whatever is cheapest for the customer will be most profitable for the utility, and vice versa. .

That changes utility behavior amazingly. It means that every week, the chief executive of the utility will call up the head of its efficiency department and say, "Is there anything you need?" because that's now the most profitable part of the utility. And as we get the regulatory incentives more aligned with customer interests, so that we really can do the cheapest things first (and make money on it), we're rapidly seeing the soft energy path emerge, out of economic logic, because efficiency is by far the cheapest thing to do.

At the same time, there's been a rapid emergence—not as rapid as it would have been if we hadn't slashed the R&D budget, but still impressive—in very cost-effective renewable supplies. So, for example, both the regulators and the utilities in California are now saying that wind power is their cheapest supply option, much cheaper than

Man must go back to Nature for information.

Thomas Paine

fossil and nuclear fuels. And there are even circumstances in which solar cells are cost effective right now. Those circumstances are turning out to be a lot bigger than we thought. They may apply to practically everyplace, if we do honest accounting and count all the benefits.

Politically, a soft energy path would be a lot more democratic and accountable than what we're accustomed to in the energy system. People would be quite free to make their own choices, and would have the information and the ability to respond to the price signals they see, because they would be able to finance efficiency on exactly the same terms on which a utility otherwise finances a power plant. You can pay for it over time, at the same interest rate. A lot of utilities already do this by financing, leasing you compact fluorescent lamps at twenty cents per lamp, per month, on your bill. Your bill goes down because you save more than that much worth of electricity, but then you get to pay for it over time just like a power plant, and you can decide which one you want. I think the kinds of political conflict we've become used to in energy, whether to drill in the Arctic Refuge, whether to build a power plant down the road from you, and so on, would essentially go away if we did the cheapest things first, because we wouldn't be building those damaging and controversial sorts of facilities.

A soft energy path, I think, would facilitate a more Jeffersonian trend in our society, but it doesn't cause one. That is, I don't see it as a vehicle for social change, but it certainly could be consistent with change in a direction I think is rather healthy. I should note also that we're not assuming in our analysis any change except improvements in the amount or quality of services people get. So your beer would be as cold, your shower would be as hot and tingly, but you get them with a quarter as much energy by using quadruple-efficiency refrigerators and shower heads; substituting brains for kilowatt-hours. It is possible to save energy by changing behavior and lifestyle, and some of that may be desirable, but we're not assuming any of it.

If we did take economics seriously, there's no question we could get all, or nearly all of our energy from appropriate, renewable sources in, say, forty years. In fact, by that date, the five national labs that work on renewable energy have said we could actually have somewhere around half as much energy, and two-thirds or more as much electricity as we use now. However, even if the economy grew

> "The soft energy path is more decentralized and thus more in line with the ideals of Jefferson?"

considerably, and especially if we wanted to, we could be using energy several times as efficiently as now. So that supply would be plenty to run the whole country very nicely and we'd be living happily ever after on our energy income. Of course, we only have one set of deposits of cheap oil and gas to get there from here. It's kind of like a bridge to the energy future we want to get to. If we burn the bridge before we cross it, we don't have another chance to get there, because the cheap fuel (and the cheap money made from the cheap fuel) will be gone. Then the transition becomes extremely difficult. We would have just backed ourselves into a corner.

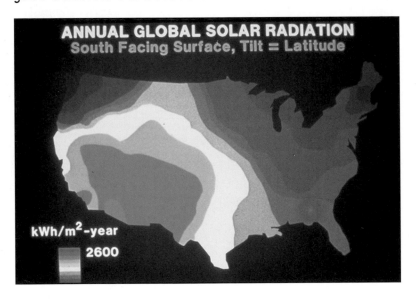

Key Statistics in the Photovoltaic Mosaic:

* Time it takes for sunshine energy falling on the U.S. to equal fossil fuel energy consumed by the U.S. in one year: 40 minutes.

* Estimated area of photovoltaic solar energy cells needed to produce U.S. annual consumption energy: 58, 060 square miles/land area of Georgia.

* Cost PV energy, 1960: $2000 per peak watt.

* Cost in 1975: $70 per peak watt

* Cost in 1993: $5 per peak watt.

We are using fossil fuels at 250,000 times their rate of formulation.

The Green Architecture of David Sellers, Prickley Mountain, Vermont.

Hunter Lovins

The Rocky Mountain Institute

My mother . . . has an abiding love for natural things and beauty in the world, and is always seeking ways to make people
feel and be better. They always said, in figuring out whether or not a day was well spent, "Did
we leave the place a little better than we found it?"

"can you trace the roots of the founding of the rocky mountain institute?"

Rocky Mountain Institute was created out of Amory's and my discussions as to how we could be more effective in the world. We had previously been batting around the world, working in about fifteen different countries, kind of living on a 727, and had decided to settle down. We decided to come here to Colorado and we were posing the question to each other, if we're no longer traveling and cross-pollinating the energy grapevine, what will we do? And I said to Amory, "Why don't we create an institute? Pull together a group of people who we want to work with—colleagues, friends—and be able to chase around some questions that we haven't had the time to look at, such as: What really is security? What is it that makes people be and feel secure? What is sustainable agriculture, and how do you achieve it? How do you do sustainable, locally based economic development? And how does energy affect all of these?

Amory's reaction to the notion of creating an institute was that he did not want to be an administrator, and I said, well, that's fine. You direct the research, and take care of the quality of the research and the direction of it, and I'll administrate. So that's been our division of responsibility ever since.

Rocky Mountain Institute has five program areas: energy (particularly the efficient use of energy), water (again, looking at ways to use water more productively), agriculture (trying to figure out how to foster a transition to sustainable agriculture), economic renewal (which is seeking to empower small rural communities to strengthen their economies by themselves), and, finally, security (make cars be more efficient).

In our water project, we've recently completed a couple of projects for the Environmental Protection Agency in the state of California, looking at what technologies exist, and are now on the market, to use water more productively. In some ways we're very similar to a lot of other organizations around the world that are looking at issues of sustainability; in some ways we're different. One of the differences is that we come at it from the standpoint of how to achieve it within existing institutions, such as market economics and representative government. We assume that people aren't going to make radical, fundamental changes in their lifestyle, in their philosophy, in their politics, but seek implementation techniques that are right at hand, that can get the job done without revolutionary sorts of changes in institutions.

The Institute has staff housing for ten to thirteen people. We seek to embody, within this structure, many of the concepts that we're talking about. I'm a basic redneck. If it's not convenient, if it's not comfortable, if it's not just as easy, I don't want it. So I'm a pretty good test bed for a lot of these technologies. Amory sometimes comes home with a nifty new gadget, and I look at it and sort of kick the tires, and see if it'll really work. And if it works for me, I have a pretty fair confidence that most folks are not going to have trouble with it. And there are times when I tell him, "Get that thing out of here! I don't want it!"

The Rocky Mountain Institute, Snowmass Colorado.

The Rocky Mountain Institute—the Lovins' Green Home—conserves the equivalent of one barrel of oil per day.

THE CONSUMPTION GAME

Living and working at the Institute, you're different than people living in, say, Aspen, for instance. You're living in your own design, you're doing R&D, and you're not coming out of a consumer model, as in towns like Aspen. Why are they continuing to play the consumption game, when right nearby there's an institute showing that it's got no future? How can that continue? Well, the consumption game will always continue to some extent. I guess it's an artifact of being alive, that you consume things. I guess it was Gandhi who posed the question between needs and wants, one of which is finite, and definable, and the other of which is, effectively, infinite.

Aspen is one of the world centers for the infinite desire for gadgets, baubles, fun, image... As a result, it ceases to be the kind of town that I really want to spend very much time in. It's handy having it close by, though. It is one of those world centers to which people come, partly because it has some excellent institutions like the Aspen Institute, the Aspen Physics Center, the Global Change Institute. They bring people here, so we don't have to travel as much if we want to see those people; they're going to come here anyway. On top of which, there are people who want to come from all around the world to vacation here. And while they're here, well, you know, they kind of get bored with skiing and such, and they want to see something different. They drift by here, and say, "you know, maybe I could do that in my place." So in a sense, we are able to influence the kinds of people who would not seek us out otherwise and who don't read our books, who don't read books on sustainability, but come here out of curiosity.

The course of Nature is the art of God.

Edward Young

Peter Calthorpe

Whole Systems Design

It was that beginning idea of connectedness that was at the root of all of this work.

"what influences led to the work you are doing now?"

I think in the early '70s the perspective I got was that there were some fundamental decisions that were amiss. They were technological, and they were design, and they were social; it was that complex soup of ideas, but trying to get a handle on that, at least, led me to design. The simplest and the most direct way into that was through the home, through the way people live. There you can began to look at things such as solar energy.

The idea of the domes (early on) was more symbolic. It was a gesture, an anarchist gesture really, that we would make a break with history. I don't think now, in hindsight, that's such a great idea, breaking with history. If anything, we need to reconnect to the bigger history. Ironically, the domes were a statement of a kind of hypermodernist, hyperengineered, hypertechnocratic solution, which really turns out to be dead wrong. But the philosophy behind it, I think, holds true over a whole generation, twenty years of work. [And that philosophy] is to think of things as whole systems. There is no such thing as waste. Everything comes from somewhere and goes somewhere else. [It's important to see a] larger interconnected fabric and also to see frugality itself as an aesthetic and social good.

The Solar Connection

The experimentation with solar [showed us that] buildings have to be seen in their context. They have to be connected to their surroundings, which is the antithesis of what modernism proposed as it took over from the beaux arts and the romantic movements in architecture. The modernists saw the building as isolated from its

118

environment and its urban context. It was an object in space. It became a piece of sculpture in space, and that's the way the modernists thought of it. As a matter of fact, the great credo of modernism was form follows function—in other words, the form of a building isn't the product of its environment or its urban context (i.e., the community of buildings), it is the product of its internal workings. It was a very, very individualistic philosophy—the building, like a person, is an individual that expresses itself in a very private way. This is the way I am, independent of community, independent of environment, and independent of history. All those connections were severed in architecture.

Solar was a beginning way of saying, "No, buildings are connected to their environment." At the time, we weren't thinking about how buildings were connected to their community and how they created or frustrated community. But it was that beginning idea of connectedness that was at the root of all of this work.

The most wonderful places in the world that you've ever been, it wasn't so much that each individual building was so extraordinary, but just that the fabric of the whole town was extraordinary—the way the buildings responded to the climate and to one another to make a whole out of a neighborhood or out of a village.

This problem of the specialist versus the generalist is really at the heart of this, and I keep saying we need generalists, we need people that think about the whole system. You don't optimize one small piece, you optimize the interaction of all the pieces. There are eco-

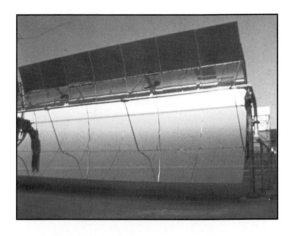

ABOVE
A solar farm in Europe.
BELOW
The first solar dairy farm in Switzerlnd.

nomic dimensions, environmental dimensions, and social dimensions to all design problems. So that the social dimension began to be recognized, and, simultaneously, we began to understand how buildings affect the whole city fabric. It turns out that the patterns that we weave in our community design, the way buildings relate to one another, the way the public world is formed, the quality of the street, the size of the street, whether it has porches versus garage doors, whether it has street trees—these are all fundamental to how lots of people can change the way they live their lives.

Finnish integrated solar design.

NEW SOLAR HOUSING

TOWARD A NEW COMMUNITY DESIGN

What I see in the way we design communities now is profound isolation and segregation—not just racial segregation, but age-group segregation; the elderly are in retirement communities, families are in subdivisions, singles are in condos, everybody is segmented. Our political system is becoming a reflection of this. We have special interest groups, we don't have citizens. That lack of connecting fabric is absolutely reflected in the physical character of our communities, in the fact that the buildings are disconnected, and that the buildings are specialized, but this is really what modernism and modern technology is all about. You specialize, you segregate, and you standardize. We have a kind of mechanistic way of treating community development, where each piece is standardized and isolated much the same way we treat products.

"when are we going to design better communities?"

121

Somebody moving at the speed of a pedestrian cares about the quality of the environment. When you're going along at forty miles an hour in a car, you really cannot perceive the lack of quality in the environment. You know buildings are large, everything is overstated, everything is blaring at us much the way TV does. The pedestrian [pace] slows people down and allows their sensibilities to surface again.

The work evolved from, I guess, in my early twenties doing this kind of—at that time, it seemed revolutionary—domes, as a way of making a really big statement of alienation and separation from mainstream culture to more practical concerns about passive solar in buildings and then realizing the larger question of community design. In my thirties, I started working on that, largely theoretically, at the university, because there was no developer around that was interested in anything like that, not a planning group. Then, luckily, at the end of the '80s, or about '86 or so, after publishing that book with Sim Van der Ryn about sustainable communities, we started to have a few people get interested. It happened in a very interesting and instructive way.

Rather than doing the traditional thing "environmental specialists" do, which is opposing development piecemeal anywhere it turned up, because typically, most development is really destructive to the environment and to community, one environmental group in Sacramento took a proactive stand. They said, "Not only do we oppose sprawl, but we want to support . . ." and they wrote a white paper about what it was they thought they could get behind. Now the gridlock between development and the environmental community was such that few of the developers looked at their white paper and said, "We can live with this. This is probably a good idea from a marketing standpoint. They're talking about mixed-use, walkable communities."

Such synoptic vision of Nature, such constructive conservation
of its order and beauty... is more than engineering: it is a master-art; vaster than
that of street planning, it is landscape making:
and thus meets and combines with city design.
Patrick Geddes

122

They [the environmental group in Sacramento] had gotten some of the stuff that I had published when I was doing the theoretical thinking about pedestrian pockets, and so they got together, and a very progressive developer took on [the project]. It was out of that kind of alliance, between the environmental community and the development community, that something finally happened. Once it had, people really started to take note and listen to it.

All the municipalities and cities in the United States are at a point of high frustration. They can't afford more sprawl, they don't want it, their citizens don't want it, and yet they know they need some type of growth because communities are growing. [Our project] seemed a way out for many, and so we've had a lot of opportunities since that one kind of watershed event. Then, of course, the more you do, the more people think it's a credible idea, and the more you can do. So we've gone from doing one project here in Sacramento to designing a whole set of guidelines for the city of San Diego, and doing a

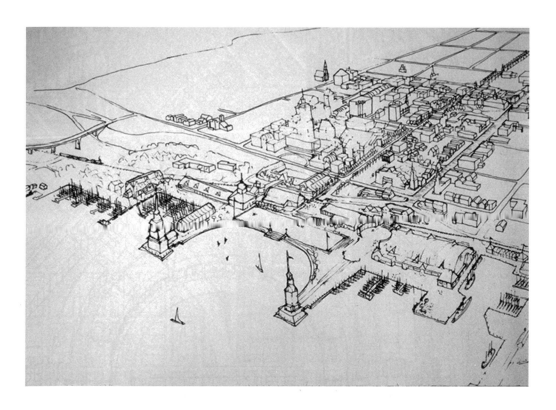

Drawing by David Sellers of a mixed use settlement.

123

regional plan for the city of Portland, and a general plan for the county of Sacramento.

People understand that they're at a standstill with standard patterns of development. They want to move toward mixed-use, walkable environments. And so what you have, running on three legs simultaneously, you have the environmentalists saying this is a better way to make development happen—those [environmentalists, that is,] that are intelligent enough to know that they can't stop development, they can only direct it. There are a lot of very myopic environmentalists who think that the only job is to stop development. It's what I call the Marin County environmentalist, who stops it in Marin County so development goes farther to the fringe of the metropolis, Sonoma County, and people end up commuting farther, and the people who pay are the poor and the working poor, because they're the ones shunted way out to the fringe where they're then saddled with a huge commute. They're not solving an environmental problem, they're protecting their property values.

Find your place on the planet, dig in, and take responsibility from there.

Gary Snyder

NEW PATTERNS FOR DIVERSITY

Anyway, so there's an environmental community going on—the enlightened ones—understanding that a new pattern needed to exist. There are developers who, you know—it's their job, just like the environmentalists have their priority—they have to think about marketability and economics. It turns out, and I think this is inherent, it's not just a lucky coincidence, that it's more marketable. This is a way people would like to live. Surveys done recently of people who've moved into our communities and communities like them, show that this is what people are looking for: communities. They're looking for a way to get out of their car, they're looking for an environment that's aesthetically and environmentally more coherent.

This idea of focusing back on traditional urban structure, understanding the quality of making a good street, a good plaza, understanding the hierarchy of public and private buildings, this goes back to that first modernist principle: buildings have to orient not just to the climate and to the sun, they have to orient to the public domain. Buildings form the walls to our public rooms. They have to participate with one another to identify public space.

Public space is environmental space: interesting overlap. Now, the idea of pedestrian pockets was a bit too specialized; it wasn't diverse enough. When I really came to confront the development community, in saying, "let's build these things," they said, "you gotta be crazy, we couldn't market 100 percent multifamily, no matter what." And I realized they were right. The most important thing in a community is diversity, that you have everything from wealthy, single-family owners to apartment dwellers, and they should be part of the same neighborhood. They shouldn't be the wealthy in a country club community over here, and the poor or the single people in an apartment complex somewhere else downtown. That kind of segregation has to end. So in our communities we've been successful with planning for huge diversity of housing types and housing costs.

Eighty percent of all development in the last twenty years has been suburban. It's obviously subsidized and directed by some major programs, such as the federal highway program and FHA loans, but it still represents a fundamental force and direction in the culture. But even within that context, I think that we can create places that are more urban.

A drawing by Malcolm Wells of a Chattanooga futurable.

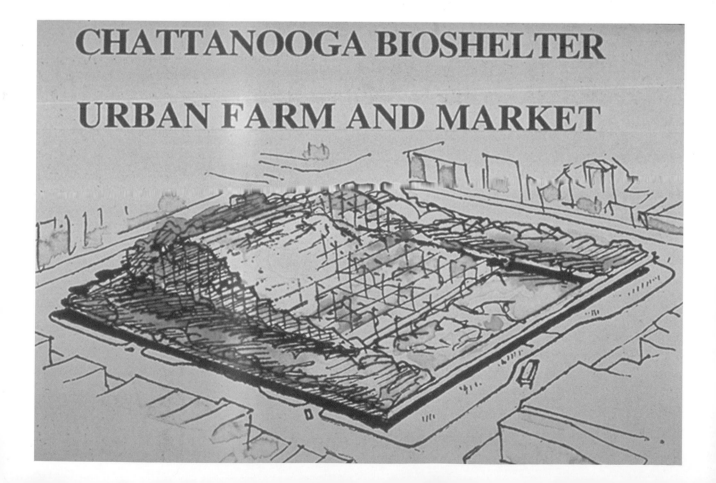

CHATTANOOGA BIOSHELTER

URBAN FARM AND MARKET

Hazel Henderson

Redefining Wealth

If you have any kind of information that is a split-second ahead of the trading screens around the world, then you have, by definition, a tremendous amount of money, and the money is always following the information.

"can you talk about the Relevance of Fuller's definition of wealth?"

I think that Bucky Fuller's definitions of wealth are very insightful and certainly are advanced over today's definitionsHis definition of a kind of channeling universal energy would be the one that I would most prefer because it does get across the idea that, for we humans on this planet, all of the energy that we use does come from the sun. Bucky understood that very well. But you know there is this thought today in our industrial society that energy is anything that is dug out of the earth, whereas what Fuller introduced was the idea that human knowledge could help us to use energy less wastefully and more elegantly. He also made us understand that we really were the energy source, as well, and it was our mindpower that could be an energy source.

I think my own view of wealth is also love. One of the errors that economists and a lot of futurists make is that they think that somehow human beings, because they are so clever, can get cleverer, and cleverer, and opt out of having to do any physical work themselves. The problem with that is that there is, as all women in the world know, an irreducible amount of physical effort that goes into nurturing the next generation. There is no way you can alternate changing a baby's diaper. There is an irreducible amount of this kind of manual work, for which you need reframing.

I like a spiritual reframing of this kind of work, the way Buddhists are with the idea of sweeping the temple garden really being a spiritual practice. For me, having a child and taking care of a child, in spite of the fact that it slows you down and there isn't anything you can delegate, is very much a spiritual practice. As we come to rebalance the roles between males and females and move into gender-partnership kinds of societies, and [as] men do more and more of the nurturing of children (as they are doing now), we get a slightly more balanced and less arrogant view of our place in system.

AN ECONOMY BEYOND THE HALL OF MIRRORS

Conventional economists really mistake money for wealth. This is a problem. Yet, as we know, even in economic textbooks, they are very sure to explain what they call the "money veil," i.e., they know the difference between the "real economy" and the "money economy." When you try to quantify everything in money terms, you lose all sense of what's valuable, because, of course, there are so many things that really cannot be quantified in money terms.

"we don't hear too much from economists about such distinctions. why?"

Today we have this international global casino, with about five hundred billion dollars' worth of currency sloshing around this planet every twenty-four hours. All these issues are becoming crystal clear. Bucky would have loved to see all of this that is going on today, because, in essence, money has simply been revealed as information, and money and information are interchangable. My operating assumption is that, on the whole, I would rather have information than I would money, because money now follows information. If you have information about what is going to happen to currencies in the future, what is going to happen to investments in the future, if you have any kind of information that is a split-second ahead of the trading screens around the world, then you have, by definition, a tremendous amount of money, and the money is always following the information.

So that's one level of it. But that's the most crass level and the more important level of it is that, in trying to assign money values to everything, we define the wealth of a nation—and whether a nation is making progress—by whether the gross national product is going up. That also is coming to be seen as ridiculous. I always like to say that trying to run a complex society by using this one measure of whether the gross national product is going up is rather like trying to fly a Boeing 747 with nothing on the instrument panel except an oil pressure gauge—I mean, no way. You need all these other gauges along the instrument panel; you need to know what the altitude is, and whether there is any gas in the gas tank, and all of those other things, and so in a sense that also has been revealed as nonsense.

As you know, there are many other attempts now by economists to reformulate the GNP. What my argument with the economists still is—even those very well meaning ones who are very good friends of mine, like Herman Daley who has his new ISEW, which is an Indicator of Sustainable Economic Wealth Fare, and there's one that has come out of the United Nations now called HDI, or Human Development Index—the economists' approach is still that you can sort of go behind closed doors with the other experts, and you can weigh all of these various factors and come up with one aggregated number, where you can put all the apples and oranges together, and you come up with what to me is an insane level of aggregation where nobody can understand what it means. So my approach is to unbundle these various indicators. Many of them will never be able to be quantified in money, like the purity of the air, or the purity of the water, or the hectares of land that are lost through deforestation, and desertification, the species loss that is going on around the world.

None of these things we can put numbers on, and, so far, my viewpoint is that my country's future indicators will allow a kind of development which is culturally specific. Every culture has its own value system and its own priorities and goals, and they ought to be able to roll around, and have the kind of indicators that best represent their goals and values. If you have these indicators all in different dimensions, and maybe it takes fifteen minutes to read the "State of the Country" report, as it were—at least this way it allows ordinary

WEALTH; The measurable degree of forwardly organized environmental control, in terms of quickly convertible energy, capacities and performance ratio system capabilities per capita, per diem.

R. Buckminster Fuller
World Design Science Decade, Document 2

citizens to do politics. So you have the health indicators, and the people who are interested in health can follow the health indicators; and you have the air- and water-quality indicators and other environmental indicators, and these environmentalists can follow those indicators; and you can have the indicators on child development, and you have indicators on military-versus-civilian budget ratios, and people in the peace movement and who are concerned with social development can watch those indicators. I think that we are beyond the stage now where we can allow experts, particularly economists, do those weightings through some kind of mathematical formulas, where basically all that they are doing is expressing their own values rather than values of the general public.

"what about expressing the ultimate abundance of the natural universe?"

THE LESSONS OF SCARCITY AND ABUNDANCE

These issues that economists frame as scarcity, and the abundance of the universe that Bucky Fuller talked about, are very, very crucial at this period, as we are going from a transition from industrial societies to what I still hope to be the solar age. I thought the solar age was going to happen in the 1980s, and so I wrote my book, Politics of the Solar Age, ten years too soon. But now people are beginning to really understand what we mean about a solar economy, where we shift to the daily income from the sun instead of digging out the earth's capital. Bucky Fuller talked a great deal about that, too.

For me, it's been a very interesting exercise to try to help Americans to understand that their abundance was bought at the pain and misery of so many people on this planet. Of course the same can be said about colonial Europe, where you had this thermodynamic imbalance, where colonial countries and the United States ended up gobbling up an enormous amount of the planet's irreplaceable resources and leaving this tremendous deficit in the Southern Hemisphere.

When I was writing both Creating Alternative Futures and Politics of the Solar Age, I felt that people had to first learn the lesson of scarcity of the rest of the world, and [learn] how the way we had constructed and designed industrial societies meant that we were using these irreplacable resources in a very unfair way.

Wealth is what Nature gives us and what a reasonable man can make out of the gifts of Nature for his reasonable use.

William Morris

OPPOSITE
The Jersey Devils
design and build
approach to
architecture enable
them to truly
understand the
Genius Loci of the
site and thus bring
a new form of
wealth into the
landscape.

My point really was that Bucky was right about the ultimate abundance, but that it did require what he called a "designed revolution" particularly in industrial societies, so that we minimize the amount of energy and materials [we use]. I always loved his concept of miniaturization, that as you went more and more in that direction, you could truly say that the abundance that the Americans and the Europeans had achieved would no longer have to be at the expense of three-quarters of humanity, which was the situation, you know, when I first started writing about all of this in the '60s.

The whole idea that we can have this ultimate abundance, in which Bucky and I totally agree, was [based upon] the input of knowledge, and [I have believed that] as human know-how increased, we could redesign our societies—although my caveat always was that I wanted to counter this very glib idea that so many (particularly men) had that we could end up with a completely ultimate society where nobody would have to do any physical work. There again, we had to always emphasize the fact there is this kind of irreducible physical work which has to be done, mostly to do with nurturing children, and that, of course, would require the balancing, the rebalancing of societies to [foster] partnership between the genders, so that the nurturing of children would be shared.

Our understanding or lack of understanding of this point—what wealth really is—will have a whole lot to do with whether or not man is going to survive on the face of the earth.

Buckminster Fuller

CAPTION ON PAGE 130

J. Baldwin

On Tools

A whole group of tools is like an extension of your mind in that it enables you to bring your ideas into physical form.

> "what is the significance of creating an evolving tool shop?"

When I started making geodesic domes, of course I found that nobody knew how to make them and I had collected a bunch of tools over the years to help me take my ideas into a concrete form, to try them out and to try living with them. I found that when I had somebody else make things for me, something got lost in the translation. So I learned to use tools and I bought the tools as I needed them, most of them used, and I finally put them into the truck because I found that a lot of places like the New Alchemy Institute, Fallons Institute other places that were doing interesting work with solar energy and green houses and so forth, and I saw that green houses had good use for the domes, Fuller's domes. They often worked from grant money and they could never get grants for tools, so by having a portable shop I could bring a whole bunch of tools to the job and get things done that way. And I found wherever these tools arrived, a lot happens. Right now they're kind of roosting at the neighborhood shop.

The parts for 37 geodesic domes have been made in here and the New Alchemy Pillowdome was fabricated in here, not the pillows, but all the rest of it was and with these tools. It's a set of tools that's intended to be maximally flexible and constantly improving and they're set up in a way so that you don't need much of an introduction to the shop to be able to use it. I'm not afraid at all if somebody says may I use your shop. I say, sure you can. Almost anyone can find their way around in here very easily, and Liz went to some extent to make the place woman friendly so it didn't have this intimidating macho high school shop feel to it that some of these shops do.

When Fuller remarked that good hardware was one of the few irrefutable proofs of clear thinking, I took that to heart and I'm not famous for good workmanship, but most of the work that comes out of here is sort of proof of concept work. I call this place a three-dimensional sketch pad and it's important to carry out the ideas to the theory, all the way through practice because you learn as you go when you start making the thing, the object, whether it's a geodesic dome or just a joint for a dome, let's say. if it's anything. As you start to make it, you learn a lot about it that you didn't know. Also I found, and Fuller also knew, that diagrams are one thing, but it's very easy to lie with a drawing, lie to yourself, but when you start working in three dimensions the lies have to cease because there the thing is, and if it's the wrong size you soon know that it is and you can say, I think this should be a little bigger or obviously this isn't strong enough even though it says in the blueprint that metal this thick is sufficiently stiff, it turns out that it isn't when we actually do it. It's an old adage actually that tools are extensions of your mind. Like pliers are just a very strong fingers and a hammer is just a very hard fist, but I found that a whole group of tools is an extension of your mind, in that it enables you to bring your ideas into physical form. Actually, what you're doing is, you're adding so much energy to the idea that other people can see it, is my theory.

I tried to integrate the shop with the people that would use it, thinking very carefully of the ergonomics of it, much in the same way I've learned biologically what human beings are. The whole shop sort of ends up being my hands, it's just like your hands do what your mind has thought up. The shop just makes my hands more capable. The shop has sort of an atmosphere that at the very worst doesn't prevent innovative thinking and the execution of the ideas and I would hope that most of the time it would actually nurture the ideas and makes them so easy to do that you can not only try them, but you can try versions. And it's very important to try versions of things, iterations is the right word That's what sophistication means, sophisticated design or a well developed design is one that you've tried different ways of doing it. It's so easy to work in here that we do just that. It's not a hassle. I deliberately designed the place to be hassle free, and the way I integrate working in here is the same way I would integrate working outdoors, as a farmer outdoors or something, except the system in here obeys

Knowing is not enough; we must apply. Willing is not enough; we must do.

Goethe

133

physical law. It's not very biological. But I'm integrated into it rather than it's owner. I don't show it off, but I'm a part of it. Without somebody in here, the shop is nothing. If I was outside without the shop, I couldn't even drive a nail, so it's a symbiotic relationship. Most people don't think of shops that way.

J.B.'s mobile rapid deployment system.

J.B. in the shop.

HAROLD COHEN

So the struggle, the search to make a buck, to get the honey... is Bucky's parable.

So the struggle, the search to make a buck, to get the honey which is the money, is Bucky's parable. Corporations, in order to do that, are going to spread and reseed and refertilize. A lot of things around the world in production will come about because of this great need to make money.

The issue is that you can make money by doing good products, being moral, and, in fact, if you can use less material, you make more money. So this effort for the bottom line, he thought, would help make it possible. Bucky used to tell a wonderful parable. There's the bee, the bee goes around and he is always trying to make a little something, so he goes around, and he's buzzing here and he's buzzing there, going around, buzzing bee, making honey, honey is money, money is honey. [Then] he'd say: "While you're doing all that, you're fertilizing all the flowers."

© Thomas Slagle

The gratification of wealth is not found in mere possession or in lavish expenditure, but in the wise application.

Miguel de Cervantes

William McDonough

Designing for Interdependence

We can actually design things that produce more than they take over a long period of time, so they become like a tree. They produce more energy than they might need, and they give something back to the community.

"can you illuminate the ways in which the ideas connected to ecological design reframe the role of the designer contributing to the common— wealth?"

Rather than use the word sustainable, I think the way we can approach this is to talk about the condition of prosperity. What we're actually talking about is prosperity. We're talking about bringing value to things. And the value can be perceived both on a short-term basis and on a long-term basis. As a designer, I can bring value to something by giving it the ability to last a long time, for example. I can create heirlooms. I can also create buildings that have adaptable purposes, therefore I've brought value to [the building] so that when its purpose is over, it still has residual value. I can bring value to something in design by having it attend to, perhaps, five different agendas at the same time.

Our roof structure for the Frankfurt project, for example, does five things at once, much as a bedouin tent does: it illuminates; it ventilates, it heats water, it heats space, and it protects you from rain. So by having five different agendas attended by one object, I can make that object very valuable, because I have five budgets over which to amortize the cost of what I'm doing. I can afford to do something much better, and I can leave something behind that has a multiplier effect over the years, because it's that many less gallons of oil that are being purchased every year, so the economics become quite fascinating. There's a great deal of economy involved in those kinds of decisions.

So we're leaving something better than the way we found it. In fact, in some cases we can actually try to go beyond the neutral location and get to a fecund location. We can actually design things that produce more than they take over a long period of time, so they become like a tree. They produce more energy than they might need, and they give something back to the community, the way a tree would absorb solar income and provide more than it's taking. When you apply this to the level of the city, you find phenomenal economic effects.

If you focus on human need first, as your design agenda, rather than desire, you can find astonishing values being brought to bear, because we take care of the fundamental principles first, which frees up a great deal of enterprise and a great deal of income for other purposes.

As people who are responsible for designing (which means that we're imagining the future), if we don't deal with these things, then, in a sense, we're being negligent. Negligence is defined as knowing that something has a dangerous effect and going ahead and doing it anyway.

We realize that designers do have a special role to play, just as Peter Senge at MIT's Sloan School of Management has pointed out in his learning laboratory, where he brings in CEOs and asks them, "who is the leader on a ship crossing the ocean: captain, chef, or crew?" His answer is that it's the designer of the ship, because everyone on that ship is affected by its design. So we need to recognize that designers have to take leadership roles; designers have to try to turn this supertanker back into some form of sailboat and connect back to what Emerson called the Aeolian kinetic—what he missed on his return voyage.

The notion of independence is critical. I think that we do need to be independent of things that are destructive. But I also think we have to recognize interdependence. I think if Thomas Jefferson were alive today, he'd be calling for a Declaration of Interdependence. When we look at interdependent notions, we find, for example, an economic model that we're essentially working from capital reserves instead of current income, in terms of energy. Since ecology comes from the roots oikos logos, which are the ancient Greek words for household and discourse, we can have a discourse about our household. Our household economics are terrible. We are working completely from capital reserves, for all intents and purposes, and not working from any kind of current income. Solar energy is the currency of solar income, and we have to design our habitations and our systems to utilize current income.

That's fundamental to any kind of practical agenda. Even my

> "how important is energy independence in terms of our culture's design agenda?"

grandmother, who saved aluminum foil, understood things like this. We can see the urgency of this, and we can perceive it as war. I think it is an urgent need, because, the fact is, we're killing our children. We may not realize it, we may not be aware of some of the persistent effects of our actions, but it really is about what we're leaving behind for someone else to live with. With certain characteristics of, say, radioactive waste, we're asking future generations to be incredibly diligent and have a very high maintenance program. It's not necessarily the most wonderful thing to pass along, [not to mention] the potential danger.

Energy is eternal delight.

William Blake

When I was in Jordan working for King Hussein, I lived in the Jordan Valley with [the] bedouin. One day we were walking by a village that had been flattened by the Israelis. . . . It looked like a pool table, an adobe block flattened into the desert surface. I looked down and I saw this child's skeleton pressed into the blocks. I looked at this Sheik who was with me and said, "Oh my God, there's a child's skeleton here!" He looked at me incredulously and said, "Don't you know what war is?" I said, "I guess I don't." And he said, "Well, war is when they kill your children."

So we are talking about a war, in those terms. We have to stop making machines for killing, and we have to stop making killing machines. If, as an architect, I can accept the fact that I may be in a position to have an effect on people's health and security and long-term value, I have to ask questions. We're finding terrible things in terms of volatile organic compounds in sealed buildings, [and I have to say to myself,] "Well, perhaps I'm making a killing machine."

When you really think about a living machine, you then start to take on this issue of urgency, because we actually may be doing things that are in the end more destructive than productive. And that's a design problem like no design problem.

Early rendering for Gap Headquarters.

Heinz Foundation interior.

William McDonough's rendering of the first solar house in Ireland.

Chapter Four

The Galactic Explorer Perspective

All form is an effect of character.

Emerson.

The enduring search for new and bold forms requires a
Galactic Explorer perspective. The hum drum everyday television
mind of the late 20th Century American has no place in this realm.
The whirling dance of creation demands vast spaces of possibility.
There is a larger game to play. The Jewels of this voyage return to
us exciting forms that foster the regeneration life.

Can we utilize our technology in the service of repairing
our relationship with mother nature? As John Allen articulates:
"Evolution and the technospheric, biospheric conflict,
whether or not that's going to resolve, is probably
the number one drama of today, if you look at it
from the standpoint of theater and drama."

To make this a magic theater of fertile illumination
will involve "seizing the key images, myths, archetypes,
eschatologies, and ecstasies so that life won't seem
worth living unless one's on the side of the
transforming energy" as poet Gary Snyder so aptly puts it.

The material in this chapter gives us clues on the myriad ways in
which a new design language, "a new iconography", in James Wines'
phrase, can make the world a more buoyant place to be a spiritual
being in the human form.

C.Z.

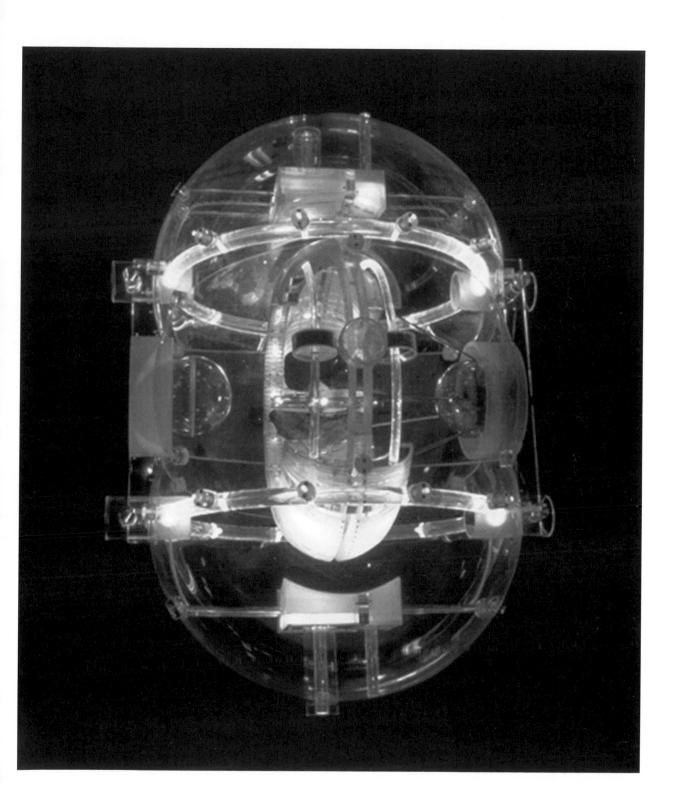

Paul MacCready

The Galactic Explorer Comes to Visit

Everything is thought of just in terms of humans. If you take a little broader view, it makes you think a bit more about the rest of the species.

"what are some of your metaphors for getting into the "big mind" on design issues of our time?"

A way of looking at some at some of these broader issues is to pretend that you're a galactic explorer that visits the earth every hundred thousand years or every million years. It's an interesting zoo to look at. You don't have any particular connection to any of the creatures on it. But you find it's beautiful to watch and fun to watch.

When you look at it in this broad way, it helps you get away from the human priority that we put on everything. We're trying to save the rainforest now because we might lose some insects or plants that might be good medicines for us in the future. Everything is thought of just in terms of humans. If you take a little broader view, it makes you think a bit more about the rest of the species. Humans are just one, newly arrived species. Where we're wiping out other species of flora and fauna (one every four minutes), now that's really something to worry about. So you start with a galactic explorer perspective, and it sets things right a little bit. You realize that sure, we're humans, therefore we have human cast on our thinking, but that doesn't mean that it's right or important, it just means that obviously that's the prejudice that we would tend to have.

This galactic explorer will come and visit. Say they do some paleontological digs ten thousand years from now, when they come visit. They will certainly encounter two layers. One layer under the earth that represents the great extinction, the end of the age of the dinosaurs sixty-five million years ago. Another layer, that we are right in the midst of, will certainly be just as distinct. A layer just representing maybe a hundred years before us and a hundred years after us: We will have consumed all the fossil fuel that was readily available, all the fossil water that was available, that had been getting stored up

for tens or hundreds of millions of years. [The layer will show] the huge changes of flora and fauna. Maybe there will be some nuclear debris seen. I don't know what they will see; all I know is they will see a layer of great distinctness, and that's what we're in the middle of. But we tend to think of the world just going along. This year is like last year is like the last decade. That's not it at all. We're right in the middle of this layer that is rather analogous to the extinction that wiped out so many living things sixty-five million years ago. You see this as you take the galactic point of view.

A Galaxy

I did not set out to design a geodesic dome. I set out to discover the operative principles in Universe. For all I know, this could have led to a pair of flying slippers.

Bucky

The Sunracer in action, Australian Outback.

The dream becomes reality: Paul MacCready with his engineering marvel, the now available GM Impact.

On launch day, the Sun Explorer spreads its wings for the world press.

> *What is demanded is a change in our
> imaginative picture of the world.*
>
> Bertrand Russell

Brendan O'Reagan

Thinking in Interplanetary Terms

If we are fortunate enough to actually think correctly and keep our minds clear of the wrong assumptions and ideas, then there is a natural sort of synergy between us and nature.

"what kind of thinking was going on when you were working with buckminster fuller in the 1970's?"

Synergetics, was in a sense, the core of Bucky's thinking, in terms of both his philosophy and his metaphysics. His practical sense about engineering all came together in that body of work. And a lot of it had to do, literally, with how he thought the universe was constructed. That is something that is normally the domain of physicists and cosmologists, and though Bucky didn't formally enter that kind of thinking from that direction, he was really asking the kinds of questions that people in quantum theory were asking, that people in basic physics were asking: What is the nature of matter? What is the nature of time and space?

[Bucky] was convinced, because of his geometrical arguments, that time and space were structured in very specific ways, and that the geometry of time and space was, in fact, a geodesic geometry, and that the ways in which atoms and molecules were held together was in terms of the forces that he described in his tensegrity models. He believed that the ultimate particles of matter were not the neutrons and electrons, in a sense, but that they in turn were made up of fundamental modules, which he called the A and B particles, initially, and then modules. So this was a view of geometry that extended right down into the microphysical realm, this was nature's geometry.

Synergetics was his way of trying to articulate all that, and, in particular, his way of pointing out that whatever our models were, they should be ones that involve the whole system, [that involve] that synergy—the unpredictable relationships between things that does not result from their linear addition. One and one equals two would be the linear approach. But one and one equals three would account for the synergy, the unexpected interaction of the parts. His geometry was really aimed at trying to include that.

Bucky, in a way, had a very strange view of the human being, in the sense that it was a very dispassionate, almost cold view in some ways, because he felt that we were a function of the universe, that we were here to create order and to manifest a certain kind of "negentropy," which was a very technical kind of view of the person. It wasn't one that gave meaning to passion, or to emotion, or to caring, even though he was a very passionate, emotional, and caring person. But his passion was devoted to caring for the planet as a whole thing, as a whole system, spaceship earth and all of that. Our role was really to, number one, to stop messing that up, I suppose—but if we became as intelligent as he thought we could be, the proper relationship of the human being to the planet would be one of expanding the role of the life on earth and life beyond earth. He really had a feeling that we were going to go forth into the universe in some sort of way, so it was a view that said we should manifest order wherever we were, that that was our purpose.

If we are fortunate enough to actually think correctly and keep our minds clear of the wrong assumptions and ideas, then there is a natural sort of synergy between us and nature. That was his way of seeing things, and that was part of his whole idea of reshaping the child's perception to realize that the earth was a sphere in which we were moving, and that the sun did not go down. It was that the earth rotated away. He felt that if you were . . . properly located in your environment, then you were in a better position to know what it was really about. It was like turning each person into a functioning compass, if you like. He wanted you to be as oriented from the universe at large and the stars all the way into the planet. That's why he was always so fascinated with Charles Eames's film, you know, The Powers of Ten, which was made from that book, The Universe in Forty Jumps. It's one of the ways of seeing the world from a systems point of view that continually orients you to what nature is doing. That was his basic philosophy, I think.

> "how did fuller view man's role in the universe?"

153

Bucky used language in ways that were systems-oriented, were definitely different, were designed to change your perception—designed to stop you from thinking the way that you'd been taught to think, because he felt that those were the patterns that gave you the wrong views that you had. To talk about the sunrise was a mistake. To talk about things falling down to the earth [was, too]; things fell in or they fell out. Up and down was wrong. It was in and out.

Bucky was really one of the premier planetary thinkers, and he was one of the people who really encouraged thinking about space-ship earth as a whole. He really saw, in interplanetary terms, the evolution of the species in a way that very few other people did. [His view] incorporated science, and technology, and metaphysics, and all of it. He was all in there. Nothing could be left out, and I think if people could be aware of that and remain aware of that, it would be a real step forward. I look at a lot of the ideas that are now being paraded as if though they were some great new piece of thinking about the environment, or about saving the rainforest, or some other idea that, if you look in his writing, he was thinking about and writing about in the '30s and '40s and '50s. One wonders why there isn't more attention now to what he was saying so clearly back then—the real roots of environmentalism, of ecological thinking, of systems thinking about the planet as a whole, of our interdependence. He said that there would be a north-south axis instead of an east-west axis, which is now rapidly coming about. Many of the things that he talked about as trends really are happening, and I think it would be instructive for people to go back and see what he was saying, because you know what is it they say—those of us who do not know history are condemned to repeat it. And if we don't understand or learn what Bucky learned for us, we will be condemned to relearning it by tougher means.

Bucky was really a planetary healer. He was someone who wanted to heal the earth. He was not so much concerned with individual healing. He figured that that was already being taken care of—it was understood that we needed to do that. But he wanted to generate a new breed of people who understood that caring for the earth was part of why we are here. It was taking things John Muir and people behind the basic environmental movement and the Sierra Club and so on had said. He took it through the entire realm of the industrialized society. And the whole thing was not really industry versus nature, or

technology versus nature; it was technology in the service of repairing nature, to some degree. Some people say that he was a classical
technocrat of the '30s, and to some degree there was a utopian
vision of nature there. If you look at those old films of H. G. Wells,
"Things to Come" and "The Wonderful World of Tomorrow" and there
was that hilarious one, "The Wonderful World of 1960", I don't know if
you ever saw that one—but I mean, in a certain sense, there was some
of that. And people said it was naive technocracy. Well, so be it. It was
well motivated and it was well driven, and I don't think it was aquisitive
technology—it wasn't saying let's have more of it for the sake of having more. It really had another larger purpose, and that was to make
technology evolve to the point where it could be about the issue of
caring for the earth and seeing it as a whole system.

*Paolo Soleri leading
Bucky on a tour of
Arcosanti.*

*Synergy means behavior of whole systems unpredicted by
the behavior of their parts separately.*

*

*Because Synergy alone explains the eternally regenerative
integrity of Universe, because synergy is the only word having its unique
meaning, and because decades of querying universities around the world
disclosed only a small percentage familiar with the word <u>synergy</u>, we can
conclude that society does not understand nature.*

Bucky

Pliny Fisk

Systems in Continuous Evolution

Once we're understanding those worlds within worlds within worlds then we understand that what we're doing affects everything. That understanding has got to be brought into everyday life and into design methodology.

"how is the art of design science connected to a biospheric understanding?"

In systems theory, particularly, there's a big difference between open and closed systems. An open system is the ability to participate with the environment, the ability to be responsible for what you're doing, instead of making some cocoon that says I'm going to do all my neat things inside this thing. Now if it ever could be a situation where lots of people could have biospheres, you can easily see outside going to hell, while inside is being a perfect environment. It's a perfect intro-duction to the biosphere.

The biosphere is a system that is continuing in evolution. It doesn't give a damn whether we're here or not. It's evolving. It's a liv-ing system that's often, these days, called Gaia, which is a whole living being in itself. It's very difficult to pull Gaia apart and analyze all these things because it depends totally on an integrated system. It's home—it is possibly the only home that we're ever going to have. If you talk to people in the area of astronomy, and you ask, "How do you categorize our system, and the possibilities for other systems? And what is the chance that we're really going to connect to somebody else?" They'll give you the most extraordinary statistics that say there's an infi-nitely small chance that there is another sun and another planet at the point of intelligent evolution that we can ever have contact with. The idea of the frontier in space that our minds are totally adjusted from our past our brains, our cultures, our storytelling, and all those reli-gious beliefs that place us in worlds of impossible futures that defy the basic laws of the way things work..

So, whether we like it or not, this is it. Once we understand that this is it, this is what essentially we have, then we have to take a very different view of this planet and of ourselves.

From a design science standpoint, we have biospheres within biospheres within biospheres. This region that we live in, in central Texas, is a biosphere in the sense that it's an ecological system. It works because it is fitting within a watershed, with certain vegetation, minerals, soils, and so on. To understand that system, to understand a house as a system within this system, to get ourselves in the frame of reference where responsibility can take place in understanding what home is, that [is the goal]. It's really part of a rule that's beginning to appear in the sustainability movement: Do what you can at the smallest possible scale that you can. If you absolutely cannot do it there, then all right, go to the next scale. There is a back and forth glue between context and connection.

What becomes very important is where you are at a house level.

Pliny's "aesthetics of the unfinished" green form prototype house. Austin, Texas. 1996

What is your immediate community? What is the cluster of housing? What is your neighborhood? All of those things are going to gain much, much more importance, because what you're doing, from a life-cycle standpoint of energy, of materials, is shrinking those things down to where your feedback loops are so close that you understand immediately what you can or cannot do; where things are coming from and where they are going.

At CMPBS we have had to work at several levels at once because we are going through (as a society) a critical transition period - a period of much catching up. At one level, we do considerable indigenous material research that connects to our central Texas grassland home. We design and build public demonstration buildings for public and private clients. We function at the city level in policy terms developing things like the Green Builders Program for the City of Austin: at state level we were contracted in 1994 to rewrite the Architecture and Engineering Guidelines for our State of Texas: at the national level I co-chair the committee responsible for overseeing development of the Environmental Resource Guide for the AIA. Presently, EPA regions, watersheds, states, planning regions, counties, cities, Sectors, neighborhoods, clusters, sites, etc... . Our mapping and our design methodology is a way of hitting responsibilities at the levels of responsibilities of all societies' actors. If your site is the whole of the U.S., what is your level of responsibility?. All the rules are beginning to come out in what this game has got to be.

The idea of ecosystems in ecosystems, and this dependency on the next and next scale, is a very good basis, in any region, to look at as a managerial unit that can really understand itself and understand its metabolism. It has a structure for decision-making—it has any number of techniques that enable that kind of thing to happen. What's going to occur probably, is very much like what old cities were. The concept of what we call "city gate" (really picking off of the old idea of a city gate), which was a control valve: What came into the city? What left the city? Why do you want these things to come and go? In our system it's going to deal much more with flows. Now, when we say a road is a ring road and another road is the connector between the rural and the urban area, that's a very important, noble point to connect that region to that city. It's that point that we call a potential city gate, and that city gate really is involved with a whole new series

158

The Greenest Building on Earth?

There is nothing more difficult
to take in hand, more perilous
to conduct, or more uncertain
in its success than to take the lead
in the introduction of
a new order of things.

Niccolo Machiavelli

Some of the vocabulary of green forms.

of businesses that relate specifically to that city and that region. There's an ecology between those businesses—how they cooperate, how they're using the by-products from each other in order to create other products.

That could be what our enterprise zones are, or what we call enterprise zones now, but put into an ecological sort of context, the whole idea of green building, which is, seemingly, a big topic in the movement these days. Do green builder homes support regionally connected business. Does something when it is called green, connect boundaries of nature's performance? These are the kinds of questions that the EPA contract is trying to answer. What is sustainable?

What happens in the sequence of thinking is very important— you cannot lose your train of thought, because what you're trying to do is understand your context. If you understand the region, green building comes out of that region. It doesn't come out of the fact that you're doing so-called healthy products that can then be distributed left and right over all regions and all places around the globe. It says that green building is the metabolism of your place.

The rating system for our green builder program in the city of Austin (which, by the way, [received] the only Earth Summit award given in this country) was based on the life cycle: Where is something coming from? Can you track it? Is there a [local] business that is doing that? All the way through to the death of whatever material, product, or energy form, showing that there are businesses at that end also taking care of those things, and showing that that loop is occurring within our place. And if that loop, [that is, the entire life cycle], is occurring in our place, the rating, potentially, is very high.

Nature does not complete things. She is choatic. Man must finish, and he does by making a garden building a wall.

Robert Frost

John Allen

The Cosmic Drama

It's a very, very classic Greek drama that we're seeing unfold, but magnified on a planetary scale.

who were the key influences behind biosphere 2?

Both Lewis Mumford and Bucky Fuller were great influences on this project. It goes back in American history to Whitman and Melville. Whitman is onward and upward. On the other hand there's Melville: the ship is sinking and Ahab goes down in a fight with Moby Dick. Mumford emphasizes all the ways that things could go wrong. Fuller emphasizes all the ways that things can go right.

Of course the crucial points in Bucky's philosophy, the two main evolutionary factors, are ephemeralization and synergy, which are the basis of his positive viewpoint. In other words, doing more with less, increasing the metaphysical or information component vis-à-vis the physical component. Biosphere Two is highly ephemeralized and it's highly synergetic. That is, we designed a system—a total system—that has properties unpredicted by the component parts. Now, naturally, that's a metaphysical quest. You don't put tonnage in to get synergy.

Another of Fuller's key concepts, comprehensive anticipatory design, is something that we worked with very much. I think it's one of his most extraordinary concepts. All three words are important: "comprehensive," "anticipatory," and "design." In a sense, Biosphere Two is comprehensive anticipatory design for a twenty-first century society.

I have many colleagues that prefer different arts than poetry, or maybe are primarily scientific, but, for myself, the old distinction is that poetry deals with the mysterium. There's the mysterium fascinans, and the mysterium tremendum. The mysterium fascinans is what fascinates us: it's beauty. The mysterium tremendum is the one that makes you shake.

I think biospheres and space have these two fundamental poetic qualities. If you catch this aspect, the surface aspect has glamour in the deepest sense of the word: beauty. And at the same time, the price of failure in biospherics—to species, to genera, to phyla, perhaps to the whole biosphere itself—is tremendous.

Theater is something that you use to navigate through the cosmos. To my mind, the highest poetry is that written in a dramatic context, for its developing character, and showing plot lines or conflicts. Evolution and the technospheric, biospheric conflict, whether or not that's going to resolve, is probably the number one drama of today, if you look at it from the standpoint of theater and drama.

In dramatic terms, the biosphere is the protagonist. This is what, originally, the Greek drama started with. There was only the protagonist, and then Aeschylus introduced the antagonist. Then Sophocles introduced the third actor on the stage—that would be, in these terms, the noosphere. And the chorus is us.

So you look at it dramatically. I mean it's a very, very classic Greek drama that we're seeing unfold, but magnified on a planetary scale.

> "how is theatre related to the way you think about the design process?

The controversial Biosphere II aims to integrate humanity, technology, and nature.

ABOVE
Biosphere II's roof, an octet truss structure ,
was inspired by the work of Buckminster Fuller.
OPPOSITE, ABOVE
The experimental coral reef and ocean simulation system.
OPPOSITE, RIGHT
The Savannah.
OPPOSITE, LEFT
A banana tree.

Harold Cohen

Making the World Work for All Humanity

*So to make the world really work,
communication is the first thing.*

"does
design
have a larger
purpose?"

Human beings are a very, very, resilient animal. We live in the arctic, the tropics, can go up, down, inside, outside. Because of that adaptability, [humanity] is all over the world, all over the globe. And because of its history of environmental survival through different support systems, humanity has developed culture. Culture is the way human beings have learned, through history, to survive, raise families, and understand their own natures, as well as the nature of that which surrounds them.

The one thing that Bucky did predict was that communication was going to shatter the "bell jar" that kept people controlled. Communications that go around the world make it possible now to tune in to other cultures, other people's idea. As we sit and talk, this room looks like it's empty—it's not empty at all. In this room, there's Chinese, Japanese, languages from all over the world are in the air because of the wave phenomena, and all I need is the right thing to tune in. So all people, all over the world, now, with very little, can tune in and communicate with each other, and it is that communication skill and ability which is shattering predictions by politicians and economists.

When I go to South America, which I do quite often, there are human conditions that are just unbelievable. I've been in the jungle where there's a car battery, there's television, they listen to radio, they have Walkmans. I hear this music—it's [being run on] a battery, a solar battery. And [these people] are very angry. People are angry in Russia, because they see other things going on in West Germany, East Germany, north, south, the battle between the haves and have-nots that Bucky always talked about. That's possible because people are now realizing that the earth can be used in a way which makes it possible to raise a family, not to be sick, to be able to have time to laugh and enjoy life, instead of working until you drop because you're so exhausted from diarrhea because you've lived all your life with two or three different parasites.

So there is a revolution going on which is going to make the world work. Some of it is coming about through some very disastrous means—Jesuits taking machine guns in South America, people killing themselves so that perhaps others can survive. There's still 30,000 people "disappeared" in Argentina, Argentina's a mess. So are Brazil, and Chile, China, Russia.

To make the world really work, communication is the first thing. But then again, once people learn that, then the question is, do they go to governments to solve their problems? Who do they go to? Governments are going bankrupt, they're in debt, whether it's the Russians, or us Canadians. We're in terrible trouble. We spend so much money in "killingry," and as Bucky said, we need to get into "livingry." Will the government get into livingry? Probably not. But there are corporations, whose bottom line is money, who can see that livingry is a big payoff. Products that can go around the world—like a telephone, or like a radio—can be made in Mexico, or Korea, or Taiwan, or Detroit. They're useful and people will have them, so the idea of mass consumption will now make it possible for Bucky's dream of livingry to go worldwide, because there are a lot of customers who are poor and injured. If the world were all middle class, and living in perfectly wonderful housing and healthy, it wouldn't work.

Unfortunately, it's going to work because the world is in terrible shape, and people are dying all the time of terrible diseases, and inadequate food, and poor shelter, and a lot of other things. And so this communication revolution—which you're a part of now by filming—is now going to be available. The spirit for change has come about by the human desire to have something better.

It's a struggle for wanting to live and wanting to share, and Bucky talked about that—making the world work, and having enough to go around, because there is enough. And if you design it well, using less will make more, so less is more, to make one pound, by design, serve three different purposes rather than one. It isn't because you've heard about Bucky that this will work, it's because, in order to be efficient and meet the bottom line, [companies] are going to have

Structurally and formally all the Architecture was in lovely shape, but humans were not fully understood; Design did not serve survival.

Richard Neutra

to produce well, do more with less, satisfy customer needs.

In this kind of competition, who's going to make it work? Corporate structure! The large international corporations are going to be the great moral leaders. Bucky talked about it, and I thought he was crazy, but it's true. They have no allegiance to countries, or national or political parties. They are an organism that was not predicted in the fifteenth century. An international corporate structure. Here in Buffalo, the Marine Midland Bank was bought by the Shanghai Bank, and we have Chinese newspapers here, and the Wall Street Journal's in Chinese and we've got the Asian Journal, and we got all this stuff here, in Buffalo, because it is international. Banks don't go to sleep, because when I'm asleep somebody else is working and it's daylight, so this whole global concept is being supported by a reasonable degree of wanting to make money.

Bring me men to match my mountains.
Bring me men to match my plains.
Men with empires in their purpose
and new eras in their brains.

Sam Walter Fass

Papago Park, Phoenix/Scottsdale, Arizona.
(Martino/Pinto, 1992)

A spectacular example of art and ecology merging to bio-remediate a dying landscape.

Duane Elgin

The Universal Liturgy

Everything that's happening everywhere in the universe is connected with everything else, everything we do, in the most profound sense.

"what do you think thomas berry meant when he said we need to see "the universe as our liturgy?"

Thomas Berry really takes the position that the universe is our teacher. He's a theologian and he says the universe is our liturgy. Written out there plainly before us is everything that we need to know, if we will simply look carefully at the universe. So if we understand the universe—and by that I mean not only material, matter, and organizing principles in physics, but also biology and the other life systems that surround us—we can then learn the basic organizing principles of the universe and reality, and we can then begin to model our social and ecological systems around those. We can learn our way into a living that really is workable, is meaningful, is harmonious with the cosmos as a whole.

Everything that's happening everywhere in the universe is connected with everything else, with everything we do, in the most profound sense. That's what Bell's theory was saying, that beyond the speed of light and separation, this is the whole essence. If two particles are connected or disconnected so much that they cannot communicate at light speed, then how can they be connected?

What they're finding is that they are connected. The basic principle reveals that there is something at a deeper level about the universe and its connectivity which transcends light-speed separation, so that physicists are forced to say that beyond the laws of four-dimensional, materialistic physics, there's something else going on here. And that pushes us into mind or consciousness. I prefer to think of it as mind. In my cosmology, consciousness always has an object: and it always arises, with an electron, to a human, to a plant, or animal, or whatever. There's always an object with consciousness.

Mind, on the other hand, is this deep life energy out of which both matter and consciousness simultaneously arise as co-evolving systems. So we're really pushed to look at this deep life energy, or mind, or whatever you want to call it, and to see that it is giving rise to this whole cosmos, moment by moment, as integrated creation. Whatever we learn is really fed into the holographic memory of the whole system, not only on this planet but over the whole cosmos. We're learning on behalf of the cosmos.

When you think that there are a trillion galactic systems (which is the best estimate now), each one with billions of stars. Out of those billions of stars, roughly half probably have planetary systems in which some kind of life could possibly evolve. When you look at the ocean and you see that there are life forms which are functioning without the benefit of photosynthesis—they're just drawing on the heat energy of the deep ocean vents—you say you wouldn't even need to have photosynthesis for the basis of life. You can function maybe on chemical-transforming, energy-transforming processes. I think the likelihood, the probability, of life throughout the universe is very, very high.

I think for us to actually physically encounter and communicate with other life forms we need to evolve to the status of a mature species. I think people would be blown away by the encounter with another civilization; our sense of species identity would be obliterated. What I think is happening right now is that we are evolving a sense of species identity. We're evolving the capacity to self-sustain and to learn our history as a species. Once we can maintain ourselves, we can begin to look at the origins of the human experiment—what have we done, what's the culture. We can celebrate all that, we can acknowledge all of that, and then we can discover our own creativity and create our own projects. And at that point we can then begin to interact with other species, civilizations without the integrity of our species identity just being blown away by their advanced state. In the best sense we would, as Joseph Campbell says, evolve into an ecology that is appropriate to the character of who we were and what we learned here.

Man becomes great exactly in the degree to which he works for the welfare of his fellow men.

Mahatma Gandhi

John Todd

The New Alchemists

There is another underlying theme, which was borrowed from the teachings of Taoist science, of which I was a student, that is that science not practiced out of a context of sacredness or responsibility was a devil's bargain.

"will you Recall For us the origins of the new alchemy institute?"

In the late 1960s there was a strong sense of revulsion against science. A lot of thinking people thought that most scientific activity led to destructive ends—pesticides, herbicides, the triumph of the industrial culture over nature. It was our feeling, very strongly, that the revulsion was legitimate, but that science needed to be seen in a much more exquisitely whole light, as a science of assembly, where knowledge could be reintegrated around a whole theme of reverse stewardship.

From the very outset, we saw all of science as a kind of pigment in this great canvas we hoped to be able to paint. This canvas had to do with reintegrating society into a genuine partnership with nature. I was a young college professor, promoted too quickly, still in my twenties, to associate dean of 19,000 students. I was made the head of this new Center for Environmental Studies and I was realizing that a university department, for example, wasn't going to change the paradigms. We were talking about fundamental change.

At the time, Nancy Todd, who co-founded New Alchemy Institute with me, and Bill McLarney, a third co-founder, and I, were very taken

Nova Scotia Ark, Prince Edward Island, Opened by
President Trudeau in 1976.

"We asked ourselves the question: Is it possible to grow the food needs of a small group of people in a small space without harming the environment and without enormous recourse to external sources of energy and materials on a continuing basis? The whole idea was: Could we design a system that is self-sustainable and capable of functioning as a system?

John Todd

with the notion that most of the way society goes to try and improve a bad situation is basically to work on the coefficient's structure of the system alone.

Through our friendship with people like Gregory Bateson, we realized that, technologically, we're a completely addicted society. Let's say that we're addicted to internal combustion—the way we would solve the problem of using too much gas is to make it more efficient. But there was nothing in the society that would allow us to ask the fundamental question, "How would we get around?" The same was true of food production—using too much energy from halfway around the globe, or simply poisoning the hell out of the planet.

So to make things better, people were saying, "Well, maybe we should use lower impact strategies." But no one was asking the question, is the way we raise foods—shuttling food several thousand miles before it ever reaches the table—does it make sense?"

New Alchemy was really begun to go back to first principles. There is another underlying theme, which was borrowed from the teachings of Taoist science, of which I was a student, that is that science not practiced out of a context of sacredness or responsibility was a devil's bargain. If you think about it from that point of view, if science were practiced in that context, nuclear power wouldn't have developed the way it developed. I don't think modern society

The basic concept of ecological design as being a powerful tool—perhaps one of the most powerful tools of this century—had been pretty much proven by the late 1970s. A lot of what had to be done in the 1980s was to prove that these could work in an economy which was not foreign to our time. . . The bulk of my work has to do with dealing with toxins in the environment which are damaging to people.

John Todd

would have developed the way it has developed. So we had to change the rules. There were all kinds of great minds floating around to which one could turn for inspirations.

The name was completely unpremeditated. I was sitting in San Diego and turned to Nancy and said, "It's New Alchemy!" And she said, "Yes." It just sprang up out of the unconscious. So those are the origins, I guess.

LIVING MACHINES

It has been a long journey from the original idea to the sophisticated living machines that we've developed today to provide food, waste treatment, fuels, climate, heating and cooling, architectural integration. All those things that have become possible weren't even visible in the beginning. An enormous amount has happened in this brief span of twenty-two years.

There are a series of lessons, which I think led to the development of an ecological science of ecological design. The first lesson was when I was asked by a community in the mountains of Tecate

Early experiments in Living Machines, Cape Cod.

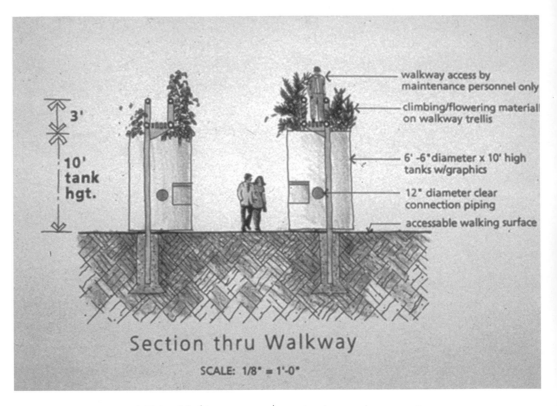

walkway access by
maintenance personnel only

climbing/flowering material
on walkway trellis

6'-6" diameter x 10' high
tanks w/graphics

12" diameter clear
connection piping

accessable walking surface

3'

10'
tank
hgt.

Section thru Walkway

SCALE: 1/8" = 1'-0"

A Living Machine promenade coming to your town soon?

[California], north of the Mexican border, to help them become self-reliant. These were mostly middle-class people who felt that humans were living too heavily on the planet, and they were looking for a lighter model. Again, very much characteristic of the mood of the times—a mood, incidentally, which is welcome at any time, but which happened to be very dominant then.

So I went out with Bill McLarney, and Nancy Jack Todd, and a group of people to this beautiful site high in the mountains. And these people said, "How can we capture our own energy and recover our own moisture, and are there ways of integrating with this quite difficult, semi-arid place?"

We had degrees and boatloads of academic credentials amongst us. And we stared at this land and realized that we'd been tricked. That our knowledge was abstract. That none of us could make a piece of the world work. And that was the beginning of the beginning.

Our response to that experience was to learn all we could about that place, its microclimates, geology, its botany, its zoology. As we studied it, it began to tell us what the latent potential of the area was. Working in that particular spot, we began immediately to move into bodies of knowledge, some of which were thousands of years old, of civilizations that worked with very few resources but did extraordinary things. What did they have? What were their sciences like?

So we looked at stuff going on in the Middle East, and we looked at stuff going on in the ancient native civilizations, and, all of a sudden, this site just simply opened up the whole idea of an earthly science that had to encompass the most advanced ideas and material engineering. We had to know about chemistry, we had to know about light. We had to know about intelligent materials, even about things like artificial intelligence, communication, everything.

THE DREAM OF BALANCE

But it had to be recast in a new light, this dream of balance. One of the beautiful things about using ecology as a model is this concept of balance, this concept of all kinds of strange things that technologists don't think about, pulses—day and night, seasons, cold, warm—how to design all these things so that they dance with each other to create a whole system that self-designs, that becomes intelligent. All of a sudden you are talking about a technology that is alive, a living machine.

So meditating deeply on the question for a while, we began to realize that there is only one model. The one we knew worked over time and had the attributes we were looking for was planet earth. So the very first experiment was to create, much in the fashion of the alchemists of old, a microcosmos, a miniature earth. To do that we had to simulate the dynamic processes of the earth.

For beginnings, we had to create an atmosphere that is part of this earth. And in order to create an atmosphere we had to think very much in the analogue of the river or the stream. We had other species, including the one here behind me, which were capable of living off the bottom of the food chain, off the microscopic algae.

God is an infinite sphere whose center is everywhere and whose circumference is nowhere.

Pascal

177

Living Machine bus stop.

The microscopic algae, in turn, were providing the gases to drive this microcosm. Everything about it was global but, again, in the traditional alchemical sense of the world, it was miniaturized. We did not try to literally simulate an ocean. We simulated the ocean's processes. We did not literally try to simulate a river. We tried to simulate the river's processes. This is the difference of what we do and perhaps a lot of what you have seen at Biosphere Two.

Getting back to the whole cycle, the seventy percent water then had to feed terrestrial ecologies thirty percent. Now you can begin to see the water providing not only a climate but providing the nutriment and the moisture for multidimensional terrestrial structures providing fruits and vegetables. Then, as the process began to evolve, the whole idea of dealing with pulses, the great regulators. We began to superimpose on these systems wind engines, which sometimes would blow, sometimes would be still, again, sometimes contributing to the system.

As this science of assembly—I was trying to get the relation-

178

Living Machines integrated into a public promenade.

ships right—came together, a whole series of extraordinary possibilities began to emerge. They were very productive, they were beautiful
to be in, and they worked. We didn't set out to try and race and create world records of anything, but along the way these systems began
to evolve. They were doing just that. But we always played that down.

That original experiment blossomed out into four or five different directions—into the direction of food, into the direction of
housing, into the direction of climate control and regulation, into the
direction of waste treatment, and finally into the direction of the
whole idea of designing a village which is in fact an ecology.

There was a wonderful gathering that was held in 1980 in which
a number of truly wonderful people, including some of the people
you've talked to, came to try to visualize this dynamic system that
would be alive. It even led to working with sailing ships or ocean arks
which were in themselves ecologies designed to take materials that
were missing in one part of the world, or where ecologies were
degraded.

> "In what
> ways
> can the
> discipline of
> ecological
> design
> transform
> our
> civilization?"

179

But the basic concept of design, of ecological design, as being a powerful tool, perhaps one of the most powerful tools of this century, had been pretty much proven by the late 1970s. A lot of what had to be done in the 1980s was to prove that these could work in an economy which was not foreign to our time. A lot of work subsequent to that was to deal with that. The bulk of my work has to do with dealing with toxins in the environment, which are damaging so many people.

SIGNIFICANCE OF ECOLOGICAL DESIGN

From where I stand, ecological design and ecological engineering are about as radical a discipline as you can get. Because what they say at the very outset is that human beings are going to be partners with other life forms. Now your average designer in a studio, or your average architect, or your average engineer isn't going to think much of that. But what I am proposing is that ecological engineering has the potential to transform how we run our society.

It's possible, using ecological engineering, to create living machines that will generate the fuels we will need in the future, that will transform our wastes, culture our foods, regulate our climate, and integrate our buildings with the larger world. That's an extraordinary thing to say, but it is true. We've already proven it in most of the areas that I just mentioned.

So what's a living machine? How is it designed? What does it look like? It has engineering components. It has material components. It has living components. And they are all completely integrated. The engineering in them is both familiar and different. The ecology in them is completely unfamiliar. The use of materials is familiar to a few people, but is basically unfamiliar—namely, materials that are intelligent, that change their properties with the conditions around them.

The best way to describe the science of this ecological design that leads to living machines is to say that living technologies have their fundamental power source from the sun, and inside all of them are photosynthetic activities. That's a must, so that there are tiny cells capturing radiant energy and transforming that into growth and gas production. Where it goes from there depends on the needs of the

We define ecological design as "any form of design that minimizes environmentally destructive impacts by integrating itself with living processes.

Sim Van der Ryn, Peter Calthorpe

society and the ecological engineer.

The other interesting thing about a real living machine is that it must have, in my opinion, three distinct ecologies. In other words, a living machine—let's say that's providing foods for you or treating all your wastes, it doesn't matter—has to have borrowed ecology from a pond, it may have had to borrow ecology from a forest, and it may have had to borrow ecology from a marsh or a meadow. There must be at least three of them interacting with each other.

But if you produce these three, you put them together (let's say you have a machine you want to grow food; it could be fish, vegetables, all sorts of things), [the resulting machine] has the ability—this is another extraordinary aspect of living machines—of being very long-lived. There is no reason why you can't create a living machine to, say, produce foods for an automobile, if you will, that can last for thousands of years. All the spare parts are alive. All the spare parts are self-designing. All the spare parts are interacting as the external variables change. One of the things we find about designing these systems is that we can't know a fraction of what they know. That's why I call it a true partnership. I mean, they know more than we do.

What the human ecological engineer does is two things. Say the organism is for waste treatment. When you set up the living machine you don't know what organisms will recombine in the presence of the waste. So you get thousands of different species of organisms from all kinds of different aquatic environments and you seed them preferably every season, or four times a year. They begin to recombine in ways to adapt to your waste. It can be as deadly as hell. They'll figure it out. You can't. But you must honor the system by making sure the cast of characters is there. The other interesting thing about living machines—and this is the part that particularly the genetic engineering types find very difficult to understand—is that all the phylogenetic` levels need to be represented. Not just the bacteria and a little algae, but the higher plants and the trees, the mollusks, including the clams and the snails, the fishes, the vertebrates. They all have to play a role.

And it's interesting. The more dangerous the role they have to play, the more ancient the organism. So, when I am working on a Superfund site or a toxic waste site where most of the compounds are carcinogens, the first phase of the living machine—the organisms

Fundamentally you start with the sewer. The sewer is the background to any plan.

Bernard Maybeck

181

that are in it—are the cynobacteria, the most ancient forms, and the ancient anaerobic, phototropic bacteria, the ones that were here on earth before there was an oxygen atmosphere. The design process is one that has, in part, taken place in the wild and is brought into this new domestic, if you will, environment.

The other aspect of all of this is the materials. Ninety percent of our thinking is what I call gossamer engineering. This is the kind of thing that Bucky thought a lot about—membranes, intelligent membranes. I'm much more fascinated by hang gliders and windsurfers and these ultralight phenomena because those, combined, say, with some of the computer-based electronic integration possibilities, are really where the future is going. It's not going to be mass transfer or mass combustion. It is going to be these delicate, intelligent structures. By intelligent, I mean able to change their properties so that they are one state when the internal state inside the machine is one way, and they are another state when the external [state] is the other way. That is really the most sophisticated materials chemistry. From our point of view, it's where the action is.

THE BENEFITS OF REGENERATIVE DESIGN

The real news in all of this is that if living machines are allowed to develop in the twenty-first century, we begin to break down (and this was what Bucky was getting at) the old inequities between north and south and rich and poor; they don't exist in the same way in this new context.

The tropical world is so poor, and the northern world has some of the mineral resources, the libraries, and knowledge to bring to bear. The arid areas, now so "impoverished," have certain kinds of intelligence that are brought to bear in this age. So living machines actually can do as well in Beirut as they can in Iowa. This kind of concept of an ecological design is breaking down the global inequities. It strikes right at the heart of so much of Bucky's thinking.

We know and have already proven that living machines could reduce the amount of space that humans require by 90 percent. In other words, we could give back the wilderness to itself, by miniaturizing the processes that sustain us. That's extraordinary.

One of my goals would be to give the wildness back to the planet and the humans could then live with relatively little impact on the wild. It would be nice to be able to walk through wilderness from Cape Cod to San Francisco, with a side journey to an elegant, sophisticated city—maybe a day and a half downwind—every now and again, when one had the feeling for it. And that is really all possible.

William McDonough

Architects will recognize the need to go back to practicing an ancient art, which is the design of buildings that are sensitive to the human agenda and the natural agenda.

"Buckminster Fuller felt that architecture is the most comprehensive discipline. Can we hope to see architects assuming more of a leadership role in the future?"

I like architects. Most architects are actually people who have signed up for a profession that's very low paying, very demanding, and yet very rich because it really is the meeting of technology and art. [Architecture] has a very rich agenda, and I think that that's understood when people get into it. I think that what happens with the way the system is presently structured, is that we get put in little boxes, and we get focused on certain things, and we only get paid for what's in that box—and actually it's the line between the boxes that we have to be aware of, and that, I think, architects are in a position to be aware of. It's no accident that [Thomas] Jefferson was also an architect because it's all about synthetic thinking.

I think architects have more and more of a role to play because even the methodology that architects use to think through problems has been found to be very valuable in terms of longer- and larger-term agendas, in terms of systems thinking, in terms of pulling together a great number of variables into a coherent whole.

So the architect does have a significant role, and should take a leadership role. We do need to be paid more for what we do. We do need to be seen as more valuable, and I think over time that will happen, but it won't happen as long as we focus on things that aren't necessarily related to what people really need. This notion that you heat a building rather than heat the people in the building is a fundamental one. Why are we taking the demands of the buildings or of the system before we take the demands of people? I think that there's a lot of frustration in the world when people see that we're really servants to the system instead of servants to real human needs, and real natural

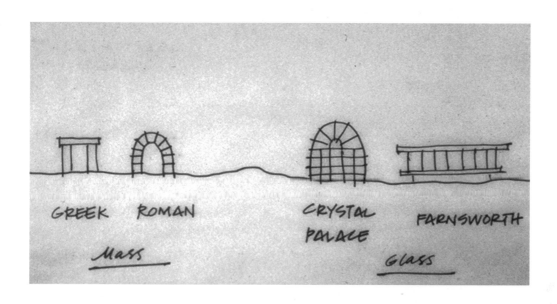

GREEK   ROMAN

Mass

CRYSTAL
PALACE

FARNSWORTH

Glass

CAVE   ADOBE   TENT

Mass   Mass   Membrane

*Tradition is
the alphabet.
Form is the
language.
Architecture
is the poem.*

Richard England

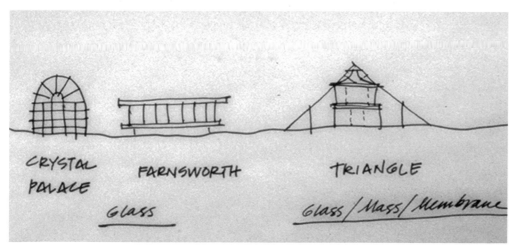

CRYSTAL
PALACE   FARNSWORTH   TRIANGLE

Glass   Glass / Mass / Membrane

needs. So there's a great deal of frustration there. I think that can be busted open and needs to be busted open, pretty quickly.

Architects will recognize the need to go back to practicing an ancient art, which is the design of buildings that are sensitive to the human agenda and the natural agenda. I think it'll happen because people are going to ask for it. We're already seeing that. The demand is there.

Professionalism often implies that you know all the answers to something. We're at a point where we have the marvelous opportunity to reexamine everything we're doing and to turn this whole thing on its head. We have whole new ways of thinking about the making of things. So we're not acting professionally in the conventional sense, in terms of you come to me, ask me a question, I give you the current professional response. Instead, I have to stop, I have to think, I have to wonder, I have to look around, I have to explore, I have to come back to you with a considered opinion, based on a great number of parameters that haven't been codified. If you asked, "How do I flush a toilet, where does it go?" a professional would say, "You have a septic tank, you have a leeching field, it's this big." That's the end of the professional response. But I may look at that and say, "No, there are other ways to do this that make more sense." So in that sense I'm practicing, I'm not acting on a purely professional level in the traditional sense. We have such amazing opportunities, and we have to examine them. The point that we're at now involves a great deal of invention—careful invention.

We can no longer say there is nothing new under the sun.
This whole chapter in the history of man is new.

Thomas Jefferson,
in a letter to Dr. Priestley just after his accession to the Presidency in
March, 1801.

186

Heinz Foundation Office.

Environmental Defense
Fund Interiorscape.

James Wines

Developing a New Iconography

Architects like Le Corbusier and Frank Lloyd Wright, in their time, anticipated tomorrow. They anticipated the direction of the future.

deal of invention—careful invention.

Every art form, to be relevant, has an imagery, or an iconography, or a source of content—that's what makes it exciting. For some artists, their imagery is so profound that it can bridge a century. Someone like Samuel Beckett, for example, wrote about ideas that did, in fact, become the umbrella over our entire civilization: the sense of desolation, the sense of loneliness, the sense of a kind of apocalyptic scenario. He sensed maybe fifty years ago where this century seemed to be going psychologically.

The same is true of all of the arts. Architecture is not alone. Architects like Le Corbusier and Frank Lloyd Wright, in their time, anticipated tomorrow. They anticipated the direction of the future. The problem, of course, in all art forms, is that the pioneers often steal the show. In other words, they do all the things that are most interesting in the beginning, and the residuals that are left over are usually not worth exploring, or at least they're minor explorations at best. The Russian Constructivists, for example, because they really believed in the image of the machine and the image of the factory, their iconography, their images, are exciting and dynamic and new. Neoconstructivism now is, at best, a style. One can be incredibly adept at manipulating stylistic things. But how exciting are they? So when I speak of imagery, I'm really talking about the search for a new language which is more appropriate and more in touch with the world that we are living in right now.

> "what do you mean by a new iconography?"

188

Sketches of alternative, ecologically driven public spaces by James Wines.

James takes on the greening of two national icons, the White House and Manhattan.

The city should be an organization of love... the best economy
in cities is the care and culture of them.

Lewis Mumford

"what is it going to take for architects to break out of the power of tradition and start leading us into this ecological age?"

I think the problem with architecture is that it sort of dumped the old order, meaning the beaux arts and the tradition of decoration on buildings, which you did at the beginning of the century. Architects jettisoned all of that. They just tossed it over, throwing out the baby with the bathwater essentially, in favor of this new imagery of the new age, which at that time was technology, and engineering, and so forth. In the process, of course, it became academic, and it became void and deprived of any relevance. You just can't repeat something over, and over, and over, and over, and over again for the millionth time, and expect it to contain any of the energy of its original inspiration.

So we're at a threshold now, I think, where most sensitive people are rethinking the fact that architecture says very little to people, that it's basically the manipulation of abstract shapes. Some of the postmodernists tried to bring back some kind of historicism. There was a little period about five or six years ago when everybody was running around putting pediments and columns on buildings. But that, again, was a manifestation of style and not of a gut-level reaction to a kind of changing world. It seems to me that the gut-level reaction is: How do you deal with this incredible flow of information? We are just besieged by contact with the world. Film. Video. These are the art forms of our time. In fact, architecture seems a little static by comparison to all of this. How do we re-recognize the earth? How do we go back and look at it as a fresh source of imagery? And if we go to these two ideas . . . I think that you can build something that is exciting; that you can communicate to people. The buildings will not look as if they had been designed fifty years ago.

I don't think the arts can save the world. One of the conceits of early modern design was that they proclaimed that architecture was in fact going to save the world. Le Corbusier once declared, "Architecture or revolution!" [He believed that] you have to build architecture for humanity, or the masses would revolt. But I do think that the arts can monitor civilization. I think they can monitor human behavior and they can offer guidelines. Architecture is certainly the most pervasive of all the public arts, and it's totally wasted.

Again I go back to my original premise: to continue to create abstract cubist designs in public spaces is to really render them merely decorative, or merely a backdrop. I don't think that was always the case. Certainly during the Middle Ages, the Renaissance, buildings served a function of being chroniclers and monitors of culture. They told you stories, they guided you in the right direction. The church, the Catholic Church, couldn't have existed, couldn't have generated the power that it did, had it not been for the images that were inherent in architecture from about the ninth century to the sixteenth century. So I'm really looking at architecture as having options in that direction of having the possibility of generating a dialogue with the public again. It desperately needs that.

In that sense, I'm sort of happy to be an artist in the midst of this. I say that advisedly, too, because I think most architects are designers, meaning that they kind of convert pragmatism into some kind of aesthetic resolution. I always say it's like a compromise of art, really, because the functional elements seem to always get in the way. To me, the function of any building or work of art is to communicate. That is the prime function of a building. Certainly it has to service the uses to which it's been placed, but that's not very difficult to do. So I'm really looking toward younger architects and artists to think about developing a new imagery, a new language for the new age.

> "what is the role of the arts in this shift?"

> Without art and architecture, civilization has no soul.
>
> Frank Lloyd Wright

James Wines' eco-redesign of a French Village.

Chapter Five

The Emergence of Eco-Design

*It may be true that one has to choose
between ethics and aesthetics, but whichever one chooses,
one will always find the other at the end of the road.*

Jean-Luc Godard

▼▲▼▲▼▲▼▲▼▲▼▲▼▲▼▲▼▲▼▲▼

Whether we want to admit it or
not, the built world
is a manifestation of the intentions of our Soul.
In this century, the subtle mechanisms of artificially
cheap land, subsidized fossil fuel energy ($84 billion per year),
and TV mediated reality, have been
the biggest contributors to the
suburban sprawl poured like marshmallow syrup on to the landscape.

The modernist notions of Zoning (originally a 19th century
German idea) that evolved out the conventional conjectures
based on low density, segregated land use, and auto-centric planning approaches. are now in deep need of being radically re-
addressed in light of ecological design principles., such as those
presented here.

These embedded constructs can be displaced by a more empowering understanding if we begin to make that majestic
shift from designing inert objects in space
to designing organisms that are apart of
living systems that give back more than they take.

This goes back to Froebel when he said "It is not a question of
communicating knowledge already acquired, but of calling forth
new knowledge". Ecological design has the power to do that by
bringing about a more sophisticated integration of Nature and
Culture.

The emergence illuminated in this chapter
has the potential to bring us buildings that
are net exporters of energy, transportation
systems that bioremediate, and cities that
harvest food, energy ,and are
natural processors of human waste.

As evolution's tail wags us towards the regenerative city.

C.Z.

He who understands this technology will inherit
the 21st Century.

R. Buckminster Fuller

Ian Mcharg

On the Origins of Ecological Design

The idea that nature could be benign, and sublime, and beautiful, and there could be an ideal relationship was a very, very revolutionary idea.

People have been engaged in modifying the environment from the very earliest of times, as they were in the irrigation of the Tigris and the Euphrates. But the formal exercise—that has its origins in Hannibal, the interior court gardens in Egypt, and Pompeii. Then we begin to see rather more complex medicinal gardens done by monks in the Middle Ages. But it's not really until the late Middle Ages that this garden form becomes quite an important thing.

At that time, there was an architecture that made a symmetrical system: great avenues lined with plants and so on. It really was a kind of green architecture. That continues right through the evolution of the great governments, the Renaissance in Italy and France; Versailles, of course, in the early 1700s, was its culmination. Can you imagine? A mile and a half long, and half a mile wide, and Louis XIV lying in his bed looking down into all of nature? Because his forte was to exercise his dominion and demonstrate his subjugation of nature, which he was doing very effectively! I'm sure that looking at this great symmetrical composition, he was a little embarrassed about the fact that he was not entirely symmetrical, with only one heart and his testicles not in true symmetry! There can be no question that this adaptation of the landscape was serious. Whether or not this is landscape architecture is a question that may be thought of as an essential one.

In the early eighteenth century, in a coffee house in London, there was this new idea that there should be an ideal relationship between man and nature. Oh, gracious! Addison, Cowley, Dire, all such people, they started writing an optimistic paper about an ideal relationship between man and nature. This was incredible. Nobody knows where it came from. There don't seem to be any antecedents at all. Up to that time, almost every development of nature was brutally savaged, and induced every kind of sinful aspect of man. The idea that nature could be benign, and sublime, and beautiful, and there could be an ideal relationship was a very, very revolutionary idea. It may have been the beginning of the modern world. This became the most important subject being discussed in eighteenth-century London, the demonstration of this ideal relationship.

© Thomas Slagle

Brendan O'Reagan

Heading for an Aesthetic of the Invisible

It is when our technology becomes invisible to nature and nature invisible to it that we will have achieved the ultimate.

"how is the notion of ephemeraliza- tion connected to design science revolution?"

One of the key ideas that was essential to Bucky's thinking was the notion of ephemeralization, by which he meant that we were always proceeding to do more and more with less and less. The idea that there was a limit on resources was, in fact, a mistake, because we could use the same material differently and more and more efficiently. Ultimately, ephemeralization also connected with miniaturization— less and less and smaller and smaller. In that sense, Bucky anticipated the development that we now call the nanotechnologies, of technologies operating at scales below 109 of a centimeter, at the molecular and other [levels].

I remember talking to him back in 1971 and saying, "Where will this idea of ephemeralization go? What is its ultimate consequence?" His answer, in a kind of partly serious and partly humorous way, was to say "We're all heading for the aesthetics of the invisible." It is when our technology becomes invisible to nature and nature invisible to it that we will have achieved the ultimate, and what he really meant, in a sense, was that we would no longer have crude methods. We would refine our interfacing with nature to such a degree that we would recycle and we would evolve in ways that we wouldn't need to do the crude industrial revolution kind of things.

He was thinking about nanotech before there was nanotech and he was watching trends, where instead of using tons of copper wire, we're using one satellite; instead of rates of information transmis-sion—nobody tracks that. I would be very fascinated to see tracking of ephemeralization from the '70s to the '90s. I have a feeling that it would be an extraordinary curve.

I think that he was part of a different tradition. What really happened for him was a spiritual experience about life or not having life at all. When he was sort of brought to the brink of self-destruction, I think, it ultimately put everything into very sharp focus for him about why we live in the first place. His view of being on earth to be of service is very similar to the views of great spiritual thinkers. It is not very similar to what drove the great physicists or scientists, except perhaps towards the end of their lives. I think they all tend to become metaphysical toward the end. Bucky was metaphysical at the beginning and all the way through, in a sense.

So, in a way, he was internally very conscious of the metaphysical origins of his drive to be of service, but he didn't want to talk about it, because he didn't want the metaphysical side of his being to take over how people saw him. He wanted people to focus on the physical and the useful ideas that he was putting out for people to work with and design with. He felt if he talked about the metaphysical side too much, it would work against him being taken seriously. He was very cautious and astute about that.

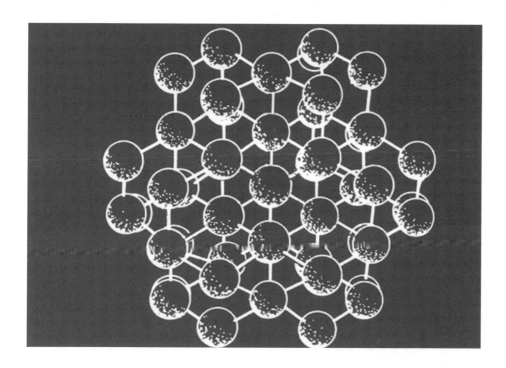

Driven by the force of love, the fragments of the world seek each other that the world may come into being.

Teilhard De Chardin

William McDonough

The Multiplier Effect in Design

Development should be seen as something like the development of an idea, you intensify it, you make it more rigorous, you make it richer, you make it better.

"how does design thinking affect the economy of a place?"

Talk to companies like Walmart, K-mart, and 7-11 about the multiplier effect, because, ultimately, things can be recycled within a community. These facilities can start to see themselves as part of a community, model themselves that way; they can become the center for recycling, for example, they can give something back, they can be designed as housing of the future.

The Walmart we're doing in Lawrence, Kansas, is designed to be converted into housing. When it's finished . . . you've changed the demographics, you've changed transportation plans, but all of a sudden when they've finished with the use of it, instead of saying we're gonna desert this and go build another big one, it becomes a part of a community. So you can start to model things like that. You can also model on conservation—there's a multiplier factor to energy conservation. A lot of people don't realize that when you put in a solar collector, and you produce the equivalent of a dollar's worth of oil, using renewable energy in its place, that's a dollar that is not leaving the community every year. So every year that dollar shows up again.

Once you start to model the multiplier effects, you leave short-term thinking. You start to wonder, "What would the multiplier effect be here?"—in the city of Chattanooga, that freed up five million dollars a year that was going out for energy—and you start investing that, year after year. See, it's not a five-million-dollar, one-year hit, it's five million dollars a year. It has interest. It amortizes. It builds.

So you can start to model these things that way. You can have communities start to think in terms of their development, get them involved in this larger pattern, where they look at their development opportunity and instead of saying, "Isn't it wonderful that someone is

202

Central "agora" at the Environmental Defense Fund office in New York City.

coming in here to provide jobs"—which is the way they look at it now—"and therefore it affects our tax base and we'll have some work for people," you really have to study an enterprise before you insert it in community. You have to evaluate the community assets and ask, "What is the net effect of enterprise on this community?"

So the sorts of things a community should consider first are what is our water [system], what is our local economy, how is our health, how's our school system functioning, and so on. Once you've done that, then you bring in enterprise and examine its real effect on your town. So you can say, should we zone for a 7-11 down there on the corner? Well there's a question; it's not just that we get a 7-11— we get four jobs, but what happened to Mom and Pop and Fred? So you look at your local town and ask, "Do we need endless cups of cof-

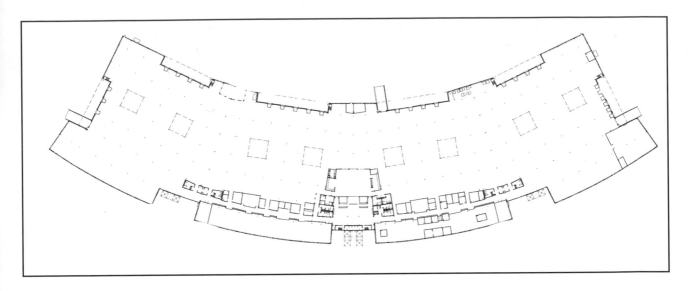

Main floor plan, Herman Miller SQA Factory.

fee? . . . What is the effect on our community by having this thing happen here?" And you just look at it, model it, and say, "Yes, it makes sense" or "No, it may not make sense." Because, in the end, it may actually be more destructive than it is productive.

I think one of the problems with Bucky's domes, for example, is that they dealt with the notion of efficiency and the efficient use of materials, but they didn't necessarily encompass all the agendas that go along with habitation. . . . [Similarly,] I think the reason that the solar building failed as a large-scale event was that people were designing solar collectors for people to live in, rather than houses that were sensitive to climate and culture. So solar buildings still represented the same engineering mentality that created the problem in the first place, and I don't think we can solve our problems using the same methods that created them.

So what does this imply when you're designing a building? The ancients understood very kinesthetically, very directly, what it meant to put a house on a site, in the sun, using local materials. Their resources were, essentially, only those at hand and they understood them in very sophisticated ways. So we can now look at what we do and ask, "What were the generic characteristics of some of these ancient buildings, before the large sheet of glass, and what lessons can we learn from them?" We find special things—for example, buildings often [had] generic characteristics and were designed around human proportioning systems. That was because they didn't have all the bells and whistles that we can apply today on a mechanistic level, and they had to work with natural energy flows. And we find that Soho, in New York, for example, still exists as a neighborhood, because the buildings there weren't designed around mechanical proportions, they were designed around human proportions. They had high ceilings so that hot air could rise in summer, they had good ventilation – these places were workshops and they had gas lighting, so they wanted the bad air to go up—they had very tall windows which allowed the daylight to penetrate very deeply, because they didn't have artificial lighting the way we do today. The buildings had a great deal of thermal mass,

The view along interior "street", Herman Miller SQA Factory.

which means that their comfort levels could be basically static—they could preserve heat and they could preserve cooling. You find that those buildings have great long-term utility because they can be applied to many human purposes. As the use of that neighborhood changed from industrial, to commercial, to residential, let's say, it could apply itself to all those various human needs, and therefore the neighborhood continues to exist.

So one of the fundamental principles is to design for the long term. Think about energy, for example—the amount of energy it takes to make a building is so intense. A steel building, for example, has the equivalent energy embodiment of pouring four and a half inches of oil over every square foot of the building—just to make the building. If you see that as a mortgage on the capital reserves of the planet, then you would want your amortization period to be as long as possible.

One way to extend your amortization over that human effort would be to make the building adaptable to many human purposes, so it could be there for a very long time, preserving culture, preserving community. As a designer, it means that if we take on a generic design—a warehouse, an office building, retail space, housing—we really should be designing them all around the proportions of housing. That way, when their current use may no longer be necessary, they're adaptable to other human purposes. One of the terrifying prospects today is that our visions are so short term that we make office buildings that could never be inhabited. They're sealed; they're steel structures; they're not appropriately proportioned for living—you could have corridors that are sixty feet from a window. But we're seeing laws changing. In Germany, for example, [there are] rules that you can't be more than 8.5 meters from a window—that's only 25 feet. They're focusing on this issue of what it means to inhabit a place. So we see those kinds of issues coming in and starting to affect our design. We are designing a day care center in Frankfurt, for example, to be housing of the future, in case its use ever changes.

Ideas perish as soon as they are compromised... Build in fantasy without regard for technical difficulties. To have the gift of imagination is more important than all technology, which always adapts itself to man's creative will.

Walter Gropius

A view of the main entrance, across the constructed wetland,
Herman Miller SQA Factory.

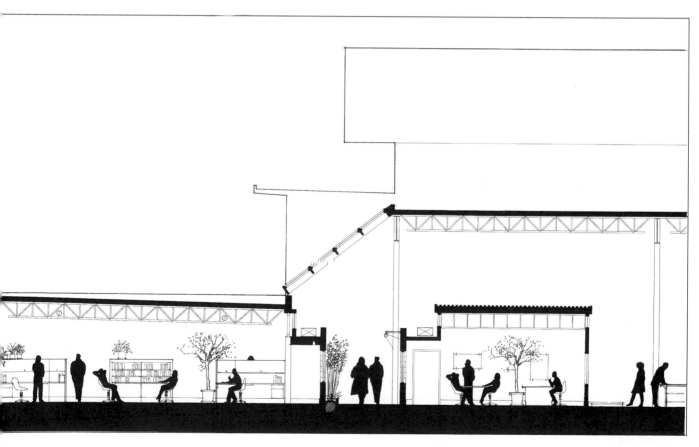

Section through offices and interior "street",
Herman Miller SQA Factory.

Carol Franklin and Leslie Sauer

Synergistic Solutions

You don't look at solving a single problem—housing for a certain group of people or providing office buildings—you look at a larger integrated whole, in which all the systems are synergistic.

"In what ways is ecological design different?"

CAROL FRANKLIN: The fundamental way that ecological design is different is that it's a wholistic approach. No problem is seen as a single-focus problem, whether it's a simple problem, like parking cars, or a larger problem, like how you place a community on a site.

You don't look at solving a single problem—housing for a certain group of people or providing office buildings—you look at a larger integrated whole, in which all the systems are synergistic. And one of the reasons that's important today is because our problems have increased exponentially, rather like population has increased exponentially, and unless we have synergistic solutions we will not have tools that are effective in solving the magnitude of problems that we have today.

LESLIE SAUER: I think one of the big differences with ecological design is that it's very inclusive. Carol spoke about the idea of solving multiple problems. It's not only a goal, it's an absolute requirement, in that the real world is by definition very complex. We have tried to simplify things to a point where somebody wins—one side loses, one side wins, or we can take very black-and-white approaches to things, but that really hasn't worked. I think what distinguishes the ecological designer is this need to really go after a solution that will work, and, of course, it means involving people. Some of us tend to treat the ecological designer as if culture and social issues are left out, but that really isn't true at all. It's really about getting nature and culture working together in ways that are very positive for people, and it makes it a very different process altogether.

FRANKLIN: This business of the integration of solutions means that when we look at something like water, water has traditionally been treated by engineers as something to control. We talk about flood control and non-point- and point-source pollution control, and we look at soil erosion control when we look at soil and water interacting. An illustration of how the ecological approach would tackle a problem like that is to see water as a resource, which means that you're looking at the entire water system of a site, and all the water uses that would involve development: potable water, storm water, waste water, all groundwater, rainwater, available water on a site. All become part of a larger system, and any solution is seen within that larger context.

SAUER: You ask about changing values. While they're certainly very important, and there seems to be a lot of growing consensus about what the new values are, I think a lot of what we have to look at is changing power. Much of what we're really interested in as ecological designers is actually empowering those people who live in a community, who are responsible for the care of the landscape, with really making important decisions about it. We find that the values that people have serve us well if we're actually able to bring them together and to find what the real consensus is. A lot of what we see going wrong is that those people who really ought to be involved in the decision-making as well as the implementation do not get involved in the process.

FRANKLIN: There is a false dichotomy that has been developed between the technological and ecological values. We are the representatives of our age, and in fact this [ecological] point of view has come about and seized people's imaginations partially because we are a high-tech society that has the tools to bring these things to people.

Restoring natural habitats, Trexler Memorial Park, Allentown, PA.

The natural splendor of a renewed habitat:

I know it's a cliche to say that it started when we could leave the earth and see it as a fragile ball hanging there. Clearly people had this sensibility long before that, but right now we have the tools to bring a lot of the understanding of our destruction and our abuse of the earth to a wide range of people, and I think that's why we're seeing a great groundswell of interest in sustainable design. Can we live in harmony with our earth? Or are the ways we live going to destroy us?

"are you optimistic that the tools of ecological design can make a difference?"

WHEN THE COMMUNITY BECOMES THE DESIGNER

FRANKLIN: I do have an enormous optimism. There's a fundamental consensus about the abuse of the earth, the destruction of the earth. The tools that we have today are showing us things like the hole in the ozone. When we bring this to people, I think that there gets to be a far wider and deeper level of concern. One of the tools of the ecological designer which is going to allow people to be more empowered is the interactive technology of computers and televisions and

A narrow
alley eco-design
transformation.
Queens Village,
Philadelphia.

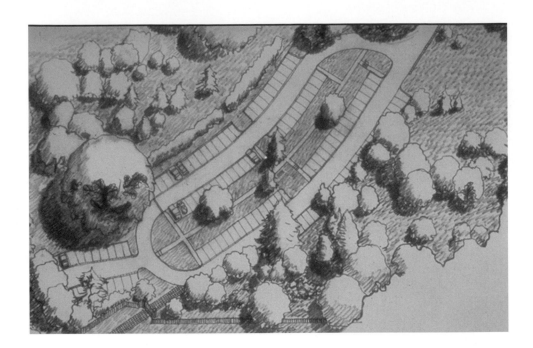

CD-ROMS. A community can be made aware of what is happening to it, of what its consequences are, and can propose solutions and see instant changes that these solutions would bring about. Then the community becomes the designer, and one of the things that's going to happen is that these tools, as they are used by what you're calling the radical designers, as they are used by communities to design themselves, are going to allow us to really understand the data, to see the key issues, to see the consequences and come up with new solutions.

SAUER: We're interested in the ecological designer with a lower case, rather than a capital D, in the sense not of the designer of the old days—who's an eminent individual, probably male, whom everyone's terribly interested in and gets very excited about—but the designer as people in a community being informed about their community and actually taking an action. We see ourselves much more as facilitators than designers, in that sense.

There's a very important element of self-design in any community. It comes from the people who are there, but it also comes from the reality of the site. In the past, we thought we could change any site willy-nilly. We are now seeing we cannot disrupt so casually, and so, in that sense, all of us are very much engaged in restoration of those

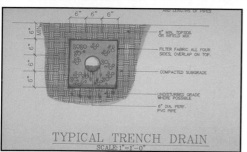

Ecological design strategies applied to parking at the Morris Arboretum, Philadelphia, PA.

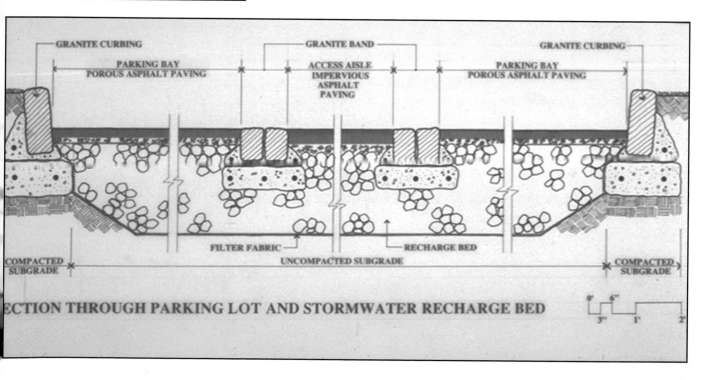

specific systems that are particular to each place and that sustain it. There's a very high degree of humility in that exercise that is quite different from what we may conveniently or frequently associate with design.

FRANKLIN: When you say we treat every site as if it's the whole planet, which I think we do, we are looking at this site in terms of the systems, in terms of the site as a whole, in terms of its larger context and, most of all, in terms of both its universal qualities and its unique qualities. Every site shares with many other sites that are like it some fundamental structural aspects, and every site has unique qualities.

Probably the most important part of the approach is that we let the site speak to us before we speak to the site. In other words, the designer doesn't come with preconceived ideas. We've talked a great deal about the fact that the community would be empowered and become the ecological designer, and that we are the facilitators.

Site plan with nature's contours in mind. SmithKline Research Campus.

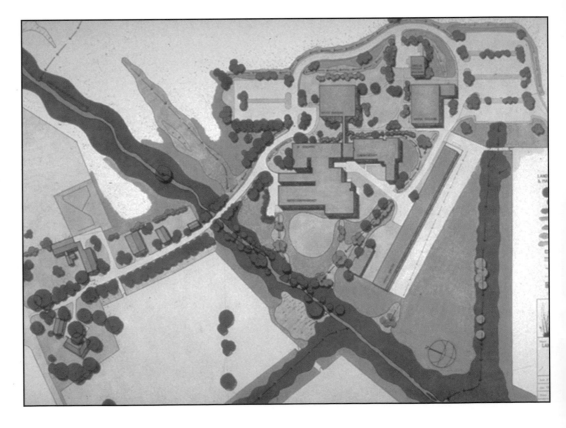

Ecological Design
Strategies are about
transforming dying
patterns into dynamic
complex living
systems.

What I think we don't want to leave you with is the impression that this is not art and there is not art and imagination and inventiveness that are deeply required to make this thing happen for people.

Inventiveness comes from surprising places. As you break down barriers and empower unexpected people, inventiveness comes from strange corners and is built on by many, many people to create the final solution—which then does not have the imprimatur of a single designer, perhaps. Again, I think this comes out of the fact that the problems are very complex and no longer can be solved by a single personality with a single style.

SAUER: The idea that we design every site as if it were the whole planet really goes to the core of the idea of sustainability. We no longer accept the notion that you can justify actions on one site on the basis of something that is somewhere else. I can destroy all the forest here because there's a forest preserve over there. Fundamentally, if we look to the real ideas of sustainability, each site must address the real problems that are characteristic of all of the globe. If I need to affect more storm water infiltration and pollutant reduction, it happens on every site. If I have to restore habitat continuity and restore forests, we do it on every single site.

---

*I consider Lawrence Halprin, Roberto Burle Marx,
A. E. Bye, and Andropogon to be the most
significant landscape architectural designers
of the late twentieth century.*

*Ian McHarg,
A Quest for Life*

Crosby Arboretum
Picayne, Mississippi.

Landscape improvement plan for the 26th Street gateway to Center City Philadelphia.

Tony Gwilliam

Comprehensive Anticipatory Design

Science is basically a logical process so we actually look at the whole picture and don't try to specialize it out.

"what is comprehensive anticipatory design and how is it Relevant?"

Anticipatory design science is just what it says. It's anticipatory—so you actually try and resolve a problem before it arises. It has to do with the whole concept of design—relating, repatterning earth's resources to bring them together in a way which is useful to us and to the health of the planet.

Science is basically a logical process, and Bucky also used the word comprehensive at the beginning of "comprehensive anticipatory design science," so we actually look at the whole picture and don't try to specialize it out.

We're looking at all the impacts of any particular behavior or repatterning that we do from the point of view of health effects and so on. So we really design that way now. But who is educated to design that way? Fuller looked around the world to see who has a comprehensive education today. He felt that the captains of the ships, before the days of radio, anyway, were trained in the defense ecologies to make decisions on the spot, because they couldn't go back and ask the king of their country. So they were educated in a very comprehensive way to decide whether to declare war or not without having to ask. Nowadays, because we have radio, we don't educate people comprehensively, because we send all the decisions back to the Pentagon, or wherever the basecamp is.

Some people are comprehensively educated. The royal family and aristocracy in some parts of the world still consider that an overall education, for what they call their top people, is important. Fuller felt that architects were reasonably comprehensively educated—they actually considered a lot of different points; they considered materials, and production, and energy, and bringing together different things, the arts and the sciences linked together.

So Fuller, for a time in his life, had great hope that the architects, internationally, would get together and look at the planet as a whole. I think he was a bit disappointed in the architects who tried and were interested in his geodesics, but really weren't tuned in—well, some people were.

Quite a few architects have followed Fuller, but they really weren't tuned in to the degree that Fuller would have liked, and so there's really nobody. Now people who are dealing with anticipatory design science are people who study on their own, through their own experience, or people who are moving from one profession to another. Maybe they started off as a doctor of medicine or something, and they're moving to another area with two or three degrees behind them and slowly becoming comprehensive through their own wishes.

The artist-scientists apparently assumed intuitively that a more man-favoring rearrangement of the environment would be conducive to humanity's spontaneous self-realization of its higher potentials.

R. Buckminster Fuller,
Critical Path

Christopher Alexander

Design for Living Structures

That ought to be our goal: the production, creation, and sustaining of life, which is a holy ideal.

"how is this emerging ecological world view hooked up with the world of architecture that you operate within?"

It seems to me that the crux of the whole thing has to do with life. In the '70s, one started out with stuff like solar energy and non-renewable resources. They were really technical problems that were brought to the fore to actually illuminate a much more problematic consciousness. In other words, I think the people who are now behind the ecological movement are spiritually affected by it, and they are emotionally affected by it, in the sense that they hope for a more harmonious, more integral world. It isn't because of some particular concern—Is gasoline a bad thing and is solar energy a good thing? Or are my bricks good and concrete bad? It's a much larger issue.

I don't think that the people who speak for ecology have yet actually made that quite clear. They tend still to be hammering on certain particular themes, some of them very, very important and sensible—sustainability being one. But when it's phrased like that, it's still a technical problem. You can say, "Well okay, so that's the sort of fashionable technical problem now." But it's not that fascinating when you think of it that way.

On the other hand, if you say there's a more general way in which we would like human communities to become a part of all life on the planet, then you're getting closer to the larger issue of life. There's a certain sort of funny thing that we see in a natural traditional environment—whether an American Indian group living in the forest or on the prairie, or a mountain village in Nepal—we see people very, very close to the earth and very close to life. In a literal sense, what they did in their communities, what they built, was an extension of that living fabric.

In some parts of the world, that living fabric was actually quite huge. There are parts of the foothills of the Himalayas that were treated like that. One of my favorite examples is southern England, which is a structure about three hundred miles by about one hundred miles that was built up over an eight hundred year period into one of the most complex structures ever made by man. It is now rapidly being wrecked, because of lack of understanding of its existence and structure as a living fabric.

What I see coming about is a transition from the twentieth century—with its preoccupation with money and technical problems and the sort of sanctification of those things. Some of the much-admired architects are people who have raised technology to huge heights. What I see happening as we open the twenty-first century is a completely different kind of awareness, where the critical thing is asking: How do you make life of which we are a part?

If you take Berkeley here, you've got a few miles square. What does it mean for this actually to be a living structure? You can ask the same question about a house; you can ask the same question about a region. What the ecologically minded people have been saying, correctly, I think, is, "We're not very good at making living structures. We don't really know what living structures are, hardly—we've gone ass backwards about it. We're not paying attention to the right thing." That ought to be our goal: the production, creation, and sustaining of life, which is a holy ideal. It's actually a religious problem and that's really what I'm trying to get at.

For all of the interest in solar energy or avoiding dangerous pesticides—all of these things are very intelligent, but they're all quite pragmatic, because they are actually narrow, little, particular, technical devices or critiques. The larger problem, what it really means to make a house have life or to make a town have life, has hardly yet been raised. I was going to say there's even a taboo about talking like that, but that isn't quite true. I think that taboo has just about run its course.

Let me give you an example. Just down the street here, we had a zoning issue. Somebody wanted to build a large apartment building, and a lot of people felt, well, it's kind of ugly, and it's too big, and it's unpleasant. They didn't like it, didn't want it. There was a lot of neighborhood resistance. So people come into the city hall after planning meetings and get up and start making objections. But the kind of

You cannot make a building unless you are joyously engaged.

Louis Kahn

objections that they feel it's okay to raise are things like there's going to be a huge parking problem in the neighborhood, or it's going to create more pollution or some sort of labor problems. Very sort of specific, narrow, technical things. And yet, there were some times at these hearings (there were 100,150 people) when what they really wanted to say, and almost never did say, was simply, "This thing is ugly! It's not harmonious with the neighborhood! We have a certain harmony in the neighborhoods right around this spot, and if you bring this thing in like that, it is going to be damaging to the harmony."

But the point is, of course, you can say that informally in a conversation, I can say that right now, to you, but to say it in front of the Board of Adjustment means that you have to be able to claim that it has legal validity—otherwise the developer is going to get up and sue you for basing the decision on that kind of concept. So people felt very nervous about saying it in such a simple, straightforward way and instead came up with all these pseudotechnical objections which could maybe be used as a basis for legal action or for forcing the developer to actually scale it down.

That's what I meant by saying that the idea of life as a real thing, or harmony as a real thing, is still almost taboo. Not in the sense that you dare not open your mouth to say it, but if you do say it, it doesn't have authority, it doesn't have weight, because it hasn't been formulated in a way that people feel has enough authority to actually force action onto that developer, or onto this person or that person, or this community.

So what I see happening in the twenty-first century is that the concept of life, harmony in the environment, and a community as a living structure, I believe, will mature to the point where we can all have intelligent discussion about it, not be afraid that it's all personal, that it's just my opinion, your opinion, that person's opinion—that actually we can gradually attempt to reach consensus about what a living structure really is and work our way toward it.

To me, the people in the ecological movement have simply laid a few foundation stones for that kind of discussion, as I myself have also laid a few foundation stones for it. It is a much bigger and more wonderful thing that lies on the horizon, bigger than any specific thing about what kind of building materials you use, or what kind of energy conservation you have.

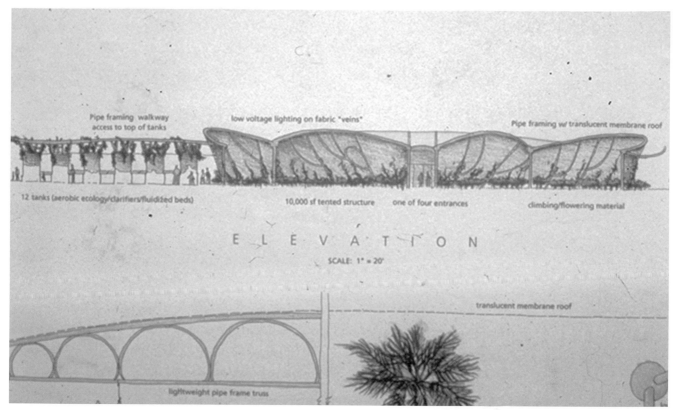

Pipe framing walkway
access to top of tanks

low voltage lighting on fabric "veins"

Pipe framing w/ translucent membrane roof

12 tanks (aerobic ecology/clarifiers/fluidized beds)

10,000 sf tented structure

one of four entrances

climbing/flowering material

E L E V A T I O N

SCALE: 1" = 20'

translucent membrane roof

lightweight pipe frame truss

Two recent examples of living structures design
(Chattanooga, Tennessee and Hopland, California).

Gail Vittori and Pliny Fisk

The Obstacles to Sustainable Design

The building codes are an obstacle to sustainable building, both from a material point of a view and a design point of view.

"what role do the building codes play in the matrix of sustainable design?"

Gail Vittori: There's definitely a long, long way to go in terms of building codes being a reinforcing element to sustainable design. Everything from the types of building materials that are considered conventional and therefore safe, to how buildings are built and, in terms of a systems way of thinking, what needs to be in a building to make it really operationally efficient. A lot of buildings that we've been working on would be virtually impossible to do within a city like Austin right now. Our intent and our efforts have been to get examples up wherever we can, rather than invest a lot of our time and energy in fighting codes to get working examples up that people are living in and using, that together provide some historical precedent for sustainable building and design in this country.

We don't have the sort of a historical background that Europe has for working with indigenous materials. We've lost and we've wiped out a lot of historical precedents of buildings in the United States that might have related to sustainable building. However, if someone were to look back and see what the longest standing buildings in the United States were, they'd see examples of four hundred-year-old rammed earth buildings, or other kinds of rammed earth buildings that, structurally, are still very sound. They would provide a body of information that says we can do this in the United States and it works.

Moving into the realm of commercial building, or in incorporated areas, the building codes are not recognizing those precedents and instead are saying, "conventional materials, basically stick construction, portland cement, all that we're all familiar with." Wherever we go, we see a repetitious pattern of that kind of building. In fact, I think if anyone were to do a serious analysis of the safety—from a structural point of view, from a fire point of view, from an indoor air quality point of view—of conventional architecture, as it's known in the United States right now, [they would see that] in no way is there a demonstration of inherent safety or quality. Certainly there isn't a demonstration of durability.

These are all qualities that in sustainability have got to come to the forefront, in terms of being guiding forces of what's going to dictate building practices and design practices in the next century. One of the ways that we're trying to shape the experience that we and other groups like us have had, is to use our hands-on experience in the buildings that have gone up.

For example, like Pliny was saying, in the city of Austin, with the Green Builder Program, can we take that body of information and wield a little more weight with politicians, and say, "Hey, we have got to start doing things differently! The building codes are an obstacle to sustainable building, both from a material point of a view and a design point of view"— in order to make buildings pay for themselves. That is, buildings that are more self-sufficient are more resource-efficient.

We have to change what is now considered conventional practice in the building industry. It's going to mean what might be perceived as stepping on some feet—of certain institutions and certain power bases in this country—but I think it's time to start reevaluating whether or not those particular dependencies are going to move us forward in a way that is going to best serve the needs of our generation and generations in the future.

Unless we start asking those questions and start building momentum toward institutional changes, I think we're going to find ourselves very shortsighted in being able to do the kinds of work that we all want to see happen. Again, like Pliny said, the reinforcement now on a state level in Texas is overwhelmingly a surprise.

It's especially important with these windows of opportunity in an institutional framework that the advances we are recommending and want to see adopted are ones that we can feel very assured are going to be positive steps forward. It would be extremely counterproductive for us to be suggesting material approaches or design approaches that we aren't very certain are going to be ones that are strong enough to really turn the tide.

PLINY FISK: Landscape architecture under Ian McHarg was a

Two recent examples of Pliny's strategy of integrating passive cooling towers into the building form.

point in life where the whole importance of the environment was brought in, but more than that, it brought in a methodology and a way of thinking. That alone—with people like Russell Acoff, and Bucky Fuller, and any number of other people—got us concentrating on [the question]: Is there a methodology, is there something that you can share—even a language that you might be able to share—as to what is this new design?

> "In addition to practicing as an architect, you also have a landscape architecture understanding. How does this shape your design methodology?"

We are working behind the scenes a lot with that kind of thing. We've been doing a lot with icons and iconography, and developing a language and structure that people can easily understand that does not change with different flows and different topics. Energy, materials, money, information, all have sources and sinks - they have life cycles which have stories, that, in their most simple forms can be sequences of pictures. We've been doing a lot with the next sensible step to that, which is object-oriented programming, where you're using pictures on the computer to actually program things. Boundaries are critical in order to develop performance models of any type. Our boundaries are the same that I briefly mentioned concerning our EPA project to develop benchmarks for sustainable building. It's very participatory, in that anybody can understand pictures. They certainly might not be able to understand the programs behind them, but they are able to mock up where things are coming from and where things are going, whether they be materials, energy, money, or information. They work and conceive of things in cyclical modes. What is the flow of those materials? What is the energy cost of doing one type of material sequence versus another? Is that material choice actually supporting your region, supporting the businesses in your region? Each icon actually represents sets of businesses, sets of vendors, sets of products. Each product possesses a performance that can function related to other products within the boundary of that particular project and at another scale for that particular region. Are those businesses handling themselves in a sustainable way by sourcing businesses, processing businesses, users, and re-sourcers. recyclers, reusers? Where are they getting their materials from? Are they managing the environment in a way that is sensible? Those things can be brought up in a very, very effective way with computer technology and iconography. Because that icon in one sense is just an image, but in another sense it's an actual picture of that person, a quick-time review of what that business is like. Or it can go into the actual performance of that building material, water, waste water. etc...

So the material part, to us, not only involves building materials per se, but involves the material flows of all kinds—waste, water, solid waste, the materials that are going into a building, the materials that are going into the transportation system outside—any of those things really relate to how the region is dealing in the material sector.

The argument is often put out that, well, materials are not really the energy sector; we've got to concentrate on energy first. It is true that if you look at energy, the cost of producing energy is our largest energy cost, but the next cost is what we do in the material environment. Ever since automation in the production process replaced people, energy cost per capita in the U.S. increased dramatically. In other words, materials are intimately involved with the energy flow in an area. What we believe—and we have some evidence to this—is that how you design the system of material acquisition, and where those materials are coming from, not only has tremendous influence

Except during the nine months before he draws his first breath, no man manages his affairs as well as a tree does.

George Bernard Shaw

from a regional energy sense, but it also has a tremendous influence on economic development. So the buildings that we do try to grow out of a region's metabolism, they're sort of a metabolic, so to speak. We build from this understanding of what a region can do, from aspects of water, waste, materials in the building.

The exciting part about the materials in the building is that you begin to apply information to where you are. Our information base normally is from everywhere else except from where you are. It deals in a world of information that essentially emphasizes what is being sold. It emphasizes who is best at advertising. It does not emphasize what you should be doing in a region because you're trying to come to grips with that region and its ecological future. That's a totally different kind of information.

So now—as Alvin Toffler, in Power Shift, and a number of other people say—information is becoming more and more localized. We essentially begin to say, "Well, it's interesting that plants of different types have enzymes in their roots. They break down minerals in soils. Can enzymes be used to do different things in the materials arena, to make certain materials more available, to cut certain materials, using biological means?"

What we try to effectively do is to understand how the most successful plants have done that in the ecological mix, [how those plants have come] to deal with those minerals in that specific place. There are very magical stories that can come out of indigenous people about how they observe birds and how they observe plants growing in very difficult terrain. They were very, very attuned to what was going on in that particular place, in order to minimize their work and maximize information about that place and its proper use, to do things in an ecological fashion. So now we're slowly coming around.

GAIL VITTORI: One of the most glaring examples that we've come across recently of how codes can serve as obstacles for achieving sustainable design work is one in which engineering guidelines actually prohibit plants from being placed in [Texas] state office buildings. The rationale for this is that it will take up too much of the employees' time to care for the plants. It is in total disregard of the benefits of plants, not only for aesthetic reasons, but for air purification reasons.

This is obviously an absurdity. Plants can be a tremendous asset to the built environment. That's one of the things that we hope to take on as we moves toward a major overhaul of the state of Texas architecture and engineering guidelines.

To the dull mind nature is leaden. To the illuminated mind the world burns and sparkles with light.

Emerson

Mary Catherine Bateson

Making the Earth Our Home

I believe that homemaking is something that everyone, man and woman, all human beings, could think of doing on this planet. Making it an environment where growth is possible, not interfering with other forms of life, restoring—all this would come under the heading of ecopoesis.

New ideas in human cultures tend to come from the margins of any civilizational pattern, often from points where civilizations meet. Then it takes time for these things that come from outside to be integrated at the center. Design outlaws are people who've gone outside the system, found their own way of doing things. Our task is the task of integration—to take those ideas and reshape them so they can apply to not one household, not one village, but offer solutions of how to design patterns of adaptation for the five billion human beings there are on the planet now.

It's a shift in perception, hopefully, an integrated shift in what we value. I like to use the term ecopoesis. Poesis is the Greek for "making," [oikos, which our prefix eco derives from, means home, so ecopoesis is] . . . a Greek translation of "homemaking." I believe that homemaking is something that everyone, man and woman, all human beings, could think of doing on this planet. Making it an environment where growth is possible, not interfering with other forms of life, restoring—all this would come under the heading of ecopoesis. Making this earth increasingly our home, and you know we don't want to mess up our home.

The organism that destroys its environment destroys itself. That's why I like the concept of home. Home isn't just a place, nor is it just a set of persons living inside it, it's an interactive system. We

> "where are we going to find the new ideas to build a more livable 21st century?"

236

must preserve the environment in order to preserve ourselves and develop new ways of interacting within that system. The role of design in all of that is that we can think about these things and talk about them. We're constantly building material objects and we've got to think more about the way we're designing them in a more inclusive way. We have to think of whole cities as organisms with their own metabolism, their own need of food and air and need to process waste.

So we look, for instance, at the concept of an organism or an ecosystem, and then we say let's think of a whole city like New York on that model. Instead of trying to turn New York into a more efficient machine or factory, let's look at it as a living being, as, of course, we now look at the planet as a living being.

In the industrial age, the effort was to design systems, artifacts that were fully understood: you knew exactly the engineering principles that you were using. [But] through most of human history, human beings have depended on working with systems they didn't fully understand. They tried to heal their bodies without knowing all the details of physiology. They planted crops without knowing anything about the biology of the soil. So human technologies through history have been based on a collaboration with living systems that were not fully understood.

Now we live in an era of tremendously powerful science, but I think we've gone too far in believing that we could design fully determinate systems. Instead, we have to design with other living systems, allowing for a certain ambiguity in that process, and because we know that the outcome will not be fully predictable, we also have to have systems for evaluating midstream, shifting course, reshaping things that have been built with one understanding, modifying them for another understanding, so we don't get locked in. If you believe in a determinate technology where every relevant factor is known, you design material objects that lock you in instead of designing for flexibility and responsiveness.

THE CHALLENGE OF GLOBALIZATION

The most important thing that we learn from looking at the adaptations of indigenous peoples is how different one human group is from another. We are not trapped in a particular form of adaptation. When we look at these different communities, we can temper and develop our idea of what it means to live at peace with the natural world, but we're not going to solve our problems by replicating or imitating solutions that worked for small communities with limited technology.

So we get some ideas, we get the benefit of contrast, we get a flavor and a style, but we're going to have to find our own solutions, finally. It doesn't help to be too romantic about the fact that indigenous or primal peoples live at peace with the natural world, because, very often, when technology becomes available they are as quick to go out and be destructive as anyone else. And the problem that we face is with the huge size of human population. We have to take that into account, and the tremendous potency of available technology, and the globalization that means that every problem is interconnected with every other.

We have to find a way to adapt in the context of those problems, and that's never been done before.

The World Commission on Environment and Development in their report, Our Common Future, defined sustainable development as "meeting the needs of the present without compromising the ability of future generations to meet their own needs.

Richard Schoen,
from Sustainable Cities

Chapter Six

The New Collective Dream

"I ll tell you this, No eternal reward will forgive us for wasting the dawn"

Jim Morrison

The aboriginal people
make no distinction
between the dream life and everyday life.
Altering the urban fabric will take the strength
to dream wisely in a new bio-technical way.
Time travel to ancient lands of real and imaginary
civilizations can propitiate us to interweave a compelling blend of
natural elements in a new way with our existing technology. The
Aztecs, the Minoans, the Mayans, the Moors, the Visigoths, the
Celts—all have a gift of potent insight if we just open the door
a little bit more.

Coming back from the vast and almost
pristine wilderness of the Amazon was a return trip
I shall never forget. From the immense womb of succulent Mother
Nature, back to the walls and ceilings of Civilization. Immediately
arriving upon the asphalt streets and entering the inorganic Hotel, I
was asked to fill out a form. I paused for a moment to remember who
I was before I left on this sojourn. Then it all came back to me. I knew
I was back in the game.

The endless game of form filling seems to be the price we pay for
living in an industrial society. The question remains, who is the
architect of the forms we must live with? As Thomas Jefferson
wrote in The Declaration of Independence "all experience hath
shown, that mankind are more disposed to suffer, while evils are
sufferable, than to right themselves by abolishing the forms to which
they are accustomed".

Nature never has to repeat a form exactly. Only humans desire to
standardize and impose mass produced forms. However, we are
more than just maintainers, life seeks to transcend itself. One of the
best ways is through the growing of graceful forms in the built
environment.

Our 20th century fossil fuel driven cities can best be seen as
massive retrofit projects. From my experience of traveling the
country to make this film, old Henry Miller was right on when he
described America as an air-conditioned nightmare full of places
without soul. What he didn't fathom was that the root cause and
solution lies in the nature of our design epistemology—the theory of
the method or ground of knowledge. In other words, what counts for

240

knowledge in a cultural context. Awakening from this cultural trance is no easy task. However, it is our task of tasks, if we are to become creative stewards of the earth.

Somehow, we have systematically encoded ourselves from realizing the buoyancy that comes from a sophisticated integration with the natural world and instead created endless artificial worlds that degrade rather than augment the human spirit.

The healing work may begin to grow once we escape the ensnarlment of the abstract infotainment industries and get our hands dirty once again cultivating our own garden on the common ground of Mother Earth. Recall, the native Americans had no concept of wilderness. The systematic disconnection from beauty and restorative power of Nature is one of the peculiar baneful aspects of 20th century city life. How much new information will it take for us displace the industrial imagination that has shaped our existing world?

C.Z.

© ArcoSanti

Paolo Soleri

Transforming the Urban Condition

The urban phenomenon . . . that might take us slowly towards an awareness that the whole of nature has to be transfigured and transformed or metamorphosized in order to develop into a meaning.

"what do you mean when you characterize yourself as an instrument maker?"

Given my conviction that the human landscape, the suburban sprawl, in this country is totally catastrophic, I very much feel that in order to be effective in transforming society and transforming priorities, we have to start with the landscape, the human landscape—which means observing what Los Angeles has been doing to the human species, and then decide maybe that's not the way to go.

The development of a new instrument is fundamental to developing a new society. I keep insisting what we are doing here [at Arcosanti] is basically building a new instrument, without the pretense of ever transforming society by directly working on the society itself. So we like to build, let's say, a piano (that's my metaphor) and then the musicians will come and will make use of the piano to play their own music, any music, all sorts—from the very frivolous to the very serious.

Looking into the performance space at Arcosanti.

<u>LEFT</u>
A profile of the Arcosanti complex outside
of Phoenix, Arizona, including the
performance center, library, and housing.

The kind of work we do
does not make us holy, but
we make it holy.

Meister Eckhart

Multiple views of Arcosanti's
Earth Form Architecture.

Dreamer of dreams, born
out of my due time
Why should I strive to set
the crooked straight?
Let it suffice me that my
murmuring rhyme
Beats with light wing
against the ivory gate,
Telling a tale not too
importune
To those who in the sleepy
region stay,
Lulled by the singer of an
empty day.

William Morris

Maybe the one thing that tends to diverge here a little from Fuller is that I worry very much about the isolation of a very complex system, like a human being or family, being put on a very beautiful corner of this planet and then being tied to it, through all the technologies of information and knowledge. That I find very, very dangerous, counterproductive, because we are very vicarious and very cooperative animals, though it does not look like that most of the time. We need the interaction, which is not possible, is not feasible, through the remote information network. Interaction has to be physically, tangibly, flesh-like present; that's important to the city. The city is an instrument for learning and for fulfillment because it is where all those individuals are able to create a culture. The electronic-cottage concept is escapist, fundamentally, and very destructive, ultimately. You can imagine eight billion people on this planet adopting that mode: it would be a catastrophe, a nemesis, an apocalypse.

Lewis Mumford was under the spell still of the urban European city, under which I am also. His solution was an intermediate or a hybrid, which is probably the way to go. My objection to the American dream is basically that it advocates this single home with its own little territory wherein you have the fulfillment of the individual and the family. Expand this notion, this democratic notion, to eight billion people and then you see catastrophe is inescapable. That would mean for instance, sixteen billion automobiles. Energy, material, resources, destruction of the landscape, ecological demise—they are coming with it.

A parasite doesn't want to pay for what it's getting. If you kill the core, which is what the city surburbia does, it doesn't know what to turn to. Surburbia needs the urban, but it doesn't want to pay for it. They don't want to pay in taxes, they don't want to pay in contributions, in dedication, in work. There is no self-responsibility there; it is a typical position of parasitism.

"what do you mean by the suburban phenomenon being essentially parasitic?"

Probably suburban phenomena came about as a consequence of a number of factors. One was that with the development of wealth, people felt the need of leaving the city, the industrial city, which was, at the beginning of the century, pretty grim. When the automobile came and pushed out the horse society, then we really had the means of developing this dream and making it a reality. So we are just at the beginning of the exodus of the citizens into the suburbia network.

When that was limited to a few, a small percent of the population, it looked like the way to go. When it became the bulk of population wanting to move out, it became the nightmare that we're in now.

THE TRANSCENDENTAL URGE

The fundamental value of the human animal is not in collecting things. It is in developing an inner growth that will appreciate things, but also will appreciate something more subtle than things, which is ideas, the aesthetic, the notion of equity, the notion of transcendence, the notion that we might need to find the reason why we exist. Churches are something you go to on the weekend, now and then, if you remember about it. Now our temples are the marketplace, the stadium, the bank.

I believe in technology more than what it appears. I am not an engineer or a scientist or technologist, but I believe that technology is at the base of everything, and I count as technology the biotech-

> "the role of aesthetics in the human journey?"

> Integrity is the deepest quality in a building.
>
> Frank Lloyd Wright

A look inside the solar apse

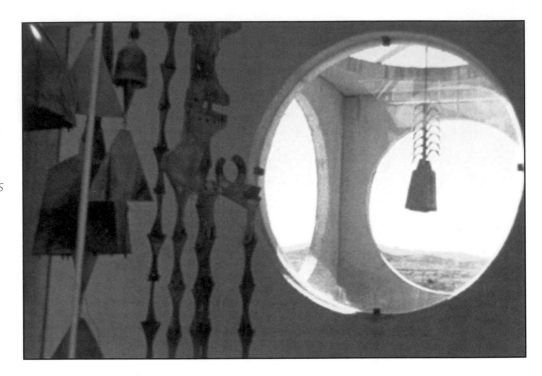

A view from Arco Santi, including the world-famous bells cast at the craft studios.

nology that preceded our technology. So from the very beginning of life, you have the biotechnology of matter becoming animated and developed for about three and a half eons, taking life from a very primitive, relatively simple event into the highly complex event of today. Without intrusion in biotechnology, through what you might call the hardware technology, we made a tremendous jump into the future. In our way we made something that was very subtle into something that was very crude.

So the enthusiasm for technology, for me, is still limited by the fact that, compared to biotechnology, our technology is still beyond redemption—almost. That's why we have to be so very careful in how we go about using knowledge to develop technological devices. I like the automobile, but I think it has been a very damaging invention altogether. Possibly Fuller had a similar mind-set, he being an inventor and a very, very sharp inventor. He saw technology as the resolution of our problems, and I tend to agree with him, but it has to be a technology-to-come. The misuse of our technology now, it makes so much for troubles, one wonders.

We are very much a throw-away society: [eager for] the quick fix, to do something, use it, and then throw it away. We accept the notion of obsolescence; it's part of our life—everything becomes obsolescent under our eyes, from automobiles to razor blades. Everything has a very brief life and then is dumped.

What distinguishes the aesthetic is that it is almost the opposite. Aesthetic is that which does not become obsolete. The [higher the] aesthetic quality, the more there is the rejection of the notion of obsolescence. To be surrounded by things which are obsolescent is part of reality, but we need also an injection of that which is not obsolescent.

Art objects, the great music, poetry, literature, sculpture, movies need to present us with these alternatives, because we pretend, we assume, or we have the illusion of not being obsolescent ourselves. If we are surrounded by obsolete things, we might end up by saying: "well, it's inescapable, everything is obsolescent, including me."

The church tried to say; "No, no, no, God will take care of you or you will take care of it through God." But that's just a not very inter-

> "what distinguishes the aesthetic understanding?"

A view into the unique world of Arcosanti

Views of medieval European cities.

"how does your work relate to the state of our cities?"

esting thing to us, because we are too busy with our obsolescent worth. The more we can surround ourselves with that which is not obsolescent, the more we might gain in self-respect, self-esteem, and also knowledge, and in enjoyment of those values which are not dumped tomorrow.

Naturally, there is a point where the most subtle technology is able to transcend obsolescence. For example, we have objects which are purely technological but which are beautiful because the maker was so great in his or her mind that these things became art objects. For the Shakers or the Amish, the folk arts were basically a technology of useful objects. The work in clay, the work in bronze, the work in all sorts of materials that have come through the ages, which used to be basically an object with some usefulness—[the Shakers and the Amish] went beyond that. [This kind of technology, this craftsmanship] becomes so subtle that it has also this great dimension of beauty.

ARCOSANTI: THE URBAN LABORATORY

Arcosanti is trying to recall and adopt a mode which is very, very old: it's the mode of the small urban aggregate. The concept, the idea behind Arcosanti, is that every time you're seeking the lively, you know you are dealing with a very complex system. When you're dealing with a very complex system, you know that you are dealing with miniaturization. Technology tells us very clearly that—through the microchip technology, but more than that—any organ is an incredible astonishing example of complexity and miniaturization.

I call the work we are doing here, an urban laboratory, which is a presumption because we don't have an urban condition here. But we are attempting to take some of the topics that are listed in that book [Urban Laboratory] and see how we can work our presence here in coherence with the guidelines of arcology, which are basically that, like any other phenomenon, you need containment. When you don't have containment you have diaspora; when you have diaspora, you have got a problem.

Taking the Phoenix or the Los Angeles syndrome as an example of diaspora, we are trying to offer the alternative of containment, which means developing an animal which is able to cope with the environment, to deal with it, to have relationships which are healthy as a consequence of this containment. So containment is not isolation or segregation. It's is the ability of any process to develop enough intensity, enough energy within itself so as to communicate and to exchange with what you might call the outside.

That was much of what the medieval city used to be, or the small town. The containment there was a consequence also of defense, but there was more to it than that. It was the fact that people felt this great need to congregate and to find an environment which would be very clearly speaking about this congregation and this coming together. And through that they were able to develop the power to contact other communities and also the environment that was feeding the community.

I think that the possibility of having individuals experiencing both the urban intensity and the countryside dis-tension, disengagement, is absolutely critical for the well-being, for the make up of our beings. Trying to have both of them on the same spot and not having either one is exactly what suburbia does. You haven't got the city and you haven't got the country, you've got a mish-mash which turns out to be segregational, isolationist, elitist, on

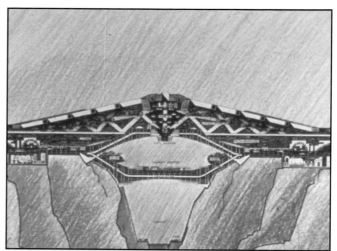

Contrasting images of Soleri's alternative arcologies.

Such synoptic vision of Nature, such constructive conservation of its order and beauty,
is more than engineering: it is a master-art; vaster than that of street planning,
it is landscape making: and thus it meets and combines with city design.

Patrick Geddes

Perhaps the first step toward regaining possession of our souls will be to repossess
and replan the whole landscape.

Lewis Mumford

and on and on, and very, very expensive—the most expensive way of going about making a living.

Last year I was invited to Italy where I was given a prize as Utopian of the Year or something like that. So I wrote an article saying that I reject utopia for the reason that utopia is for everybody, or it is nonsense. Since we know that it cannot be for everybody because it is not feasible now, then it's nonsense. Utopia is a nonsense, really a true nonsense, because we know through science and also true religion that you cannot isolate a phenomenon and say that this is autonomous, self-sufficient, and it becomes perfection. No way. There is only one self-sufficient system. It happens to be the universe. If you [believe in] God, then even that system is not self-sufficient. Since this is a given then, the utopian dream remains a dream. The only utopia which is feasible is a resolution not only of the planetary problems, not only of the human problems, but a resolution of the cosmic problem. One can play around with that idea. I've been playing around with that idea to define my own eschatology and that's the "omega seed."

Eschatology means that there might be an end. So I'm starting with the big bang—we are told it's a beginning. It seems to be pretty definite now that really there was a beginning. So if there is a beginning, chances are there is an end; so I'm banking on the fact there might be an end.

> "what do you mean by eschatology?"

If there is an end, it can be an end in failure or it can be an end in success. An end in failure—it would be that at the end of the cycle, the "big crush" would just be what you might call the material universe being crushed into a black hole or goodness knows what. The successful resolution is that, since life appeared in this very strange phenomenon we call the universe, success would be that life and consciousness have made this universe meaningful, in terms of the resolution, for instance, of suffering. Since life is becoming more and more important, and life is more and more suffering, the resolution of suffering might be an indication of success.

Total equity means that everything becomes an end, besides being just an instrument. And this end would be, typically, aesthetic. It would be a beautiful condition of equity. In fact, you cannot have a dynamic between the equitable and the beautiful, because they would be one and the same thing—that would be the omega seed.

"when does design happen?"

Design is when consciousness begins to creep in through the development of the mineral universe, and consciousness on this planet begins to try to understand what's going on, tries to reflect upon itself and begins to have a notion of good and evil. Consciousness applies its skills to be very evil sometimes and very, very violent and cruel, while at the same time developing more and more the notion of equity, and the notion of compassion, and so on. So it slowly picks up this deterministic, opportunistic phenomenon and molds it in the image of love, which is the best we have in ourselves—but it is so primitive and so puny, so infantile, that we are still struggling to pull it out from the opportunistic and the probabilistic condition we are in as part of reality.

It appears with the human phenomenon on this sort of system. It might develop to such a powerful stress as to be able to go on and influence not only on this solar system, but the galaxy, and then go on and on.

If we do not affect that, then we are irrelevant, because there is no resolution to our suffering. I live seventy years. That's it, and I'm the lucky one because I live seventy years and I did not have great suffering in my life. But what about the baby that after six months develops cancer and it dies, or what about the holocaust, what about the butchering that we are so good at?

THE ARCOLOGY PHENOMENON

"what role is arcosanti playing in the resolution of suffering?"

When I'm asked, what do you think you are doing with arcology in terms of alleviating suffering and so on, my answer is that, number one, we are to remember how puny we are—even the best of us is still a very irrelevant phenomenon. Secondly, if I believe in the premise that in order to move from matter into spirit you have to be coherent with the complexity of the miniaturization paradigm, then what we are doing is trying to make a little step in the direction of complexity miniaturization. It's a tiny, tiny, tiny step. But it is one of the steps that are trying to be in the right direction instead of being in the wrong direction. The resolution of suffering demands the resolution of the cosmic puzzle, which stands to be a violent, deterministic, and probabilistic phenomenon. If we cannot alter that condition, then the problem of suffering becomes very parochial and very relevant because it's not going to have any solution.

The alternative is to try to begin to understand how things work, and then to begin to work in a direction that might be, might give us some hope for, a resolution. My paradigm is not my paradigm; it's what is happening. Life, the inception of life is a quantum jump in complexity, and the more you move into the life escalation, the more you find complexity. To say "But now we have got to a point where we can simplify things in a way, we have again this Arcadia where we can live." is a betrayal of reality and is not going to take us anywhere, even if we can fill our stomachs. "We ate billions or ten billion of whatever, and, in addition, we had a nice time enjoying ourselves with this and that"— that's a platform. The more you enjoy life, the more you resent that it is going to go. The notion of foreverness, the notion of not disappearing becomes more and more predominant—I mean, more of an imperative. Even the most lucky, at the end of life say "Yeah, but really, really, what's going on, I mean, am I gone, I mean, tomorrow I do not exist any longer?" So the question, the big question and its resolution is not just filling stomachs and giving automobiles.

The urban effect is a phenomenon that might take us slowly toward an awareness that the whole of nature has to be transfigured and transformed or metamorphosized, in order to develop meaning. So the city is that manipulator of matter which moves us slightly more toward the mind and the spirit. It is very much an actor in the process.

It's what you might call "paraorganisms," [organisms] made of organisms that are working toward an ephemeralization of things. Keeping in mind that more and more we are told that we are not just one individual, we are an envelope that contains say, us: trillions of things, and then there are, within us, there are citizens, trillions of them helping us to maintain a system. So we are colonies. Cities are not a colony, but if you can put colonies within colonies within colonies, eventually you might get to a point where you have this ultimate seed which is the colony of all colonies.

The onion is building one skin after the other, and since the skins are almost infinite—because presence is infinite—presence has no time: it comes about and it's already passed. So the skins are infinite in number, unless all the skins become equitable because they are ends to themselves, outside of being means for the next skin. Then to talk about justice, it's fantasizing.

"how does this connect to the urban condition?"

Take Manhattan, I mean, this evil. Within it, there is so much going on which is ephemeralization, which, even though it's violent, still it's much more than Phoenix, because it has more in it indicating that there is a possibility of making matter into tangible things, and that where it's happening with such intensity it's a young animal composed of embryonic creatures—so it's full of mistakes, full of violence, full of all sorts of things.

*Arcosanti 2000
computer graphic.*

Arcosanti 2000 model.

Tony Gwilliam

Integrated Architecture

I think we should compost the cities. We've got these materials—do we actually spend our time, energy, and materials trying to keep this infrastructure together?

"in what way is the nature of human settlement changing?"

The plan of a city or a plan of a building has also got to go from the specialist, nonintegrated way of looking at the thing, where everything is separate, to integrated. So we've got to look at cities themselves again, and [decide what] we really want.

It's as if we've got a car that was made in 1948: Is it worth restoring and bringing back, or is it totally out of date? Is it better to take the materials, totally recycle them, and bring them back that way? I think we've got to look at the city the same way. I think we should compost the cities. We've got these materials—do we actually spend our time, energy, and materials trying to keep this infrastructure together? The infrastructure under New York is probably totally redundant and the cost of [maintaining] it, very high. Now the cities themselves, fundamentally, healthwise, are not reasonable. There's not nearly enough green growing area in most cities. At least part of the cities probably will be composted.

In 1200 A.D. Joachim Fiore proclaimed the post-bureaucratic age the age of the Holy Spirit in which transformed human beings no longer needed the institutional structures of church and state.

Do we need the urban? Do we need the high density of the urban with no relationship to people and nature? Can we get that high density in a rural situation? I think they have examples of that around the world. I think the traditional village in Indonesia is a high-density village with a lot of interaction between people that hasn't got the urban things. Now the urban traffic also starts coming apart. We've already [eliminated] warehouses, which we don't need in the modern industrial process—we get products direct from factory to retail outlet. We'll probably go direct from production to the home, which will probably get rid of the retail outlet, too. We'll get rid of offices, because we don't need offices anymore, so there's another building type that creates the urban environment gone. We won't need schools anymore, because, again, we can educate ourselves on earth wherever we are, and we can get experiential education. We won't need art galleries—art galleries just took art away from society, totally took art away from society and from having any validity in our life, and made it into a consumer product. So all these building types that we think of as part of the city will disappear.

I think we'll see more organic forms and allow the city to get back to its organism. And if we don't allow that to happen, it'll be destroyed by the residents through riots, it'll be destroyed through warfare and so on.

I think we should be positive about the city, reconsider it in a very deep way, and decide whether it's even valid—in a day of internets, modern communications, responses at the speed of light—or whether we're just designing disasters. Is it a natural part of our environment anymore?

It should become one continuous experience, much like Bali, where you don't have art as a separate medium, but living is the basic thing. Bali, for me, is a supportive home because the whole structure of the philosophy of the life and the way they live is totally integrated. There isn't separation. The industrial revolution, or the western sort of male-dominated society, for two thousand years, has been separative, analytical, scientific, so we've taken everything apart. It was necessary for our evolution as human beings. Now we're putting it together, and when we put it together we get synergistic effects. Well, the Balinese didn't take it apart. They're still living, basically, in a totally integrated way, with their land and their whole life.

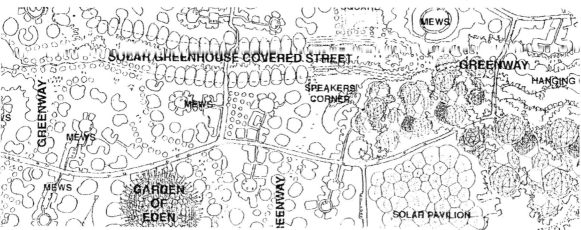

Amory Lovins

I feel it is not ethically satisfactory, as Hugh Nash put it, to pay tribute to our descendants' boundless technological ingenuity, by making damned sure that they need it.

"what do you think about the future of the city?"

Ultimately, I don't know whether we're going to see people crowding into the cities as much as we do now. You know, cities have a huge flow of resources in, and pollution out, across their boundaries. More so as they get to a bigger size, since the area grows faster than the perimeter. The city begins to choke on its own stuff, and can't get the supplies it needs anymore. I think there is a great deal we can do technically to make cities work better, even at the present humongous sizes. But they become so dysfunctional socially that I think many people are moving out. This, of course, makes further problems because some can afford to move out and some can't. I don't know what we are going to do about that, but I'm sure that the technologies for advanced resource efficiency can at least reduce, if not solve, many of the urban problems we see today.

There are in fact, exciting techniques for retrofitting existing urban buildings. Jim Sacket, in St. Louis, has a great technique for simultaneous rehab and super insulation retrofit of standard brownstone row houses. You end up with a really comfortable, elegant house that costs only half as much to own and run over its life and is much more comfortable, using only a tiny fraction as much energy as it did in the first place. The installation can even be done by semi-skilled, illiterate people. It's quite easy to do. It doesn't assume that anything is square, or plumb, or level to start with. It's highly cost effective. I think we will see more and more of that kind of technique adapted to a wide range of specific building types, cultures, and climates used to rebuild infrastructure that we had just about given up on, but that turn out to be good for a much longer lease on life if you redo them properly.

That's all based on economic arguments which I think are important. But there's a lot that markets and economics can't tell you, because they were never meant to. The markets are meant to be greedy, not fair; and efficient, not sufficient. They never tell you how much is enough. And as the economist Herman Daley points out, a boat that is loaded with too much weight will sink, even if the weight is optimally allocated. So, if markets do something good for whales, or wilderness, or God, or grandchildren, that's purely coincidental, because that's not what they're designed for. They're designed to allocate scarce resources in the short run. And they don't think about the long run at all. In fact, they discount it practically to zero.

If you really used market principles in deciding, for example, whether to have a child, you never would. It would not be cost effective to have any children, or to save anything for the long run, even the things that are priceless—particularly the things that are priceless.

I feel it is not ethically satisfactory, as Hugh Nash put it, to pay tribute to our descendants' boundless technological ingenuity, by making damned sure that they need it. I think that resource efficiency and renewables are, therefore, not only profitable and good for the Earth, they're really a moral imperative. And I don't tend to say that very much in my speeches because I can make exactly the same point

Low-to-mid-rise urban housing design within a "solar envelope".
(Knowles and students, 1992)

with the most orthodox, neoclassical economics, which is the state religion. But I think there are many people who do care about stewardship, who would find the ethical argument important as well. I hope, in time, that we all will.

> "so were moving toward a more of an energy economics based on thermo-dynamics?"

Everything had better be based on thermodynamics. Economics is a sub-discipline of thermodynamics. A lot of economists don't realize this and haven't the foggiest idea of what the Second Law says they can or can't do. Thermodynamic illiteracy is a very dangerous trend in our society. I run into a lot of economists who must lie awake at night worrying about whether what works in practice could possibly work in theory.

They don't understand the theory beyond very idealized, unrealistic assumptions about markets that don't exist and won't ever exist. That said, market economics is an awfully useful tool as long as you stay grounded in biological and physical reality. I think we also need to remember that thermodynamics is important not only in physics, but most of all, in biology. I was brought up as a physical scientist; trained to think of the world as acting like a bunch of billiard balls, in which there are no non-linears, irreversibilities, threshold effects, or all things that actually happen in complex biological and social systems. Applying that kind of physics and engineering intuition to a biological world is extremely dangerous. It is one of the worst educational fallacies we've managed to come up with.

The more we crowd into cities and get divorced from the way green things work, the more dangerous it becomes—we raise a generation of kids who have never seen a bird except for a pigeon, and never a tree but a Christmas tree. Think that milk comes from cartons and orange juice out of cans. That worries me a lot. I think, in that sense, we have (and in many other senses, including ethics) a great deal to learn from traditional peoples, who do know how things work, who had often extremely sophisticated sustainable agriculture, efficient buildings. We are not yet as good at passive solar design as the Anasazi were in the Ancient Southwest, for example. I think that increasing North/South dialogue, and the dialogue with our own native peoples, we will have a lot more to learn than we have to teach.

Anasazi passive solar design, Chaco Canyon, Arizona

Our current cityscape

Leslie Sauer and Carol Franklin

The Greening of the City

There are real opportunities now as rail corridors become open, as manufacturing corridors become available, to really put back greenways, open up stream corridors. This is what ultimately will bring people back to the city, the combination of nature and culture that will uniquely be found here.

"can we look forward to a greener city?"

LESLIE SAUER: I think the greening of the city is going to be one of the most exciting things that we're going to see in the future. We've had a tremendous depopulation of many of our cities and it's offering many opportunities for us to confront problems we may not have done before. In Philadelphia, a lot of vacant land was presumed to be valuable and we felt that people were going to be flocking back to redevelopment, flush with money, and it has turned out not to be true. This city is losing two and one-half thousand jobs a month, and the story is true of virtually every city. The city of Baltimore has seen more deforestation in the last twenty-five years, because of a mass exodus from the city, than they have at virtually any other time. This is true all over. New York has seen an exodus. The suburbanization of our cities has been devastating to nature, and we have seen, in the last twenty-five years, more destruction than in the preceding three hundred. Also, one of the great topics of today's discussions is the abandonment of the infrastructure, and with it these declining cities.

I think in the past we thought the cities were the cancer. We're seeing now that what is spreading out from them is indeed a far greater cancer, and that we've got to renew our cities, if only to bring people back to them and to enable us to really save some of the natural systems that are left. The cities are more recoverable than we give them credit for. Virtually all the restoration projects we do, we are surprised at the level of recovery in the city.

264

CAROL FRANKLIN: We cannot get away from the fact that the cities are the most complex artifact that man has created, and in many ways the cities are our greatest polluters and our greatest consumers. It's going to be here that we solve the problems—rather what we at Andropogan sometimes call going into the icebox, opening it up, and taking a new stick of butter. We have continually treated our landscape as if there's always a new stick of butter before we've fully utilized the old stick.

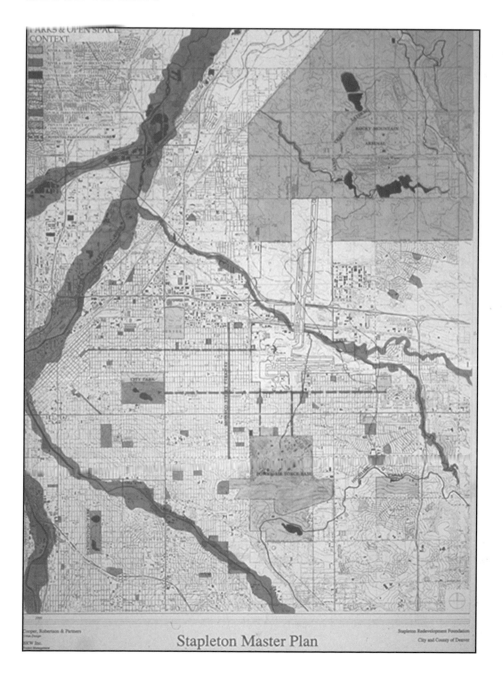

Stapleton Master Plan

The master plan for Stapleton Airport. Denver, Colorado.

And the trouble is, if you don't risk anything, you risk even more.

Erica Jong

Before and after the process of habitat restoration

One of the fundamental approaches of sustainability has got to be to go back to the places we have destroyed and to bring them alive again, by reconnecting fragmented systems and putting back the pieces, rather than going out and despoiling new areas.

SAUER: Hopefully, the way we relate to [landscaping regulations and] codes is not to take them quite as seriously as other people do. The code is really meant to be a bottom line, to catch the most venal of the developers. Unfortunately, it has become the definition of what to do, what is acceptable, and what will get through. Those of us who have been in the field for twenty-five or more years remember a lot of days, precode, when actually you could do very fine development just by selling the strength of your idea. In fact, that's a lot of what we do today, except that we look to the community to develop an idea that may or may not be specifically consistent with their codes. We find that the issues of permitting are not problematic if you really have good community support behind you, regardless of what the codes are.

FRANKLIN: Perhaps the biggest problem for sustainable development, and the saddest direction that we see, is in the government agencies. In an attempt to insure that the government is not being cheated, it has promulgated standards which go back to the original idea of integration and are very single-focused. These are focused on solving very narrow, discrete problems. We talked about flood control or soil erosion control, and the focus then is not only on very minimal standards to insure that these problems don't happen, but also, I think, on the technical answers to these solutions.

At Andropogan, the thing that we bring that is different, the thing that is so characteristic of ecological design, is a broader view. We hold the solution to a broader environmental mandate.

SAUER: I don't think the issue is that you're going to get community consensus. . . . There are always going to be a few issues on which there is general agreement, but the idea behind community consensus is really to have the community involved over the long haul and on a continuous and ongoing basis. That makes an extraordinary difference in terms of where people are actually able to go and what

"are the codes part of the problem?"

267

kinds of decisions they make. A lot of the processes that we see today involve a set of public hearings where the community speaks up, and then they're out of the loop and do not have much follow-through. The goal really is to invest in real grassroots planning.

In Central Park, where we're working with the restoration of the woodlands in the North End, everybody disagreed with everybody else on how to do it but over the years that the group has been working together, there has been a lot of communication that's gone on. Now people understand not only each other's positions, they understand the larger positions that are important if they're going to give up a special-interest perspective on things. I think we put a lot of investment into the idea that education helps overcome the small-mindedness that we like to characterize community politics with. When people really are empowered, that small-mindedness goes away.

One of the issues is that we've defined design very narrowly. And so sustainable design becomes making an architectural, and site-planning, and urban-design footprint. What we're actually talking about is changing policy, changing regulations, and changing attitudes, and this is a very long, slow process. And we at Andropogan believe that public involvement is, fundamentally, part of this process. [The process] is incremental; it is educational; and it changes policy at fundamental levels.

We were talking about James Wines and the idea that the covering of a building with ivy would be more significant than planting a tree in the city. Both the idea of planting a single specimen tree, or a row of trees in the city, or covering a building with ivy is again a single-focus solution to a single-focus problem—the problem there being to put more oxygen back into the air. I think what Andropogan is concerned with is the reestablishment of the fundamental systems that make the planet go. Vegetation is one of those fundamental systems, and a single tree or a building covered with ivy has nothing to do with the complex, diverse, interactive, dynamic living plant community that responds to specific habitats and is an interconnected system.

268

igh Plains Vocabulary
arks and Active Recreation Areas
airie Park

erspective drawing of Prairie Park

| | Small swale | | Trail | Big Swale | Sandhills prairie | | Sandhills depression |
Fence

Neighborhood | Two lane park drive with parking and trail | Prairie Park

ection of Prairie Park and adjacent park drive with sustainable drainage modifications

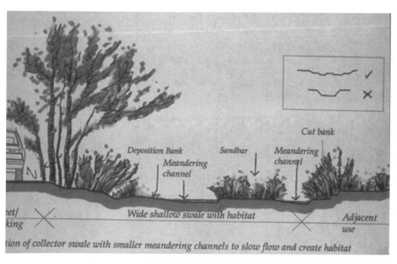

Cut bank

Deposition Bank
Meandering channel

Sandbar

Meandering channel

et/ king

Wide shallow swale with habitat

Adjacent use

tion of collector swale with smaller meandering channels to slow flow and create habitat

Natural drainage systems use predominantly open surface channels with natural vegetation, minimizing pipes and hard structures. This example of applied ecological design is more cost effective (as usual) than conventional engineering solutions.

Christopher Alexander

The Living Structure Approach to Design

You cannot produce life by the particular mechanism we have set in motion in the twentieth century to do development.

"why do we keep building boring structures over and over again?"

We've got a very simple notion that we believe is the way to do stuff. Architects makes a bunch of drawings and forget whether they're good or not and whether the people involved were contributing. Then an architect makes a set of drawings and goes with a developer to the bank. A loan is issued, a contractor gets the drawings, a contractor builds the project and, somehow, this is supposed to produce life just because the design is so good.

Now this is simply nonsense. It's absolutely physically impossible. Suppose we were trying to produce a daffodil, and we've got two contending ways of producing the daffodil. One team is going to actually grow their daffodil from a bulb and just let it open up and form the daffodil, and the other team is going to make a perfect set of drawings and is then going to use a bunch of microtweezers to put it together. Gradually, life is sort of getting rubbed off and created into existence at every moment like a fountain this thing is just gradually happening. To accomplish that on a building site is a very, very difficult task. It's quite difficult, even with a single building, just to handle the management of the construction so that fountain of unfolding is taking place.

In the case of a relatively larger thing, like a community, let's say, of one hundred or two hundred families, it is extremely difficult, because of all of these procedures that we take for granted as being really the gospel: this is how it's supposed to be done. According to twentieth-century financing and professional management, [the process of unfolding] just doesn't work, because it isn't the way that life can get produced. It was never produced that way in traditional societies, and it will never be produced that way in the future because societies, and it will never be produced that way in the future because it isn't just that it's difficult, it's impossible. It cannot be done that way.

In order to change that [attitude], unfortunately, it's not enough to change stuff on the design level. The way the whole fabric of the way communal action takes place—the way money flows in society and the way development goes on—needs to change. And I know this is a very tall order. I'm not some sort of flag-waving Marxist who wants to see the complete reconstruction of society In order for everything to be okay; I'm just simply stating a fact here. You cannot produce life by the particular mechanism we have set in motion in the twentieth century to do development.

At the moment, this is very slightly understood at best. Especially here in America, where the developer is almost a saint, sort of a holy icon of the twentieth century. And the idea of the American developer has now been exported. It's all over Europe, of course, all over the Far East, it is the norm now all over the world. This is how the environment is being built! But actually you cannot produce life like this.

The biggest challenge, by far, is to change these fundamental processes of construction and human administration so that real living stuff comes into existence. Let me just give you an example, a sort of almost absurdly tiny one. Let's take the process of a single house being built. You draw a bunch of windows, so you think you know where the windows are going to be. You start building the house. When you've actually got the floors in there, one by one, you stand in the rooms and—let's say we're here in the Bay Area—you look out the window and there's the bay out there and so forth, some trees, and the light comes in, in a certain way, and I can tell you from experience that the windows, standing in that room while it's being framed, are always totally different from anything that you thought of while you were drawing the building. If you force yourself to build what was on the drawing, the windows are always wrong. It's a tiny example, but it's true because the living reality of that view and the light and the tree and the bay and the inside of the room are related in such complex ways that it's impossible to predict it ahead of time. You cannot. It can only arise out of the situation of being in that room that you know where to put the windows.

In traditional society, that was automatic. I mean, it wasn't a big

You examine an historic form and see whether the effect it produces on your mind matches the feeling you are trying to portray.

Bernard Maybeck

we've made in the twentieth century is to institute forms of construction and development and management which make it impossible for the living tissue to develop.

In nature you see this unfolding thing happen all the time. That actually is how nature develops, even when a wave breaks. It's not only organic nature I'm talking about. Even just when a wave comes in crashing to break, you know if you track that wave every tenth of a second, at each moment what is happening in the wave is developing from what was in the wave the moment before, and the wave actually produces itself in that way. There isn't some blueprint somewhere that, five minutes before, said this wave, when it crashes and breaks, is going to take this shape. That's obviously impossible. The wave actually breaks and shapes out of itself, so that even the wonderful parts of nature that are not yet organic already have this unfolding. And, of course, organism—the forests and grasslands all have this character, right? That is the most important thing to learn from nature.

What is the analogy to draw from nature? This is the single paradigm that's most critical in nature and that we must learn to emulate in our construction of the environment.

> Inside my empty bottle I was constructing a
> lighthouse while all the others were making ships.
>
> Charles Simic

© Sean Gannon

Mike Corbett

Why Can't We Build Better Communities?

If we can put men on the moon, if we can splice genes, we certainly ought to be able to design neighborhoods that are energy efficient and have a sense of community, much like the communities that existed prior to the advent of the automobile. . .

"how did you get involved with creating village homes?"

In the late 1960s [and] early 1970s, I was building houses, designing houses, and I became very, very interested in how you could build and do something that was socially more responsive. How you could build a house that was ecologically better? It really came down to designing a neighborhood, because most of the changes that needed to be made were in the neighborhood communities—I began to think of a house just as a unit in a larger scheme. So the goal was to do something to be able to have less energy consumption, to create more of a sense of a community. In this country, the sense of community in most neighborhoods was just basically gone. Houses used a lot of energy. Village Homes really grew out of those ideas.

When we started Village Homes, there were things we knew we wanted to do: solar energy, natural drainage, edible landscaping. To do this, we had to break a lot of rules: long narrow cul-de-sacs, drainage that ran on the surface, intermixing food production with housing, smaller lots, higher densities in some places. It seems like this broke every rule that FHA had, in terms of making subdivisions. It broke all the planning rules that public works directors go with. Banks were very suspicious, because it didn't really match what they had seen before. So it was a tremendous headache. It took three years to get approval and financing for the project—enough to discourage most people. But it seemed important enough of an idea to just keep plugging away, and eventually we got it going.

The amazing thing is, once we started building it, we found that people wanted to buy it. This was 1976. We began during a recession, but we sold faster than anyplace in town, and not only did it sell well in the beginning, it sold well all the way throughout and now, as a finished product, people want to live here. Unfortunately, it costs more to live here, per square foot, than it does anyplace in the Sacramento area, because there's so much demand for it.

It has been discussed by a lot of people, a lot of people have visited to look at it, but most developers don't want to go through the headaches that they have to go through with the local public works director who wants fifty-five-foot-wide streets and drainage in concrete pipes under the streets. It's mainly just the hassle the developer has to go through that has discouraged this kind of development. To some extent, loaning institutions [raise obstacles, too], but more it is the educated, college-degree public works director who has a degree in civil engineering, and the planner who has a degree in city planning, who basically think this is something that's just too difficult for them to deal with. It discourages the builders.

I think that if there were more examples that could be built in different locations . . . it would take off, because the idea is sound. It's not expensive to build—in fact, it's actually less expensive to build than a traditional subdivision. But with just one example, it's a little hard to catch on. During the 1980s, when there was so much building . . . in the country, there wasn't really a move to do anything different, because people were making money the way they were doing it. It's actually in the last three years, where times are harder for the development community, that I've found a lot more interest in doing something innovative. In fact, I've been contacted as a planter-planner more recently to talk about this kind of design and possibly do some projects like this.

It's interesting. If we can put men on the moon, if we can splice genes, we certainly ought to be able to design neighborhoods that are energy efficient and have a sense of community, much like the communities that existed prior to the advent of the automobile, and unlike the kind of suburbia that's been produced in the last forty or fifty years in this country. So I'm very optimistic at this point. I just notice a lot more people calling me, asking me about Village Homes and wanting to hire me to do designs for them.

> The city is a fact in nature, like a cave, a run of
> mackerel or an ant-heap. But it is also a
> conscious work of art, and it holds within its
> communal framework many simpler and more
> personal forms of art. . . . The city is both a
> physical utility for collective living and a
> symbol of those collective purposes and
> unanimities that arise under such favoring
> circumstance. With language itself, it remains
> man's greatest work of art.
>
> Lewis Mumford

The beginning of any creative settlement of the land begins
at the neighborhood scale, as seen in this site plan for
Village Homes in Davis, California.

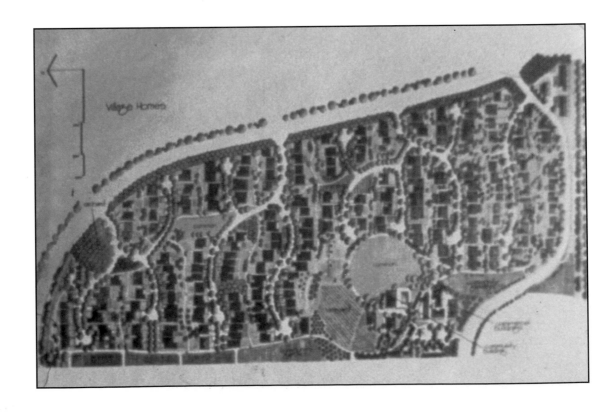

Love thy neighbor, even when he plays the trombone.

Jewish Proverb

Foot power is still the best way to explore a neighborhood.

Virginia Thigpen

Community-Conceived Designs

I think the physical aspects of Village Homes . . . are really just the surface, and they contribute a lot to what really goes on here day to day.

"what are some of the design elements that make village homes such a special place to be?"

A lot of what you notice, walking around in Village Homes, is physical layout. It's very much like a park or an arboretum, very charming, with narrow streets. Many people just walk through and, on a superficial level, think it would be a wonderful place to live. A lot of that is due to the way it was landscaped, with areas of greenbelts that are planted with food-producing plants such as grapes and almonds and other fruit trees. A lot has to do with the streets, and the fact that the streets are all cul-de-sacs, which means there's no through traffic. That also means the traffic is a lot slower, and most cars that are on the streets are there for a very definite reason. I think that the physical aspects of Village Homes, though, are really just the surface, and they contribute a lot to what really goes on here day to day. There is no fencing on the back side (or what we traditionally think of as the back side) of the house, that is, the side away from the street. The conditions on the property don't allow fencing on the common-area side. And that is really intended to be the front side of the houses, with the streets acting more like alleys. The result of that is that neighbors tend to know each other, and when you know who your neighbors are, you tend to act in a more responsible, considerate way.

More exciting than that is that people know each other's families. I know that my children are known. They're not anonymous in the neighborhood, and I know other people's children. Children having a sense of place, a sense of belonging to a community, has been shown to be very effective in reducing behavior that's undesirable in kids. A lot of the things that are going on now that we hear about can be traced back to children not feeling that they belong, or not sensing that anyone feels that they belong to them. I know children here even when I don't know their parents. That's one of the things that was hoped for, but there was no way to know that that result would take place.

When the Corbetts laid out Village Homes, with a lot of these concepts in mind, there was a lot of thought to how design affects behavior, or the psychology of design. Twenty years into it, we're certainly seeing that a lot of those thoughts are valid, and that it really is turning out to be a wonderful place to live beyond the aesthetic, beyond the physical.

There were a lot of things that Mike and Judy Corbett did that were not standard, or not conventional. Some of them involved bigger battles than others. The exciting thing about Village Homes is that they did a lot of different things. The drainage, for instance, is different. Instead of putting in an expensive system of underground piping to carry storm water away, the drainage is handled mostly by above-ground swales that look like a natural part of the landscaping, so it gives the landscaping a focus. The streets, as I mentioned, are narrower. They have gentle curves in them so you don't see a straight shot of street (which has the effect of making you drive faster). That

The joyful act of pruning the vines in an edible landscape

281

The green rooftops of Village Homes

Trees used to shade parking

was one of our biggest battles. I was sort of an assistant to Mike Corbett during the time we were getting approvals for a lot of these concepts, and that was one of the biggest hurdles we had to cross, because the engineers and public works, the people who collect the garbage, the firefighters all had concerns about narrow streets. Because they had been schooled during a time when the thought was that bigger is better. A wider street is a better street.

There were many reasons for keeping the streets narrow. One was that asphalt is made of petroleum products, so, environmentally, it's not a good material to use too much of. The streets are dark and in the heat of summer here, they do act as giant heat sinks. Narrower streets are easier to shade, and the street trees were selected and planted in such a way that they will shade the streets, keeping the overall microclimate a lot more comfortable here. I mentioned the benefits with traffic and cars. You just simply don't drive as fast if the street is narrow, and that makes it a safer place for children.

There's nothing in the planning or build-out of Village Homes that couldn't be duplicated elsewhere. Village Homes began construction in 1975. The planning went on many years before that, of course, beginning with just a crazy idea and becoming more and more practical until it really could be done. A lot of the reason that Village Homes hasn't been duplicated, I think, has to do with the vision and the determination of the developer, Mike Corbett. He had a very clear sense of how he wanted Village Homes to be and has a hard time hearing the word "no." In the minihurdles that were encountered with lawyers, engineers, city community-development directors, and that sort of thing, he heard "no" said many times, and he chose not to hear it and to proceed anyway and to plead his case, say, to the city council or whoever was in a decision-making position.

Many years later, I became a developer of sorts and tried to do a lot of the same things and began to really understand some of the reasons why most developers don't even attempt this kind of thing. A lot has to do with the legal ramifications of something like this—they are a lot more complicated now. In order to make the common-area structure work, there has to be an entity to own it and to maintain it. In this case it's a homeowners association. In the last fifteen years, homeowners associations have become very messy from the legal point of view. I once heard that 80 percent of homeowners associa-

"why haven't the features of village homes been transported elsewhere?"

284

tions have sued their developers. Now many of those are for very good reason. Homeowners have indeed been taken advantage of by developers who made promises that weren't kept. But it's become a very lucrative area for litigation attorneys. Any jury, when faced with some innocent homeowners versus, say, a rich developer are often going to side with the homeowners, and lawyers and developers are very aware of this. So we find now a climate in which homeowners associations are not encouraged as a structure for owning proper-ty and maintaining property.

We're leaning now, at least in California, much more toward a structure that allows the city to take over common areas and green-belts. Frankly, cities don't want areas that are difficult to maintain. City maintenance crews are more comfortable with conventional parks, which are turf and trees that can be mowed and maintained by relatively unskilled personnel without a lot of training. The landscaping that you see here requires an understanding of pomology, and pruning, and organic pest control, and those are just, simply, things that are more difficult. They require a lot more attention than a conventional park. The physical shape of it is more challenging, too: the common areas here meander between the homes. In some places they're wide, in some places they're narrow; they have unusual plantings, and there's often not a very clear definition, a physical definition, between where a person's private property ends and where the common area begins.

Those are all things that make it a lot more challenging to main-tain the common areas. The common areas that are shared between homes are a really critical part of what's happening here. They physi-cally lend themselves to a lot of other kinds of interactions between people, and I don't think it would be possible to have the same kind of interaction between neighbors without having that physical setting.

ENERGY SELF-SUFFICIENT COMMUNITIES

"how does Village homes deal with the energy issue?"

Village Homes was conceived originally as a community that would be energy efficient and even someday energy self-sufficient. To begin with, to make this easy to do in an environment where there were numerous builders and architects participating, all of the streets are laid out in a primarily east-west direction. Which means the lots are oriented . . . north and south. This makes it possible to locate most of the windows on the south side of the house, for capturing winter sunshine. Overhangs are designed to keep out summer sun so that we don't have unnecessary cooling loads. East and west windows are discouraged, partly through information in the community, the codes, and restrictions, and partly through just a communication of innovation between the various architects and builders who were working in Village Homes.

A lot of our cooling in the summertime is accomplished by taking advantage of the summer seabreeze that comes up from the San Francisco Bay—we're just located in a perfect place to capture that. By locating operable windows on houses on the north and south side, we're able to get a lot of through ventilation, which cools the houses down and allows them to stay cool throughout the next day without the use of air conditioning. Our summer temperatures here reach as high as 110, and are quite often over a hundred. Fortunately, at night, temperatures drop down below 60 degrees Fahrenheit. So if we can take advantage of those swings, it makes a big difference. In winter we have a lot of clear sunny days, cold but clear, in which we can take advantage of heating from the sun.

The trees help. The trees that are planted, and the way they're designed here, makes a big difference in cooling. The street trees that keep the streets shaded in summertime, lowering the ambient neighborhood temperature, are all deciduous, so that in wintertime they've lost their leaves and allow the sun to penetrate and warm the houses and reach the solar collectors for the active systems.

The vineyard and several of the orchards that you see throughout Village Homes are located in places where, in conventional planning, you could locate a house or two and therefore obviously make more money off the development. The Corbetts felt very strongly that devoting a fair amount of the land in Village Homes to

286

green belts and food producing areas that would be shared by all the residents was a very important part of the concept here.

Another thing that you'll notice as you walk around is that the lots, the houses, seem very close together, and yet on the west side of the development there's a fair amount of open space. The thought there is that houses typically take up more land than they need to, and a lot of that land is wasted with side yards and back yards that aren't really utilized very well. So instead of each house having to have its own space large enough to, say, accomplish an outside party, there are areas in the neighborhood that can be used for gatherings, for potlucks. We have a community center that can be used by residents. Each house and each lot doesn't really need to be as large as in a conventional situation.

An emerging Eco-Village in Ithaca, New York (1996)

Jaime Lerner

The Collective Dream

There's no challenge more noble than to achieve a collective dream.

"how did you get involved with making curitiba the ecological capital of brazil?"

I was a student of architecture in the time when the mayor of my city attempted to change downtown. He thought mostly in terms of building big roads and trying to widen streets that would end up killing the whole story of the city. We began to react against these changes in the city, and from that time on, it was a big fight to get the city to have a dynamic plan, especially because we usually plan in a static way, using zoning and a hierarchy of roads. The notion was we needed another idea about cities.

When we talk about the sustainable city, what we mean is the city that wastes the minimum and saves the maximum. We have to move from a linear development to a circular one, toward the rechargeable city. We cannot understand our resources as being infinite. I think we should have an eco-clock, which shows the proportion between saving and wasting. In every city we know the temperature, but we don't have a measure of how far the commitment of that city is with the environment.

If we want a human city, we have to mix all our urban functions. Mixed use, mixed income. The more we mix, the more human is the city. More and more, we have to integrate human functions; the human city will be based on a systems-integration perspective. Cities in the third millennium won't be about a Flash Gordon scenario or a Blade Runner scenario. The cities of the future—the quality cities of the future—will be about the way in which they reconcile men and nature. I think this is more important than anything. The more committed the city [is to working] with nature and [finding] ways to handle waste, [the more the place will become] a rechargeable city, a city that respects its history, its shuman scale, its part in nature.

Our societies are used to quick answers. A credit card gives you the money very quickly, the fax machine gives you the message. So our society is more and more used to quick answers and the only thing that is still stone age is central governments. The only power that you can have quick answers with is local. That's why the next century is the century of the cities. I remember a saying from Rene Dubos: "Tendency is not destiny." The exact moment when a society detects a bad tendency is the exact moment of the change. That's why, twenty years ago, we didn't have that kind of concern with the environment, and now it's changing. Why? The society detected it.

The cities can change the energetic profile of a country, when we realize how far we go with transport, or on saving energy with garbage, for instance. In our country, the foreign debt, which was responsible for the sacrifice of a whole generation, with recession, unemployment, impoverishment—when we realize that the major part of this foreign debt is related to big energy projects, this is not a question of scale, or specific problems of a city, it's a philosophy. Wasting and wasting again, building more big energy projects? What a spoiled country. We need to use the energy from the sun, and get off of the tit of big oil. This is very important for our sovereignty.

I remember a saying of Carl Paul Volberger from a celebration of the one hundredth anniversary of the Brooklyn Bridge: a monument should represent a shared cause that links the different parts of society. Cities, like a monument, should represent this shared cause. It's the only way that we could achieve a collective dream. There is no challenge more noble than to achieve a collective dream. When a city can improve its quality of life, when it respects the people that live in that city, when it respects the environment, when it prepares for the next generations, the people assume that kind of coresponsibility, and this is a shared cause—it's the only way to achieve that collective dream. How beautiful it is to achieve that collective dream of a city.

The revitalized city of
Curitiba, Brazil

*Perhaps the first step
towards regaining
possession of our
souls will be to
repossess and replan
the whole landscape.*

*Lewis Mumford
The Urban
Prospect, 1968.*

*The gentle act of
greening the city*

Chapter Seven

Writing
the
New Codes

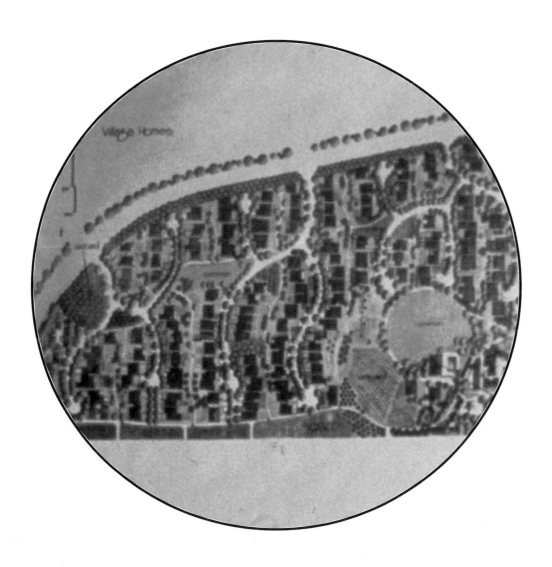

We have abandoned our role as shepherds of Being.
Louis Kahn

◆ ◆ ◆ ◆ ◆ ◆ ◆ ◆ ◆ ◆ ◆ ◆ ◆ ◆ ◆ ◆ ◆ ◆

Alas, the forms of the built environment won't finally change unless we get at the source code level. Every generation has its chance to bring new knowledge to the table as we zigzag our way into the future. Somehow the existing building codes have allowed us to produce a profoundly fragmented, unsustainable mode of being in the world. We desperately need a new mixture of incentives that impels the imagination to produce a Green Architecture and thus a more dynamic settlement that radiates the synergy between Nature, Technology, and Humanity.

If we can generate the social will to build asphalt highways to connect distant places, then at least we can re-channel our modes of thought into illuminating the Genius Loci that makes a place worth the effort to travel to. Ultimately, in order to advance the cultural DNA of our time requires that we expand our imaginations so that aesthetic concerns are at least on par with economic driven behavior, and natural law (physics) sets the tone more than the current brand of short-term politics.

This means we will have to invent a new language of form that will allow us to expand our current organizing myth (the psychological construction of reality) that the economy is the paramount force that ultimately decides what gets done. For in the end, our true debt is to the biosphere that sustains us, not the economic system that contains us.

Hopefully, this chapter will help you the reader build a more positive image of the future, and then ripple into influencing the ever emerging game plans for the 21st century now forming in the hinterlands of the benevolent design imagination.

C.Z.

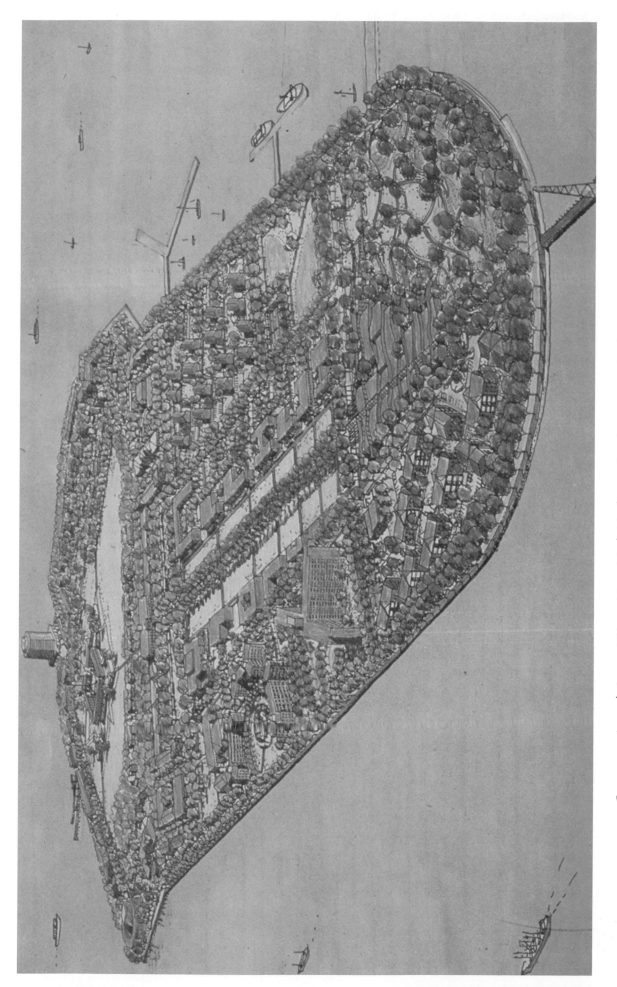

Governors Island Competition, New York Harbor. (Tourbier & Walmsley, James Wines, 1996)

Peter Calthorpe

The History of the Codes

The codes have to change, but actually, before the change happens, a consensus, a vision of a different future really has to coalesce.

The codes are really just a legal personification of the way things are done, and the way they have been done since World War II. They go back to a misguided design philosophy: the modernists believing that you need to segregate land uses. At the turn of the century, they were looking at the industrial city as a blight, and so the idea of low-density, segregated land uses came into vogue. They had a love affair with the car, and technology hadn't quite reached its nemesis and therefore was still seen in very positive terms in the '30s. So the great paradigms that drove the way we think about the built environment were formulated at the turn of the century and, largely, [from] the '30s. Frank Lloyd Wright drew his picture of Broad Acre Cities, which is really the paradigm for the suburb. Le Corbusier in Europe drew Villa Radieuse, which was the towers-in-the-park strategy of urbanism that destroyed the urban street and the mixed-use vitality of traditional urban centers, and turned them into what we see as co-op cities today, or as office parks. They became the kind of visual paradigm that became codified.

The automobile was the chosen technology after World War II. Other countries in Europe headed in a different direction: they have a different set of codes, a different set of problems. For example, Sweden, after World War II, went to a program of new towns strung like a necklace around the old urban center, connected by transit. On average, the Swedes, even though they have a worse climate than we do and are actually wealthier than we are, use their cars half as much. It's not like they're too poor to use them, it's just that they have good alternatives, because their land planning took off in a different direction.

The codes have to change, but actually, before the change happens, a consensus, a vision of a different future really has to coalesce. That vision has to be shared not just by a group of radical environmentalists, or by a self-interested group of developers, or some politicians, it has to be comprehensive. It has to be seen as the chosen way of life.

I see us at a kind of demonstration-project phase of the whole thing. Where a few of these are being built—God help us if the recession doesn't let up enough to let these places really be tested—but they need to be built, people need to live there, people need to understand the quality of life, and the trade-offs that are being made. People need to understand how well they work, and then you'll see. I believe the jury'll come in and vote yes, this is the right thing. And when that happens, then, I think, all these laws can be changed fairly easily.

Yet I'm really suspicious of the economic calculations, because, quite honestly, with the discount rate where it is, the future is inherently discounted. And because people don't know the future, they can never absolutely agree upon what the impacts are going to be, the long-term impacts, and therefore they can't find a value for them. So, inherently, economics has a short vision. Intuition and wisdom just can't play as big a role as they need to, no matter how you restructure the formulas. I'm always distrustful of that, just as I'm distrustful of the engineering solutions which can optimize things, even for the good, such as energy conservation, but still lose sight of some larger concerns.

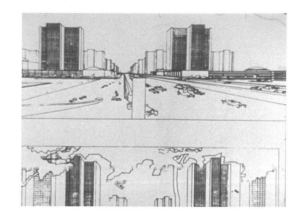

Villa Radieuse, Le Corbusier.

Co-op City, New York

The code is a series of rules and regulations made to be foolproof, but succeeds only in being rules and regulations for fools. So codes are rules and regulations made by little men to govern middle men.

Frank Lloyd Wright

297

Douglas Adams

The Infinite Virtual Address

The role of people who are the real visionaries . . . is not necessarily to be right, but is to charge people up with the idea of disposing of the sort of limitations of our expectations at the moment and trying to address the immense possibilities.

> what is the Role of the visionary?

It's very often just a question of putting something in a slightly different perspective. The most obvious and simple example from Hitchhiker is that right at the beginning of the story, you've got this guy who's having his house bulldozed to make way for a new local bypass. You think of that as a familiar event, and you know what that means. But having said, "here's a familiar event," let's put it another way. Here is the whole earth now being demolished to make way for a hyperspace bypass. Now how do you feel about that? It's the same thing. It's exactly the same thing. But we now feel differently about it.

That's a kind of trick that I'm quite fond of playing. You take a familiar thing, put it in an unfamiliar scale and suddenly it becomes vivid in a completely different way. You see it afresh.

I was very struck by whoever it was who said that, with a bit of luck, this will be the only century in the entire history of the human race that has been entirely dominated by one-way media. I suppose books, in a sense, are a one-way medium, but they're actually involved in much more active participation, from the point of view of a reader asking, "Do you understand?" The idea of television being something that you know is there to be your servant, and something that you can interact with, and make your own demands of, and that will react intelligently and smartly to whatever you need, I think, is a vast improvement on what we've been saddled with for the last fifty years, which, I think, is gradually turning all our brains to bean curd.

I think we are at a very early stage in terms of what we could be

298

getting toward. You see various interactive projects that people have constructed and, as much as anything else, they're simply trying to define how the interface works. It's like we're trying to do well. We're going through a very necessary phase of trying to determine how a brick works, when in fact you know we've got the Taj Mahal, or the Great Wall of China, or St. Paul's Cathedral that's going to be built. I think it's only when we get what's known as the "infinite virtual address space," when everybody will have continual, transparently intelligent access to that, then virtual reality will really come into its own.

At the moment, content-based software, which is what multimedia currently is, is still terribly limited by whatever the programmer has a space or inclination to put it in. So, it's not a great deal more than a different and faster way of turning pages at the moment. But I don't say that to disparage it at all, only to say we ain't seen nothing yet. We are merely dipping our toe in a vast ocean, and we've got a long way to swim.

I am certainly familiar with some of what Ted [Nelson] has been up to, and I think he's obviously a wonderful visionary, whether or not one particularly agrees with this specific point or that specific point. I think, by the way, what we're trying to envisage is so far removed from where we currently are that you actually need people like Ted who can hurl their brains way far ahead. Maybe not hit every point, but really be, as much as anything else, setting the scale of what it is we're trying to attempt and encouraging other people to see what that scale is. Because we have to lose an awful lot of our preconceptions are about how media work.

In the end, computers, as they touch every new and different realm of our lives, are going to have increasingly revolutionary effects, and there will come a point where all these minirevolutions suddenly become an immense revolution and almost entirely redefine the way in which our lives are lived. Whether that's good or bad, I don't know. I like to feel optimistic about it. I feel very excited about it— slightly nervous, as well.

The role of people who are the real visionaries, like Ted, is not necessarily to be right, but is to charge people up with the idea of disposing of the sort of limitations of our expectations at the moment and trying to address the immense possibilities.

299

THE PROSPECTS FOR INTERACTIVE MEDIA

What television has brought is a sort of artificial reality over which we have no control. If you live in a world in which you don't know television, you are completely—all of your experience is your own direct experience, and everything you do has consequences, and you know how the world works, and you know that if you do this what will be the consequence of that, and your entire life is just your relationships to the immediate world around you and the immediate people around you.

When you start having relationships instead with the people from Dallas and Miami Vice and whatever, where you actually play no part, but you see all sorts of consequences of things happening that don't really make sense, don't really touch your world, and you sort of half enter into it, you're actually cutting yourself off from your own real world. The normal sort of syllogisms of life begin to break down. The result of that is that your brain . . . becomes a lot less sharp and your experience becomes a lot less real. You're living entirely vicariously. The vicarious experience doesn't let you make sense.

The key difference is interactivity. What we have at the moment—and, as I say, I don't want for a moment to disparage it—is people doing fantastically good work at the level which is very, very basic. Compared with what I hope we will eventually get, it's merely electronic page turning. People like Ted, Bill Abel, and all these guys, you know, really are pushing the boundaries bit by bit. The boundaries are very close to us at the moment, and we have got a long way to go.

More than at any time in history, mankind faces the crossroads. One path leads to despair and utter hopelessness, the other to total extinction. I pray we have the wisdom to choose wisely.

Woody Allen

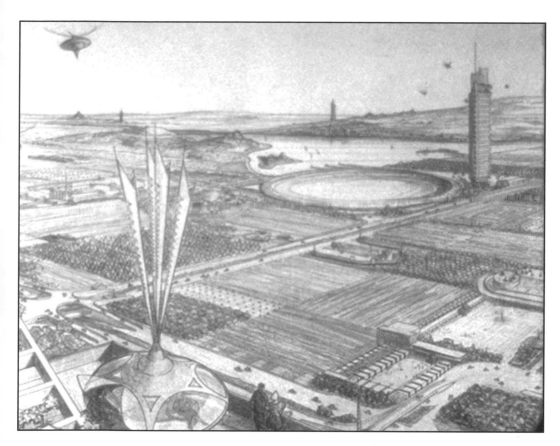

Frank Lloyd Wright drew his plans for Broad Acre City, an early
prototype of suburbia. In the 1950's Levittown became the perverted
model for the suburbs in response to housing demand after World War II

Duane Elgin

Mutually Assured Development

We're choosing a future of either stagnation, at best, or, more likely, collapse, or we can chose more ecological lifestyles, in which case we're choosing a future of mutually assured development.

"where do we go from here?"

Buckminster Fuller believed in a direct democracy, that we would move rapidly toward a direct democracy, and I take issue with that point of view. After a number of years of organizing, working with the public as well as with the various institutions, I think that is an inappropriate path to take at this point. We may evolve toward a direct democracy, but I think there's a transitional stage that is very important, and that is to use our representative democracy in a much more effective way. To do that, we have to use our tools of mass communication to provide feedback to our representatives in government, so that they in turn know how the body politic feels about these critical issues and thereby can be empowered to make decisions on our behalf.

A few years ago, in the face of the mounting federal deficit, one politician was asked, "Why don't you do something?" And he replied, "Look we're not dummies here. We know there are only a couple of ways to reduce this debt; what we don't know is how the public feels about that."

Rather than the public giving a direct remedy to the problem of a mounting debt, I would like to have the public give direct feedback to these decision-makers who are supposed to be concerned with this, day in and day out, and have them feel the heat of public opinion and the power of public opinion so that they can move vigorously to resolve some of these issues.

That's the transitional process, and I think that it's appropriate that we have the public involved, giving direct feedback to decision-makers. But the decision-makers make the final decision, and that's a somewhat different approach than a direct democracy that Fuller was talking about.

Basically, we're moving from the industrial era, with an emphasis upon material production, to the communication era, with an emphasis upon learning and communication. I think we have the technologies right now that we need to sustain ourselves as a species, but we're not using those technologies in a way that will really work for us. But we do have the communications tools to allow us to talk about how we use those other technologies, so that we can begin to design ourselves into a more workable and sustainable future. So the real challenge now is to move from, let's say, competition in our use of these tools, to reconciliation and what I would call a future of mutually assured development.

A safe and sane future touches every facet of individual lifestyles, it is just a pervasive change in every facet of living. It's so extensive. It's all in my book Voluntary Simplicity, about the changes that are involved at this point so we can chose high conceptual lifestyles. We're choosing a future of either stagnation, at best, or, more likely, collapse, or we can choose more ecological lifestyles, in which case we're choosing a future of mutually assured development. We have to really work with the abundance that is there in new ways, or we're going to tear ourselves up as a planet. I think these trends are going to converge in the next generation, in roughly twenty five years. I mean climate change, pollution, acid rain, ozone pollution—all of those, and population growth, which is expected to go from roughly five or six billion now to eight or ten billion in the next twenty-five or thirty years.

We need to learn our way into the future. We need to learn how to make a living in this new world environment, and that means we need to use our technologies differently. Instead of man working over nature, it's more humans working within nature, finding a way to cooperate with nature, using the natural abundance that's there in a much more synergistic and effective way. And I think that's also going to require that we move from a spirit of greed and competition to a spirit of generosity in how we approach the use of these tools. We need to reconcile ourselves to the limits of this finite world—if we can do that, then I think we can learn our way into a livable and sustainable future.

Expedients are for the hour: principles for the ages.

Henry Breeder

303

Paul MacCready

Education As an Odyssey of the Mind

Calling it design makes it sound a little more elegant, as though it's something they teach in college. Actually, it's what you're doing all your life.

> "can we teach design in public schools?"

First of all, the concept of design is not some narrow thing, where you're making some gadget. It's just a process of understanding some goal that you're trying to work toward using whatever tools you have. Understanding what the limits of the system you're operating with are, then accomplishing your goal. Sometimes the best way to do it is by political methods, and sometimes it takes a bunch of money. Sometimes it requires coaxing a lot of your friends to help you, and sometimes it's engineering.

So calling it design makes it sound a little more elegant, as though it's something they teach in college. Actually, it's what you're doing all your life. Kids are great at it, and wonderful with being inventive. But we tend to beat that out of them in school. The reward system in school does not give you good marks for innovation, for seeing four sides of an issue instead of one and for disbelieving authority sometimes.

Schools aren't very good at it, but people really are creative. You're creative, very creative, when you're playing in the sandbox. Everybody, when they're five or six years old, can handle a language—in this country, English, which is very complicated, with lots of exceptions. If kids are in a bilingual family, they handle two languages, and they know how to manipulate two adults beautifully. So every six year old is obviously a genius! Then they get to school, and we convince them they're not geniuses! But they really are. Some schools are better than others, or the gifted teacher is very important for continuing this enthusiasm for life and for the capability that kids have. Some kids are so strong that the school can't beat it out of them. They end up doing things that are special. When you see the art that comes from kids who are ten and twelve and thirteen years old, you realize never in their lives will they be that spontaneous again and come up with such wonderful things.

So searching for ways to kind of harness this creativity is worthwhile. That's why I'm enthused about this "Odyssey of the Mind" activity which gets youngsters to work in small teams in very creative ways, learning their interactions, but not just trying to get the best mark for themselves. This is something fun that they do after school. It isn't part of the school. They're given challenges in all sorts of different topics. There is a bit of competition, but there's fun, and respect for other teams. People who get involved in it just keep wanting to do it year after year. I bet that in many cases they get more real value out of that after-hours activity than they do out of the rest of their schooling. Thank goodness the organization is having a pretty good success. It's in seven or eight thousand schools now.

When I give talks about thinking skills for school groups, say for fifteen year olds, I do discuss a lot of the fun things, the human-powered airplanes and so on that we've invented, as well as a lot of things that kids have developed. Then I get into some more serious issues, because some of the same approach to doing these developments (looking at things a little bit more broadly) makes you concerned with the total world situation, and humanity's role in it, and where it's all going to go. I find the youngsters are attentive.

I ask them at the end of the session (rather than them asking me) about some very serious topics like "If you had to decide, what population would you want on the earth when you're my age?" That means about fifty years from the present. Not an impossible length of time, because it's just when they're my age. They first don't want to answer, because they haven't been in circumstances where they deal with such serious topics in a group. But then they kind of get started. I convince them that if they don't have an answer, if they don't decide, they've already—by default—given an answer, and it's twelve billion. They may not want that number.

Then they begin discussing it, arguing about it, and it really opens up, and then it gets to very serious issues of humans versus the rest of the flora and fauna on earth, and where the whole world should go. Two hours later I leave them, and they're in little groups, all arguing brilliantly with each other. I don't care what conclusions they're com-

Pay attention to minute particulars. Take care of the little ones. Generalization and abstraction are the plea of the hypocrite, scoundrel and knave.

William Blake

ing to; they're getting more questions. I end up rather enthused with those days, because you realize these are the kids who are the adults of the future, and they are able to grapple with these subjects. Their ideas are so much better than what grown-ups have, and they're so much more open. It does give you a little optimism to counterbalance the pessimism that may hit you on other days.

Plan for and installation of living machine learning center at the Boyne River School in Canada. The living machine serves as both a tool for curriculum as well as waste water treatment for the school population.

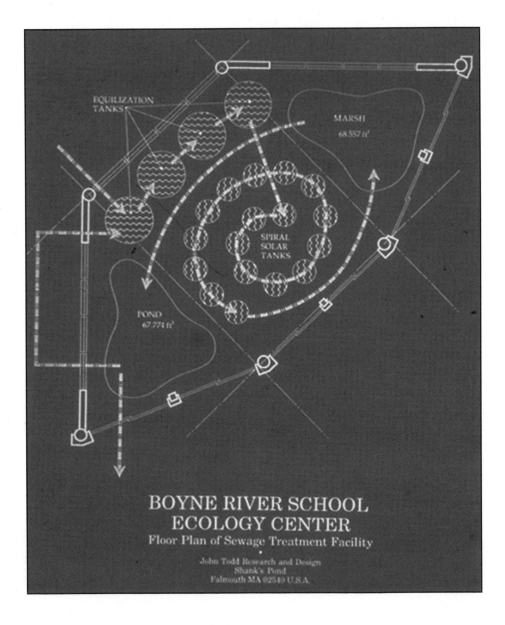

EQUALIZATION TANKS

MARSH
68.557 ft²

SPIRAL
SOLAR
TANKS

POND
67.774 ft²

BOYNE RIVER SCHOOL
ECOLOGY CENTER
Floor Plan of Sewage Treatment Facility

John Todd Research and Design
Shank's Pond
Falmouth MA 02540 U.S.A.

To learn is to change. Education changes the learner... Education at best is ecstatic.

George Leonard

James Wines

Design Education

My feeling is that you should start with the fundamental issue of habitat.

I think the most difficult aspect of education is again starting over. Education of all professions is the one most dominated by academic traditions and we've always done it this way and this is the way we're going to continue to do it. Interestingly enough even though it's supposed to be progressive it's infinitely regressive just by the nature of its own structure. So it's very hard to fight bureaucracy, especially systems that are so deeply entrenched, but I think that you can make inroads. One thing I think that has to be eliminated from architectural education, this idea of starting with the modernist paradigm and the Bauhaus idea of design. You know you start with making little boxes and little forms and putting together all of this little design nonsense. You know most design studios, elementary design education always start with putting together some little cubes and no matter which shape you put them into they always look pretty much the same and you learn very little.

My feeling is that you should start with the fundamental issue of habitat. I mean, why not go back to before there was style somehow. Really study how the first shelter was conceived and on what kind of basis in different places. So in a sense you can arrive at the basics really. Einstein said that he always loved to teach an elementary math course once in a while just because every time he did it, it brought him back to some basics that he hadn't thought about for a while, and it always gave him a new insight.

I think that's true of any art form, going back to the most primal instincts, the reason that someone painted on the wall of a cave for example. And interestingly enough, in a very short time it evolved into a very sophisticated selection of forms and ideas. And I think the reason for that was that they just had to do it. I think that students, before they design buildings, should feel they have to do it. They should have that feeling out of instinct, that they have to make shelter and understand what prompted the earliest civilizations the most.

People originally lived in caves, they decorated those caves and they finally organized communities so then they had to move out and they created a centerpiece which was usually the leadership. The role of the leader was in the center and they usually evolved in circles. The first cities always evolved in circles. So it's an interesting thing to go back to those basics. What is the source of evolution and then gradually one's designs might evolve not so much out of the magazines, out of the latest issue of PA or Architectural Digest but they would evolve out of real convictions. That's the biggest problem. The students don't tend to think about ideas in the real sense. They tend to take these heavily marketed sort of fashionable traditions and just convert them to their work.

Drawing for Shinwa Resort, Kisokoma-Kogen, Japan.
James Wines/Site. 1990.

Ian McHarg

Teaching the Ecological World View

The purpose of it would be an evolving understanding about the nature of the earth and its wonderful processes, and comedy in the present, with, then, some sort of discussion about what the future holds and what the future is about.

"how does the ecological view connect to reshaping the educational process?"

The ecological view really is the world view. It corresponds to the best knowledge in science about the way the world works. It seems to me this is the indispensable knowledge for the conduct of human affairs for every level, from the individual to the global level. I feel strongly about it. If I had my way, this would become central to the curriculum at every single level of education: kindergarten, lower school, upper school, college, and university. The purpose of all, in every single case, would be to explain to the student what a place is, how it came to be. Obviously, there'd be different levels of presentation, depending on the age of the children.

The purpose of [such an education] would be an evolving understanding about the nature of the earth and its wonderful processes, and comedy in the present, with, then, some sort of discussion about what the future holds and what the future is about. It should involve every single human activity, from writing poetry, and art, painting, sculpture, to architecture, to political science, to chemistry, to statistics. Every single subject that should be taught should somehow be incorporated into this process of producing an informed citizenry. The result should be a people, in a place, who understand about the natural processes which comprise the environment. The people who comprise the environment would understand perfectly well who they are, why they have the attitudes that they have, and see this as reasonable self-interest. They would understand the devices by which people can negotiate. This would, of course, produce an informed citizenry.

The fact of the matter is, today, you go to a cocktail party, and you ask people about the geology of their environments, they don't

310

know anything about it. They probably know very little about time and change, which is a very important subject. The unenlightened probably don't know anything about the subject at all. Nothing! They probably know a little bit about ornamental horticulture, but very little about wildlife, except conspicuous, indigenous geology. It'd be very unusual if you could find people in my circles (very old people!) who know any-thing about ethnographic history, or the communities in which they live. They're unlikely to turn to anything more formal than a newspaper to find out what people's opinions are, to see if there's any structural relationship between people, their occupations, their resources, and their attitudes toward the land. I think all of this should be the basis for citizenship.

I was once asked if I wanted to become the president of a small but quite distinguished college. I realized right at the outset that these people were going out on a limb to suggest a landscape architect as their president of their college. But I realized that I was, neither by temperament nor skill, an appropriate president of a college. And so I decided I had to do something to allow these people to get off the hook. Obviously I could not reject it. They had to decide I was unsuit-able. So I had to give them opportunities which were very, very clear to reject me. I did it purposefully. I went through this little story about producing a holistic education that included the physical, biological, social sciences, humanities, and art for producing people who are informed and civilized citizens. Of course, one of the ways that this is going to happen, we've got to reorganize the university of all the obstructions to this holistic view, the productionism of departments. And so one of the first things we're going to have to do is to get rid of all departments.

That was it, of course, because all the people who would've voted for whether I was to become president were the chairmen. They were clearly not going to terminate themselves! They were certainly not going to terminate their occupations. So that allowed the presi-dent to stay in. But one day, it's going to become possible, because, I think, we've gone as far as we have to, as far as we can, with reduc-tionism. This is not to say that reductionism should end. But I think what we have to do is wholism. It's like Humpty Dumpty:

Humpty Dumpty sat on a wall.
Humpty Dumpty had a great fall.

Modern man has developed a kind of Gallup-poll mentality, relying on quantity instead of quality and yielding to expediency instead of building a new faith.

Walter Gropius

All the king's horses,
and all the king's men,
couldn't put Humpty together again.

The whole world is really a whole lot of little shell fragments. They have scientific disciplinary names on them, and all the little pieces that people know are very, very elegant. But that's not what we need to know. We need to know how to put them together, how it works. That's the challenge to education. That's the challenge to society. We've got to do that in order to be able to handle the stream of existence.

SECTION: BARGE/LIVING MACHINE GREENHOUSE

Model by J.Baldwin for the Living Schuylkill Barge, a bioremediation barge designed to help clean the river, produce aquaculture, and be a living classroom for the Academy of Natural Sciences in Philadelphia. This project emerged out of the research and development of the film Given the state of our waters and unregenerative land based architectural forms, this kind of symbolic architecture maybe just what we need to wake up to our inter-dependence with the natural world. If you're interested in finding out more about this project, and other ones that came out of the filmmaking process--contact The Knossus Project at the address in the back of the book.

© Knossus

Mike Corbett

Reinventing Design Education

The people that are graduating go to work, and you take a project before them that's similar to this and they just can't deal with it.

I think a lot of the roots of our problem is the educational process. At the universities, I think they're really a few decades behind. There are some universities, some locations, where students are coming out with a grasp on ecological design, a grasp on interaction between physical design and a social interaction. But for the most part it's really dreadful. The people that are graduating go to work, and you take a project before them that's similar to this and they just can't deal with it. It's not the standard run-of-the-mill, and that's what they're used to dealing with and it's very disappointing.

Part of it is the fact that it is an interdisciplinary problem. You have planners in one field, landscape architects in another one, architects in another. They don't have a background in biology, they don't have a background in the things that would give you the knowledge to design something like this. So they just don't understand it. Fortunately, there is some movement in the AIA [American Institute of Architects] and there are a few universities that are doing a good job, and hopefully they'll have a good impact on the rest of the institutions.

From my standpoint, I've been lucky. I've been able to teach, I've been able to be a builder, I was an elected official, I was a developer, I've designed. I think the more experience you get of all these different fields, the easier it is to be innovative, and it's good if students can get that kind of interdisciplinary background.

The key is that universities not become so stuck in the mud. I was in Berkeley just recently. I taught there and I was, with the exception of a few professors there, really disappointed in what the students were getting in terms of an education. I know I wouldn't send my son to planning or architecture school there.

I think that the whole concept of ecological design—natural drainage, edible landscaping, social spaces that work well and make people happy where they're living, so they don't have to drive out of their community twice daily and for vacations—I think that's all transplantable to any place in this country. The design is going to be somewhat different, but the principles are the same.

Flow forms grace the landscape at the Real Goods Center, Hopland, California

For you, the world is weird because if you're not bored with it, you're at odds with it. For me the world is weird because it is stupendous, awesome, mysterious, unfathomable; my interest has been to convince you that you must assume responsibility for being here, in this marvelous world, in this marvelous desert, in this marvelous time. I wanted to convince you that you must learn to make every act count, since you are going to be here only a short while, in fact, too short for witnessing all the marvels of it.

don Juan
Carlos Castaneda's Journey to Ixtlan

Hazel Henderson

The Importance of Self-Education

There is a sense in which, if you are self-educated, you can work much faster.

"where did you learn to write so cogently about desired futures?"

I think self-education is very important in a society where the culture is collapsing and a new paradigm is emerging, for obvious reasons. It is very hard to deprogram yourself from an old paradigm. If you start off from a fairly clean slate, you have no intellectual vested interest in the past, and you don't have any emotional vested interest in the time you spent to learn all of this stuff. I feel very sorry for a lot of professors, because they have textbooks . . . they teach from and all of this sort of thing, but they are putting their kids through college on the old paradigm. And so, of course, it's very disturbing having somebody come along and say, "Hey, you know all of this is no good anymore, you know we have got to change the scorecard, change the rules and everything else."

There is a sense in which, if you are self-educated you can work much faster. It doesn't mean to say that you do not have to do a lot of studying, but that you have to have a world view as capricious as most children have when they start out. Then when they go to school it starts getting excluded, and they begin to get these signals—you have got to get a job, and you've got to be programmed this way or that way.

As a child, I was totally in love with nature, and that really shaped my world view, totally on my own motivation, following my own impulses. So the way my database grew was, of course, with that kind of cross-referencing process that we know now is the way the brain really works, where you are making associations and this reminds you of that, and then you want to read a whole lot of books in this area, and then you want to see how this connects with a whole lot of books in this other area. That kind of process is really stamped out in most school and university settings.

One of the things I loved about Bucky Fuller was that he had this delicious, divine, childlike perception. I have the same sense that I get up in the morning and it's like the dawn of creation! It's a wonderful thought that you don't name anything: you perceive things directly. I know that, for me, there is an aliveness about that, whereas when perceptions become routinized, and language begins to take over, and we are told "this is how you should react to this," and "this is the normal response that is expected from you"—when you are faced with that, it shuts down the aliveness and the life energy that we all have available, on a daily basis. And, of course, that's the source of creativity that Bucky was such a marvelous example of.

So what is this process of giving a building soul?... It starts with developing a feeling for what is the appropriate mood, then building a strong soul of a place with materials and experiences of appropriate sensory qualities. It starts with the feelings; architecture built up out of adjectives—architecture for the soul.

Christopher Day
Places of the Soul

William McDonough

A Shift from Style to Substance

In a house or an office, how beautiful is something if it makes you sick? On a planetary level, how beautiful is something if it's destroying the planet? I think people are starting to recognize that as an aesthetic agenda.

> so in the end, this is not about a new architectural style?

In many senses, we are talking about a shift from style to substance. I think stylistic issues have to range widely around the world. International style, being one style promulgated everywhere, is certainly not part of this agenda. I think whether different cultures will be expressing themselves, in their places, with their materials, with their histories, in ways that are beautiful to them, is part of the diversity question. We're also looking at the making of things in terms of what substances we are actually working with. For example, in a house or an office, how beautiful is something if it makes you sick? On a planetary level, how beautiful is something if it's destroying the planet? I think people are starting to recognize that as an aesthetic agenda.

We found that one of the tracks that we run is the issue of stress. People are under great stress, I think, because they recognize that the system is flawed and has many deleterious effects here and elsewhere. When you are aware that the harvest of mahogany, for example, is very destructive to the forest ecosystems, because there may be one mahogany per hectare, and therefore you're cutting roads and allowing access to forests and destruction, just to take out one piece of wood, [you feel stressed]. If I sit and stare at a brand new mahogany door in my office and I know anything about the harvest of mahogany, I would go into stress wondering, "Have I destroyed something by having that door made that way?" On the other hand, if we use the kind of forestry which we support—where it's indigenous peoples harvesting woods their way, supporting biodiversity, I can look at a species of wood that I've never seen before, that's incredibly beautiful, and realize that I've actually helped a tribe of people maintain their cultural space on the planet.

So it's a whole new way of making things. I can show you some materials we're looking at for making substitutes for wood, because, if you look at forestry, the sustainable forestry techniques are all involving various kinds of careful extraction.

One of the most astonishing is what they're doing in the tropics. You get 250 species per hectare in the tropics, so we're developing this database of all these lesser-known species, so we can use them. They cut a very thin strip, about sixty feet wide and maybe half a kilometer long—and the thing about a sixty-foot strip is the animals know how to get across it, because it replicates natural treefall, and the arboreal animals can still transfer across the branches because they're still touching, or they can go around it because it's not that big.

So then what we're doing is designing a system where we can ask the forest what it wants to give us, rather than telling the forest what we want.

When I was at a furniture company, a major furniture company, talking to them about designing some furniture I said: "I can't really work with you yet, because I can't work with any of your materials. We really want to design a line of furniture around a forest and what it wants to give us."

And they said: "Well, the problem you have with most of these forestry projects is that we need four million square feet of uniform material."

And my response was: "You have a design problem. The forest doesn't have a design problem."

We have design problems, so we actually have to design around what the forest needs and, in recognizing the new needs, we're creating new industries to satisfy our needs.

One of the exciting things about working the way we do is that we identify new needs, because our demands and our education grow broader and broader, and, so, in a sense, we can go to our clients and say: "We see opportunities here that may not have been perceived before, and we see opportunities for whole new industries, to satisfy the things that we're asking for."

For example, with the store we're doing in Kansas, we saw a need for day lighting. There's absolutely no reason to be using electric lighting when the sun is shining in a single-story retail circumstance. But you realize very quickly that there are certain characteristics that aren't satisfactory to many of these customers, for example, the evenness of lighting, reduction of glare, energy conservation, and so on. So rather than see that as a problem that precludes the use [of skylights], we see that as an opportunity for invention and new industry.

This one company alone, if it sky-lit all its stores, would require a half a mile of skylights, per day, for the next five years. That is an industry. So we were able to go to a major window manufacturer and say, "We want you to develop skylighting that has these characteristics: seventy-five footcandles, evenly illuminated, fewer apertures to reduce penetration, and superglazing to [maintain] energy conservation . . ."

This is spawning an entire new industry of day lighting which would cut the energy consumption in these stores by 50 percent, just on that one fact alone. And when you combine that with the other new technologies, we see the time has come to integrate a great number of things.

We couldn't have done this in the most effective way, except for the fact that the lighting now has achieved a level where we can work with electronic ballasts, dimmers that are economical, and photo sensors that allow the lights to respond to the amount of daylight that's there. So you actually get to see every bit of that savings. In the old days, they put the skylights in, but they'd leave the lights on. Now the lights have become more intelligent, the glazing has become more intelligent, and it's time for that integration.

DESIGN FOR HUMANITY

So by working at the levels we were working at, we were able to spawn that whole new industry. We were also able to look at the notion say, of wood, and insist upon only sustainably harvested wood in the structure, because it was considered important and the clients understood it and were willing to support that. So we were able to get three major forestry projects involved, only based on sustainable forestry, which sent a signal to the industry, which has a ripple effect that is quite astonishing, because this one customer alone would need half a million dollars' worth of wood every day. So that's enough to get anyone's attention.

When you go to an air conditioning company and say: "we have decided we don't want CFCs", and they say: "don't worry about it, DuPont will have it figured out by 1995," we say: "No, we want it now." When you can talk in terms of billion-dollar orders, you get people's attention, and they turn very quickly.

We also find that on small-scale projects, these things involve materials and also labor. And when you look at the cost, for example, of a wooden piece of furniture or a cabinet, the actual cost of the wood itself is not that great compared to the amount of effort to put it all together and make a building or make a cabinet.

So the extra expense, which might be two or three hundred dollars, which supports sustainable forestry in a tropical land, is of great aesthetic value to the client. It reduces their stress, because they understand that this is far more beautiful and represents opportunities that they didn't even know they had. Most people, when offered a choice of being responsible, find themselves moving in that direction. Because it has to do with the very basis of their humanity.

Set me a task in which I can put something of myself, and it is a task no longer; it is joy it is art.
Bliss Carmen

Tom Casey

The Transformation of Business

Basically, I started with a question. The question was on an index card on my desk. It sat there for eight years before I started really getting the answer. The question was: how can I do the most good for the most people while I'm here on this planet? That's the challenge we all face.

I was lucky enough to achieve, at the age twenty-seven, a level of accomplishment and prosperity. Basically, when I was done with it, I felt barren. In other words, I had got what I was chasing for all the way through my youth, and found it to be a very empty trip. I was amazed that it was so empty; that there was no sense of any value to it, or any purpose. I kind of had the feeling, " Is that all there is? This is it, this is what everybody's chasing?" I finally decided that this was not it, that the culture, if you will, was a lie. If life does have meaning, that this isn't it.

I took almost ten years off, and started studying life. I started studying things I never was able to afford to study when I was younger, like religion, and philosophy, and psychology, trying to figure out what the soul is about: What is the meaning of it? How do we get life to work? What does matter? How does one put together a rich, meaningful, satisfying life?

THE MEDIUM OF BUSINESS

A lot of people work at jobs that are meaningless and dissatisfying. They don't see any social contribution from it. They don't see their companies really making any difference in the world. It produces everything from boredom right to burn out. I see a lot of it. People asking themselves, "Is this all there is?"

I think that can be changed dramatically. I don't see why business has to be strictly a money-making, profit-making operation. I'd like to see it redefined, so when businesses set out, not to make money as their primary purpose, but to achieve some social contribution—to make some kind of contribution to the individual and the collective human potential, and as a definition of that, they also make money.

Business will not exist if it doesn't make money, if it does not return an adequate investment to stockholders. But there's no reason it can't do something larger and more meaningful while it's making money. In order for us to get on to that kind of path, we have to rethink the very context of business. What it's been about in the past isn't enough. It's not going to take us to the next level, as a society.

Business is basically a medium, just as nuclear power is a medium. It can be used for good. It can be used for harm. What effect it's going to have on society, or what contribution you're going to make to our society depends on us defining that medium, and channeling it in a way that works for us, and doesn't just make us a profit. The medium can be used in diametrically opposed ways. For example, on the individual level, you'll see people spend thirty years in business doing nothing more than making a living. Other people will use business to make a killing. Some in the middle use business to make a difference.

Very often you hear people say, "Well, I'd like to make a difference in the world, I'd like to contribute to society, but I've got to make a living." Or you'll hear younger people say, "Well, I definitely will do that down the road, but right now I've got to make my killing." What I've always played with is the idea of combining them. Why can't you make your living making a difference? Why can't you make your killing making a difference? I think that's possible within the context of the medium of business, if you open up your mind-set, and start to explore it as the medium for both making a living and making a difference.

Unfortunately, a lot of people and our institutions define business as a purely economic activity we use to make money and to make a living. I think we have to open that up. We have to break that mind set, and start enlarging the context of what business could be about in a more enlightened society. Just making money isn't going to do it.

Our worst error would lie in dreaming too small.

George Leonard

323

LEARNING TO INVENT OURSELVES

We spend our lives creating ourselves, our lives. We can recreate ourselves. We can recreate the world, including our institutions. Business is a great example of an institution that has served humanity in many ways, and has brought us from a certain level of existence to a higher one. But if we're really going to move up to the next level of human potential, the very structure and purpose of business has to be enlarged and enhanced beyond what it has been.

Generation after generation, we turn out hordes of young people who have very little clue about their higher potential as a human form on this planet. We attempt to train them, yet we teach them nothing about life, nothing about their potential. Most young people have no idea that we even have a potential. Most of them come out of school looking for a job, looking to make money, without even an acknowledgment that each of them has the incredible potential to make a significant difference in the world. That's why we're here. We're not here to make a living. We're not here to buy things. We're here to change the world.

DYNAMIC DESIGN

We need to start with a vision of the effect we want to have on the universe. If you start out with the effect that, "I want to make a contribution," then you have something meaningful to focus on. But we need to go further. What we have to do is realize an old principle that says nothing becomes dynamic until it first becomes specific. You have to become more and more specific about the effect. Only after you start getting really clear about the effect, then you extract, to start getting specific ideas from the subconscious on what it would take to do that.

I invented Humanitas basically to solve what I saw as the root problem of man's dilemma: ignorance. We've been gathering, slowly, over the last forty to fifty years (and some going back five thousand years), absolutely clear, valid, and valuable principles and techniques about life and living. But they haven't all been pulled together. Ninety percent of the people out there don't even know about any of them.

Meanwhile, in the human potential movement, all these groups are coming up with all kinds of techniques and technologies, and there's no distribution system. What I wanted was an organization that gathered, organized, and disseminated wisdom. That's it. That's the answer to the design dilemma, the design challenge. That, to me, is what it's going to take. In order for it to work, it's going to take an enormous enterprise, an enormous organization that operates on many different levels. Something as big as the Roman Catholic church of the next thousand years. That's really what we're talking about. An institution that big, that pervasive, is what it's going to take to really create change.

ENHANCING OUR MIND-SETS

What we've been talking about is achieving the individual and collective potential of the human race—what I call the global potential. In order for that to happen, many of the institutions and structures in our society have to be changed. The popular mind-set, the popular culture has to be changed. I think it will happen. The only question is, when?

I think that process can be speeded up, but until that happens, we're going to be stuck in some of the problems we have today. Corporations have to find a way to align with that purpose. Government has to find a way to contribute to that process of achieving the collective potential. Many things have to be transformed and aligned.

Unfortunately, a lot of the institutions and structures that we have today have a vested interest in opposing that kind of change. Number one, they're coming out of selfish thinking, and short-term thinking: "Well, we make a product line that is destructive to the environment, but we've got a huge investment in it, and we have no choice." Well, possibly. That kind of thinking has to be changed, and the vehicle for that is education and communication—the medium that we're using right now. We have to change the paradigm. We have to change the values of society, in order for the institutions to change. The people running them are the problem.; their mind-sets are the problem.

Until we can all get a clear vision of what the collective potential of the human race is, and until we can start building alignment

Thoughts create a new heaven, a new firmament, a new source of energy, from which new arts flow.

Paracelsus

around that, we are going to be suffering from some of the things we're suffering from today. I honestly believe that this process is inevitable. It is the one purpose of achieving human potential, the one purpose around which this entire planet and all its societies, all its corporations, all its institutions, have a natural alignment. What you're seeing is that alignment taking place. And fortunately, that process can be accelerated.

GETTING ON THE RIGHT PATH

Wisdom consists, not in seeing what is directly before us, but in discerning those things that may come to pass.

Terence

The educational system doesn't even define what your potential is, to a child. We teach them, we just bury them in knowledge (facts, figures, history, geometry) without ever talking about the collective potential of the human race. What's needed is a whole new type of social institution whose purpose is to achieve the collective potential of the human race. That was basically how I arrived at the definition of Humanitas. I started with a question. The question was on an index card on my desk. It sat there for eight years before I started really getting the answer. The question was, how can I do the most good for the most people while I'm here on this planet? That's the challenge we all face.

The path can basically be broken down into two stages. The first is transformation. Changing ourselves from the basic nature we are all born with, of being selfish, driven, getters, which is reinforced by our culture. We're all born getters. So step one is transforming yourself into a loving, caring, giving human being. Then the second stage is transcendence: having your life be about a higher purpose, or a higher calling, something other than yourself. Giving yourself to the world.

You can't find transcendence, until you've gone through transformation. One follows the other. When you go through transformation, you change dramatically as a person. When that happens, you will find a transcendent purpose for your life. Something other than about you, and your ego, and your little goals and needs. That, probably, is the philosophy, the core of the philosophy, of life, that we're here to change and transcend. Each of us contributes, in our own way, to the individual and collective potential of the human race.

Construction site of pillow dome.

J. Baldwin

Future Housing

The global dwelling service was not just intended to be a shelter, but to be a complete set of life-support services.

"is the making of the garden of eden dome on the horizon?"

The Garden of Eden dome is now possible to do, technically, and I think it's inevitable that it will be done, and it has a lot of promise. It's not the only answer for housing, but it has a lot of promise for being the basis for what Fuller hoped was a "global dwelling service." Very high-technology shelter would be available at an affordable price to almost anyone by renting the units, in much the same way Ma Bell originally rented you the telephone hardware and rented you the use of the fancy equipment downtown in the telephone exchange.

In this way, very high-tech stuff, a very high standard of quality could be propagated around the earth and, of course, the more people using it, the bigger the order would be in the factory, and the lower the prices would be, and the more efficient the production means would get. Since these dwelling units would not be based on fads, but on the use of natural principle, they wouldn't have to be redone like automobiles are when they wear out and you have to get a new one. These essentially wouldn't wear out in any meaningful way—when their small parts did, they could easily be replaced or recycled.

Fuller, of course, always had his housing as part of a major system. Even in 1927 it included the services that went with it. The global dwelling service was not just intended to be shelter, but to be a complete set of life-support services.

An artist cannot go too far out; any idea that can be conceived in our time can also be executed in our time.

Bruce Goff

A silhouette of J.B. in the Pillow Dome.

Mary Catherine Bateson

A Future That Looks Like Home

One thing that we know, as we move into this age of ecological consciousness, is that all our answers are tentative.

When I first walked into one of John Todd's bioshelters and living machines, I was struck not only by the fact that it worked, but by the fact that it was beautiful, in the sense of peacefulness that they have. I think that some of these outlaw designers, who are the pioneers of the area of ecological design, by offering us a chance to actually see and feel ecological design, even if it's very local, are prefiguring the kind of design process that has to happen in the future. It's very important that everybody should have their imagination stimulated by a chance to look at these pioneering efforts.

I think it's the essence of ecological design that it not be monolithic, that we see different communities, neighborhoods in cities, individual families, beginning to put these ideas into practice, influencing each other. We see children coming home from school suggesting that their parents start to do a better job recycling, that they could use their gray water, that more trees are needed in the yard. What you get is a process where what is pioneering now begins to be taken for granted, begins to be what feels right, begins to be the common sense of a new generation, and because it's people's common sense, it doesn't have to be centrally dictated, it doesn't have to be run by government regulation—it's run by people assuming, increasingly, that this is the way things ought to be, and the way they want them to be in their immediate environment.

If we think in terms of moving toward a society in which every member feels at home, and in which every member feels a participant in creating a home for each other and sustaining the planet as a home for other species, the last thing we want is an educational system that stamps out identical products and makes people feel alienated and inadequate. I guess what I would say about the classroom is that we should be working on making students feel at home and responsible in their classrooms, instead of feeling alienated and dominated. There are lots of things you can do in schools to teach about ecology.

Sometimes we're in a hurry and we would like to see changes made quickly that would reduce the ecological damage being done by this society. I sympathize with that, but, on the other hand, I think it's interesting that our social and decision-making processes are themselves ecological. That's what it means to be a pluralistic society—a society in which multiple points of view are argued, and no single point of view dominates all the time. And I think it's very important to support that process, to be sure that the ideas of the pioneers of ecological design are visible and available and that people can begin to see the advantages, can begin to understand how their lives will be enriched by a society that is more ecologically sound than our own.

But we should not be unecological thinkers in the sense of wanting to dictate a specific solution. That's industrial-age thinking, and, in the same way, if we want children to learn about ecology in school, we want them to learn about it as a way of looking, attending to the world around them, enjoying, benefitting from a complex living environment, but we don't want them to come out with absolutist answers. Because if there's one thing that we know, as we move into this age of ecological consciousness, [it] is that all our answers are tentative. All can become pathological unless we continue to be responsive and flexible and continue to learn what the earth is teaching us now, and what it will teach us next year and in the future.

IMPROVISING THE FUTURE

As we go about designing for the future, we're going to need new metaphors. Many of them will come from biology. Others will come from areas where human beings have learned to be gracefully flexible. One of the ones that I use a great deal in pointing out the fact that people compose their lives in original ways is saying they design their lives, and they can't design them exactly on the model of their parents. I talk about improvisation, in the sense that musicians improvise: they use familiar elements, they combine them in new ways; on the spot they modify as they go along, so that each performance is a creative process. Now improvisation gives you a metaphor for flexibility and responsiveness that wouldn't get you very far in doing the minuet, doesn't get you very far in classical ballet, doesn't get you very far in any of these patterns of behavior where the assumption is that everything should be predetermined. But if you use improvisation as your metaphor, then you can work with the assumption that you're going to respond to the environment, to natural systems, flexibly as you go along.

Now, obviously, you can't have an improvisational highway system. The roads themselves are going to have a material aspect that's fixed, but you can have an improvisation in terms of how you use them. You can change the way you use buildings over time, and you can plan for that change, the way we now have highway systems with a lane whose direction can be reversed at different times of day depending on traffic flow. So that you have flexibility in using your material systems, and responsiveness in using them.

Everything is interconnected. I don't believe that we're going to modify our behavior toward the natural world unless we modify our behavior in the social world. As long as you have large numbers of people who feel cheated, or oppressed, or exploited, they're going to seek compensations that are potentially destructive. We have to work toward a model that includes social justice and a sense of membership and community for all the human beings alive on the planet, in order that those human beings would treat the trees, and the animal species, and the air, and the water with a different kind of justice and live at peace with them.

So we do have to design communities, we do have to think about ways of participation. In designing a future, we have to think of a future that will be on the one hand clever, effective, and functional, but it also has to be appealing. People have to be offered a life they want to live—they have to be offered pleasure that they can embrace. One of the reasons that I like the term design is because a designer has to meet these two criteria. One criterion has to do with effectiveness: it can't fall down. On the other hand, there's an issue of comeliness: somebody has to want to live in it. We have to have a future that looks like home to us, all of us.

You know the most important thing that we learn from looking

Without adventure civilization is in full decay.

Alfred North Whitehead

at the adaptations of indigenous peoples is how different one human group is from another. We are not trapped in a particular form of adaptation. When we look at these different communities, we can temper and develop our idea of what it means to live at peace with the natural world, but we're not going to solve our problems by replicating or imitating solutions that worked for small communities with limited technology. So we get some ideas, we get the benefit of contrast, we get a flavor and a style, but we're going to have to find our own solutions, finally. It doesn't help to be too romantic about the fact that indigenous or primal peoples live at peace with the natural world, because, very often, when technology becomes available, they are as quick to go out and be destructive as anyone else. The problem that we face is with the huge size of human population that we have to take into account, and the tremendous potency of available technology, and the globalization that means that every problem is interconnected with every other. We have to find a way to adapt in the context of those problems, and that's never been done before.

THE CYBERNETICS MOVEMENT

You can look in rock for fossils of ancient organisms, and what you find are the forms of bones, skeletons, shells—but you don't find the process of living of those organisms. We build as if we were building fossils for the future. We're building shells, but we have to, in our designing, think about the processes, the passage of time in relation to those shells. What kind of living is going to go on in them? One of the very important breakthroughs that supports design today is the kind of thinking that was developed in the cybernetics movement, which was a tremendous breakthrough in being able to think of process, particularly those processes which are self-sustaining and self-correcting, because these are the kind of systems that we want to construct. Not fixed shells, but systems that have the possibility of repair, of maintenance, that are sustainable, and today we have a whole language of process for thinking about that.

Human beings have always looked at nature for analogues, and come up with some marvelous ideas by doing that. We know far more about nature today, and one of the things that we know that our ancestors didn't is we know about full cycles. It isn't just that we know about the growth of the tree: we know about the decay of the fallen leaves and the wood in the soil, and the bacteria in the soil that our ancestors couldn't see. So we can look at the forest and see the full cycle of process. Now it's that cycle that has to be part of our consciousness and included in our designs, and it's that kind of thinking, in terms of self-corrective cycles, that has been so original and important since World War II.

But you know, it's funny. Even though you know intellectually that you have to think in terms of cycles, it takes a long time to incorporate that awareness in your behavior. We all occasionally just treat a tree as if it were a steel pylon, or a lawn as if it were wall-to-wall carpeting, and try and make it behave that way instead of thinking of it as growing, breathing, dying, subject to illness. All of that sense of cycling in the natural world has to be built in to our sense of the human world. This is one reason why the transition we're going through at the moment is so important. Because we are, hopefully, getting away from a time when people felt they were building permanent monuments to human power and control that would be fixed. This is not what we need. What we need are patterns of adaptation that can ebb and flow and respond and be flexible.

It's odd, you know. People in cybernetics talk about control, but the concept of control in systems theory is responsive control. The capacity to change direction. That wasn't what people who thought they were going to rule the earth wanted to do: respond and change directions. They wanted to control in the sense of dominating, in the sense of determining what was going to happen.

One of the metaphors that I use in my writing is the shift in styles of dancing. It used to be in ballroom dancing that one person led, and that was the guy, and one person followed. But in the kinds of dancing that people are doing today, you don't even have to be with a member of the opposite sex. You can dance by yourself, you can dance with a friend of the same sex, you can dance with a partner of the opposite sex and people take turns mirroring each other, improvising, going off on their own steps—it's not modeled on the notion that always there has to be somebody in charge. Instead, it's essentially improvisatory, creative, and responsive. Just a simple thing like what people do on Saturday nights reflects, in a way, a change from a world that attempts to be determinate, a world in which you can always identify who is dominant, to a world that is cooperative and interactive.

> It seems to us that the human condition is poetic, that is to say that for it man lives freely and without end in the vigil and courage to make a world.
>
> Alberto Cruz
> Co-founder of the
> Open City
> Ritoque, Chile

Juan Purcell illuminating the features of Open City, Chile

Poetry and Architecture combined in Open City, Chile

Photos by
Cousineau

AfTERWORD

R. BVCKMIN9TER FVLLER

R. Buckminster Fuller (1895 – 1983): comprehensivist, poet, inventor, design science explorer, architect, geographer, geometer, ambassador for the future, "cosmic surfer", the "Leonardo of the 20th century", author of 27 books and hundreds of articles (also the subject of countless articles and books), holder of over 25 U.S. Patents, and recipient of over 50 honorary degrees, 30 honorary fellowships and 150 awards and medals: lived a life of design dedicated to making "the world work for 100% of humanity."

R. Buckminster Fuller's life work as a "Comprehensive Anticipatory Design Scientist" began in 1927, when he set out "to do my own thinking". To do this Fuller took the most comprehensive approach to problem solving, considering specialization to be an ineffective, as well as socially and environmentally irresponsible approach to design: "I simply started with the Universe. I could have ended up with a pair of flying slippers". Fuller's 1927 4-D house attempted to bring the innovations of mass production and the performance of new alloys, such as high tensile-strength duraluminum, into the design of Shelter. His entire career as a designer would revolve around this idea of bringing the potential of technology's frontiers to the service of "livingry" rather than "weaponry". Over the years, Fuller developed the "4-D" house into the Dymaxion House: the centerpiece of his idea of a global livingry service. The Dymaxion house was to be an air-deliverable, "autonomous dwelling machine" which would take care of its inhabitant's physical needs while being extremely resource efficient: human waste would be automatically packaged for recycling; water was sprayed in powerful fog mists which did the cleaning with a fraction of the water; the Dymaxion house was also self air-conditioning and self dusting (passively designed, without the use of electricity). Although still working with the tools of the Machine Age (Fuller was a "card-carrying machinist"), by considering the biological needs of total humanity in his designs at the same time that he considered their environmental impact, Buckminster Fuller would pre-figure many of the goals of Sustainable Design and indeed, he inspired every designer in this film.

In the midst of the Great Depression, Fuller designed and built the Dymaxion Car: a model of aerodynamic streamlining and high performance efficiency, almost 50 years before the Energy Crisis of the 1970's forced Detroit to re-think their approach to automotive design. In the 1950's Fuller developed his Synergetic geometry—a non-Euclidean geometry which attempted to model the way nature's energy transactions occur. Synergetics is also an attempt to model the principle that "the whole is greater than the sum of its parts"—and Fuller's term Synergy has become synonymous with this holistic approach to problem solving. Fuller's research in Synergetics led to the invention of the Octet Truss, the Geodesic Dome and Tensegrity— the strongest and lightest clear-span structures ever devised. To date over 300,000 geodesic domes have been erected worldwide. This geometry also led to Fuller's Dymaxion Map, to date, still the most accurate cartographic projection of the earth's landmasses. Fuller developed this map because he believed that in order to think clearly about the entire earth, one must first be able to see it without distortion.

While the litany of Fuller's design accomplishments could go on, his greatest legacy may be his effect as an educator. In literally thousands of invited presentations, Fuller inspired two generations of students to re-think the way we design things, and to consider the whole earth and total humanity in one's work. These presentations (often lasting over 10 hours) evoked a sense of participation in a larger adventure; that of becoming a more conscious and responsible member of the human family and the earth as a whole.

B.D.

ESSAY: Jay Baldwin

TEACHING

COMPREHENSIVE

ANTICIPATORY

DESIGN

SCIENCE

In his book, Critical Path, Buckminster Fuller calls upon humans to fulfill their purpose as an anti-entropic force in the Universe. He encouraged us to become Comprehensive Anticipatory Design Scientists. To be optimally effective, undertake the most comprehensive task in the most comprehensive and incisively detailed manner. He asserted that an appropriate education will enable designers — those who apply the generalized principles of the Universe for the benefit of all — to "assume as closely as possible the viewpoint, the patience, and the competence of God." A big order.

Designers develop and apply technology mainly in the form of products. As is always the case, any technology can be used in both beneficial and destructive ways. Insisting that humans are intended and equipped (designed!) to be successful on Earth, Bucky said that the destructive effects of technology, whether deliberate or inadvertent, are the result of ignorance. That ignore-ance, as he sometimes pronounced the word, stems from an insufficient understanding of the interconnections that lace everything together into a whole. A lack of understanding is one sure sign of an incomplete education.

It should be no surprise that Gregory Bateson's famous 'patterns that connect' are ignored, misunderstood, or even missed entirely by people otherwise considered well educated. Our society rewards narrow, specialized knowledge with PhD's, prestige, professional licenses, and occasionally with significant money. Administrators, faculty, and accreditors of schools — especially universities — are themselves products of a system that encourages the most intelligent students to specialize, just as they did. Curriculum developers forget that Nature has no departments.

A student attempting to acquire a broader education that puts a specialty into a larger perspective is usually encouraged to develop an individually tailored "interdisciplinary" major. Snaring a degree may prove annoyingly difficult. The student is put in the Academically precarious position reserved for generalists — people who know a little bit about a lot of things. Generalists rarely garner respect and the consequent goodies.

But Fuller did not advise a generalist's education, having all too often heard snide jack-of-all-trades-master-of-none remarks from his own detractors in academia. He called for comprehensivists, though sometimes he did use the term generalist, averring that "Man is born to be comprehensive." (Wholistic is the more popular word at this time.) Comprehensive and general are not the same thing. Comprehensivists attend relationships and patterns. To be truly comprehensive is inherently impossible; who can understand everything? But you can certainly try, assuaging your frustration by regarding the attempt as a never-ending quest that hones a sharp intuition that marks a good designer.

How does one become a Comprehensive Anticipatory Design Scientist? Bucky recommended this curriculum in 1967:
1. Synergetics
2. General Systems Theory
3. Theory of Games (Von Neumann)
4. Chemistry and Physics
5. Topology, Projective Geometry
6. Cybernetics
7. Communications
8. Meteorology
9. Geology
10. Biology
11. Science of Energy
12. Political Geography
13. Ergonomics
14. Production engineering

Today, he might have added the study of Chaos, Complexity, and Fractals. Of course, he didn't expect that anyone would become an expert in more than a few of these areas, but he did say that to be effective, a designer needed to be aware of the major concepts, and know the best source of the latest knowledge in each field. Since no individual could deploy state-of-the-art knowledge in all of the subjects, a need for teamwork was implied, with the designer/innovator acting as a sort of symphony conducting the ensemble towards successful implementation of a design.

Bucky also emphasized the need for self-discipline. Specialization and the resulting fragmentation of knowledge engender an oversimplification that puts image ahead of substance in both teaching and learning. Moreover, the perfectly understandable goal of security tends to displace innovation as professors and students alike maneuver to reduce their vulnerability. It is easy to be intellectually lazy.

Designers also need courage. Innovation is inherently risky, and explorers are always exposed to possible failure. Even elegant new design is rarely as reliable as the last of the well-established old, and thus may fail to be accepted. Except under severe threats that encourage sharp thinking as a matter of survival, defense of image and a secure career is also likely to discourage the information exchange and cooperation that leads to true innovation. How did Bucky get around these barriers when teaching?

Bucky taught always by invitation at hundreds of universities around the world. In the 1950's I participated as a lucky student in several of his seminars at the University of Michigan. He practiced what he preached. Synergetics came first, as you might expect. The subject was not taught anywhere and he had not yet written his two Synergistic books, so his oral presentation, along with hundreds of convincing slides, was the only source for us.

We were an apprentice crew and he was the captain, sailing our ship towards the same destination. Once the performance requirements of the design were established we organized ourselves into teams that rapidly acquired the needed information and materials — often from primary services. We then fabricated the prototype, actually experiencing the industrial processes involved. Bucky was a hard taskmaster, assuming that we would work twenty-hour days as he had trained himself to do. Most good designers I know have been apprentices of one sort or another. It was a good way to teach and a good way to learn: the best that I have ever experienced.

There is a new interest in this method of teaching and learning as the need for Ecological Design becomes critical. Nature cannot be fooled — Ecological Designers must be comprehensive, anticipatory, and scientific. Teachers who realize this are working on ways to develop skills and to inspire a wholistic way of thinking. It is largely a matter of spirit, but it isn't altruistic, it is practical. So once again, Bucky has turned out to be right. Anticipatorily right, you could say.

ESSAY: David Sellers

ANTIQUES
OF
THE
FUTURE

There is enormous momentum for the industrialized world to continue on it's current path The auto-centric view is easy to understand, it serves the short term commercial needs and greeds well
but falls hopelessly short in terms of offering a compelling and
successful configuration of civilization which can last for thousands of years. Most of America is choked with zoning codes
which foster isolation through lot size, set backs, and use sepa-
rations. The permitting process due to its time consuming nature
and detailed review limits evolution to wealthy developers most
of whom have little motive above the bottom line. These situa-

tions deliver to the public
look-alike suburbs, imper-
sonal environments which
have been sanitized to pass
the minimum codes. The general public buys it up with little to see as alternatives.

Biological Waste Treatment at Yestermorrow School
© J. Connell

Occasionally it occurs
to me that the best thing would be another oil shortage, use it all
up and go on to a better world. With the proven global warming,
petroleum needs to be replaced with a more sensible configuration of settlement.

No doubt every planet with civilizations going through emerging technologies,
overpopulation, and scarcity of resources
will suffer through the same ordeal. I kind of
see it as an emergence of a new golden age,
The Third Golden Age. Third because it is the
last chance to get there and because it is
either a golden age or the third world war.
The latter doesn't seem worth thinking about
so I look to the features of an age that can
last for hundreds of thousands of years —
lasting until a collision, solar flare-up, or
other magna-scaled event which another
start for Earth.

WIO-Riverhouse Trombe Mural
© J.Connell

Natchez St. Pavilion, seaside, Florida
1992 ©Jersey Devil Design/Build

Given this vision, my glimpse into the future suggests that the best and longest lasting source of energy for the earth surface is gravity. In the simplest terms, it is available in the form of heat. All we have to do is drill down for it. There are areas of super thin crust where the heat is a short distance down and in unlimited quantities. These places are the Niagara Falls of the long term. For example, the geysers in California or the hot bed fields in Nevada. The effect of pollution free energy means electric powered vehicles, a blend with renewable resources and a rethinking of our relationship with the natural world.

Yestermorrow Design/Build School © J. Connell

Regardless of the sources of power and the savings and the efforts for conservation of resources, there are likely to be specific and important common threads through all the visions of the future. For example, regional, site-specific settlements which emphasize the pedestrian and structures made of materials which are grown, harvested or mined locally — structures which are built to last for hundreds of years, which are shaped, molded and formed as an extension of the artistic development of our senses. The highest order in the use of materials — and this is the main distinction between man and the other species which co-habit our world — is permanence. When a material is finally available for use in a structure, building, or product, the degree to which it lasts is directly related to the artistic input in its formation. The buildings and artifacts which are preserved for prosperity are those embodied with form and life with the craft and Art of the times. These are the most efficient and lasting as they don't require additional mining, energy, and construction to keep the uses going. It is when we build cheaply without care that the products are torn down, maybe recycled and another work is put in it's place with additional energy and further degradation of resources, atmosphere and history.

Football House, Woodside, CA 1976
©Jersey Devil Design/Build

We need to build the "antiques of the future", the new inputs to the Historic Register. This requires a change of consciousness and willingness to act sensibly while evolving a new form for civiliza-

Hill House La Honda, CA 1979
©Jersey Devil Design/Build

tion. Although there have been several instances of a high Art order in settlement (Ancient Egypt, Greece, Rome, etc.), each was on the burdened shoulders of slaves, women and children doing all the work with no benefits. I see the image of the future offering an artistic, healthy, safe world for everyone...everyone. In configuration terms this means villages which are connected with permanent transit links such as light rail, spaced with mixed wild and nurtured land uses, pedestrian focused and made to order for the place with a landscape, energy and art input by the users and participants.

Montessori Island School, Lavernier, FL 1996
©Jersey Devil Design/Build

Speculative building to anonymous users has built-in ineffectiveness as the materials selected, the craftsmanship applied, and the landscape it is connected to are not participants or connected to it's formulation. The result is something which will neither last nor be cared for beyond the lifetime of the mortgage. In spite of this power there is an unstoppable, enormous, reemergence of craft and love of materials and the making of things. This will overpower the careless and cheap, replacing it with long term vitality with it's uniqueness, regional identity and feisty creativity.

Hill House La Honda, CA 1979   *©Jersey Devil Design/Build*

Yestermorrow School Fenestration Study 1987 © J. Connell

Palmetto House, Miami, Florida 1987   ©Jersey Devil Design/Build

347

ESSAY: John Connell

TOWARDS
A
DESIGN
CURRICULUM
FOR THE
21ST
CENTURY

INTRODUCTION

Though usually wary of living too much in the future (or in the past), the opportunity to consider a design curriculum for the 21st Century is just too interesting to pass up. From an evolutionary perspective, design may actually be the most profound of all human behaviors. It amounts to our best attempts to configure things the way we feel they ought to be. But that's design, the activity, which is quite different from design, the profession. The profession is in disarray at the end of the millennia just when it is needed the most. Here's why the design professions, and the schools that shape them, must re-invent themselves.

WHY WE DESIGN WHAT WE DESIGN

Humans, as a species, have survived and prospered (almost into a global blight) because of their unsurpassed ability to make whatever they "need". While other successful species develop a perfect fit with their ecosystem contingent on wings, gills, speed, agility, teeth, photosynthesis, etc., humans[1] simply fabricate what they need to inhabit any corner of the earth, regardless of climate or other nat-

WIO-Riverhouse North Porch © J. Connell

ural resources. We do it by making[2] stuff. Where a bear needs fur, we make clothes; where a cheetah needs speed, we make vehicles; where birds fly, we make planes; where predators hunt, we make agriculture; and where many species maintain territory, we maintain society.

---

[1] At first glance humans seem an evolutionary long shot. They can't run very fast, fly or swim. Their teeth rot and fall out, their skin and hair are unreliable and offer little warmth, their eyesight is medium at best and goes downhill quickly. If left outside for more than a few days, humans perish from exposure!

[2] Elsewhere I use the word "making" to suggest *design* and *building* fully integrated into one seamless process. Here I expand the definition to include the realization of any idea whether it be physical or ephemeral, premeditated or reflexive, individual or communal.

348

At the close of the 20th century our culture of technology has left no corner of the world untouched. Humans can access and inhabit the rain forests, the Antarctic, the bottom of the ocean, and now even outerspace. Whatever other poetic reasons there may be for these scientific adventures, the overreaching motivation is a relentless planet wide(even galaxy wide) quest for natural resources to make stuff. This is not a conspiracy or a plot. We cannot blame governments or industry for developing this plan. This is just humans being humans. No blame. You might as well accuse birds of taking to the air just to pile up frequent flier miles.

WIO Riverhouse 1992 © J.Connell Humans will use and abuse natural resources in the same mindless way a salmon will swim upstream — even if it is polluted. It's just basic evolutionary momentum. Humans make stuff to survive and they will keep doing it even when it threatens their own well being.

Now here is where design should make all the difference. Design is the non-mindless approach to making stuff. Design is the act of making things in a very particular way. It is the process whereby humans can express intentions through the things they make. For instance, a vehicle can be designed to be fuel efficient or really fast, or just cool to look at. It depends on the intention of the designer. Similarly, a house can be designed to be energy efficient, or to be non-toxic, or reflect the lifestyle of the occupants — or, more commonly, to sell quickly. Again, It's a question of intention.

Ecological Design, for example, intends to make built environments using materials and methods that don't compromise the future viability of our world. The specifics of this design intention are still being explored. Paul Hawking suggests a commercial model that derives from nature. Our current notion of waste must be re-engineered to become 'food' for other commercial processes. Meanwhile, Bill McDonough offers the Hannover Principles to help guide all nations as they design sustainable pavilions for the World's Fair 2000. For McDonough, sustainable design includes considerations of soil, soul, and survival. Persistent toxins must be totally eliminated. Materials or methods that compromise any species' quality or quantity of life are not considered sustainable.

McDonough and Hawkins are excellent representatives for sustainable design, but they are only part of a much larger tradition that includes Buckminster Fuller, Paolo Soleri, E.F. Shumaker, Hazel Henderson, John Todd, Peter Calthorpe, Sim Van Der Ryn, and a multitude of others. Why is this design agenda still unfulfilled? Why, as we go into the 21st Century, is it still newsworthy when someone makes an environmentally responsible building? Probably because the design professions have really accomplished very little with their efforts to implement sustainable social change.

FIFTEEN MINUTES OF FAME (FIFTEEN YEARS OF BLAME)

The designers currently interested in developing a new design agenda are numerous indeed[1]... but not really too numerous. We hear about them way out of proportion to their true numbers because they make excellent news stories. When a designer (and client) go out on a limb, it's newsworthy. The designer is interviewed and the impression is left that a whole new understanding may be dawning (a.k.a. — a design style or fad). Although a little misleading, the sequence is probably pretty good. Even though the press wants a 'scoop' more frequently than the world actually gets a design revolution, risk-taking needs rewards and some of these buildings truly are refreshing.

Yestermorrow School 1989 Welding Class
© J. Connell

Talk is cheap in the design world; it is almost a verbal art form. Any designer that actually builds according to their rhetoric deserves a little press. A built structure is the acid test for any new body of design ideas. It is a brave undertaking because the first demonstration (usually the most media worthy) is rarely without flaw, con-

[1]Bill McDonough, Pliny Fisk, Michael Reynolds, Helmut Ziehe, John Todd, James Wines, Peter Calthorpe, Sim Van Der Ryn....Just to name a few who have attained some degree of renown. Hundreds, even thousands, are known for their more local efforts.

tradiction, and even failure. There is no shame in this since trail-blazing always comes with unforeseen problems, but it shows which design theories can really withstand the tests of time.

The designers that survive this reality test usually become leading speakers for the design community. They are followed by the press, the glitterati and the academic community. Why then is their influence so short lived? Why has no one been able to lead the design community along a sustained course in the manner of William Morris, Le Corbusier, Walter Gropius? Surprisingly, the answer is because they lead by object lesson.

Pioneering designers, when they build structures that demonstrate their ideas,

Baja House, Baja, California Mexico 1989   ©*Jersey Devil Design/Build*

expose the Archilles heel of all current design schools — they over focus on the object at the expense of the human activity that takes place about the object. The great buildings of so many designers are extolled by the press only to be found wanting when occupied. User confusion, if not outright dissatisfaction, is common. In the worst cases there are even follow up news reports about how so-and-so's prize winning building has flopped.

AN OBSOLETE AGENDA FOR THE ARCHITECTURE PROFESSIONALS

To understand the frustrating plight of today's architects, one need only visit the schools where they took their training. The basic underlying curriculum in design schools has changed very little since it came over from L'Ecole Des Beaux Arts with Richard Morris Hunt around 1850. Hyper-focus on the designed object prevails while the effects on human behavior and society are only given lip service.

Simply stated the studio curriculum operates as follows:
1. a design problem is assigned
2. each student draws, drafts, and models a solution
3. the faculty evaluates the different solutions
4. the evaluations are comprised of ongoing 'crits' culminating in a final jury or review.

Yestermorrow School 1990 © J. Connell

Whether the design quality is low, average, or exceptionally high, the discourse always focuses on the designed object. How does the object respond to the design problem? How does the object exhibit meaning? Is the object the right color? The right proportions? The right materials? Is the object part of a history or tradition of similar objects? etc. etc.

There is nothing inherently misguided about concentrating on materiality and "objectness". After all, we are talking about a design curriculum and primarily one designs and configures material objects. The difficulties arise when designers attempt to implement social change through the design of material reality. Human behavior is a moving target. Material reality, though malleable, is a mostly inertia bound instrument. So buildings and other designed objects frequently lose their initial relevance and meaning as our society evolves. The ideas and meanings expressed in architecture, industrial design or city planning can't always track the latest issues of the day.

This phenomena has been wonderfully presented by Stewart Brand in his recent book, How Buildings Learn. Brand documents the fate of several buildings as they endure changing social conditions. He notes how buildings with highly specific designs (i.e. highly meaningful and expressive) tend to suffer more than generalized vernacular structures. In short, peoples' needs change and if the buildings don't accommodate, they will be changed as well. But this is the easier part to remedy.

The bigger problem is how very little of the meaning expressed through designed objects is actually understood by the user/occupant/public. Architectural expression is amongst the most inscrutable of all art forms; right up there with music. The general public (i.e. the users who "don't know much about art, but know what they

352

like") know even less about architectural design.

If designers harbor any hope of making a difference in the next millennia, their first challenge is to reconnect with the public. For too long the architectural profession has been satisfied with designing buildings that make sense primarily to critics and other architects. The architecture profession seems to have lost its way. Posturing

Baja House, Baja, California Mexico 1989
©Jersey Devil Design/Build

and showing off for its own press, the meanings of many buildings must be explained with text lest they appear to have no meaning at all!

Blame for this situation must be jointly awarded to the profession and the academic system that trains the profession. Architecture schools populate their faculty with designers who are as well known as the school budget allows. These curricula and faculty dispense with basic design and support issues quickly while spending endless hours promoting their own work and vision. Students often take the impression that successful design need only communicate with other designers. The occupants, users, and general public are considered rather like the code, budget, and mechanical systems — necessary but messy considerations. This oversimplification in assessing design solutions naturally leads to inhuman and irresponsible buildings (though pretty). Frequently the buildings that are most celebrated by the press and awarded by the profession are the very ones that do the most damage to the environment and to the quality of the users' lives. As for any general cultural or societal meaning that these buildings might have, it is more than lost on the occupants and public who are doing their best just to use the building as advertised[1].

Now to be fair, the design of buildings has become staggeringly more complex. To expect any single designer to foresee and solve every technical and programmatic issue is probably no longer even possible. Moreover, conditions are changing too fast for even a good design solution to last for very long.

---

[1] Try this experiment. Give any design magazine (this does not include Architectural Digest) to a friend who is outside the design professions. Ask them to comment. Most will admit that they know it's "design" because of the eye catching shapes and sexy materials. Ask them why these shapes and materials are used. Most won't have the slightest clue. Indeed, for many it is the disorienting lack of meaning that is the final litmus test: It's so confusing, it must be design!

CURRICULUM FOR A MEANINGFUL ARCHITECTURE IN THE NEXT MILLENNIUM

Our built environment requires the use of more natural and spiritual resources than any other human behavior. Without question it is in this area that our viability as a species will be determined. Although human beings can presently survive and prosper in just about any ecosystem, the time is very shortly coming when so many of these ecosystems will be abused that our continual survival will actually be in question[1].

There can be no question that sustainable design, construction, and principles must become the foundations of our actions as a global civilization in the next millennia. This is a difficult reality to imagine from the present day situation of the haves and have-nots. Competion for natural resources (i.e. free enterprise) means individuals and small groups tend to put short term gain and special interests before long term welfare and the general good. If we are to survive and prosper in the next century, the long term good of the whole must once again be valued and balanced against short term special interests.

This is hardly a new idea. It has been the underlying premise of all civilization. Historically every culture has relied on religion and social mores to remind citizens of the larger shared values upon which their society was based. Religious and civic agendas were effectively kept before the people by means of built form: iconography, architecture, and city planning. Unfortunately, at the end of the 20th century these tools have become increasingly co-opted and ineffective. The production of widely meaningful[2] objects, buildings, and communities remains an unfulfilled challenge for the designers of today.

To remedy this situation requires changes in the schools and institutions in which designers are trained. While the design of compelling material objects should continue to be of the utmost importance, it can no longer be studied as an end in itself. The following curricula suggestions represent a minimum specification if the design professions are to regain the ability to express profound issues of civilization, society, and culture.

[1] No news here. This has been studied since 1969 when the Rome Club published their *Limits of Growth*. The World Watch Institute continually monitors our odds of surviving as a species and publishes regular State of the World Reports. Lovelock's Gaian hypothesis also supplies a context in which we can easily understand the end of human survival without the end of Life on this planet. Indeed, it is ultimately the human species that is most endangered as we enter the next millennium.

[2] "Widely meaningful" is meant to suggest that these objects could be understood by those not in the design professions and without the latest media or marketing hype.

1. All buildings must be designed in the context of a finite resource world.

    Design solutions that use materials inefficiently, or in ways that damage off-site situations, are the essence of short term thinking at the expense of our long term viability as a whole. Independent of symbology or formal content, this kind of solution sends a very real message to the public sector — "waste is O.K. if you can afford it". Since everyone knows this is fundamentally incorrect, credibility of all designed objects is compromised. The basic equation that should suffuse all design curricula in the 21st century: Good Design = Integrity of all the Parts and Whole[1].

WIO Riverhouse © J. Connell

    If energy or other resources are consumed by a building's daily existence it has become patently clear that the building has no long term viability. It is simply not good design. Buildings must become energy providers. Good design does not depend on the despoiling of one location to enhance another. Good design enhances a location by managing its energy budget and giving back to the surrounding area.

2. Materials and methods must be understood as ethical constructs (see also #6)

    Future designers must understand materials well beyond their physical properties, cost, and availability. All materials are either harvested from nature or manufactured from materials harvested from nature. This includes organic materials (woods, fabrics, petroleum products, etc.) and inorganic materials (minerals, chemicals, metals, etc.). Before a material is available to a designer it must be collected, shipped, configured (refined or manufactured), packaged,

WIO Riverhouse Frame 1986 © J. Connell

[1] Paul Hawkin exemplified this eloquently when he stated that, as in nature, waste from any process becomes food for another process.

inventoried, shipped again, and then installed. Every step in this sequence requires energy and human investment. In the future designers must understand that these are the true dimensions of a material.

Certain materials are inherently more energy intensive or require larger human involvement to bring to market. For example, mining and refining certain ores produces toxic tailings, manufacturing certain polymers embodies great quantities of energy, other products require dangerous work sites. Justifying the use of such materials will require consideration of all effects prior to their arrival on the construction site. Future designers

Yestermorrow School Professional Course
© J. Connell

Red Cross House and Pottery Studio, Islamorada, FL 1991
©Jersey Devil Design/Build

must also understand how materials behave after they have become part of the building. Materials that are toxic or in any way compromise the quality of life will simply be unjustifiable in a "designed" building. They will never be used, except by oversight, and even then the designer will take responsibility for replacing them (see #8 below).

Materials that must be shipped great distances will acquire high embodied energy quotients. Properly trained designers will avoid the use of such materials as they would exhaust the reasonable energy budget for the design. Moreover, importing of materials to make a "splash" will be seen for what it is — a failure of design skills. Instead, good design will be characterized by the innovative use of locally available materials (see #3 below).

3. Regionalism

In the future all notions of a "universal style of design" will be replaced with regional aesthetics, materials, and methods. Successful expression of a location's unique character will be the mark of good design. This will include an understanding of local materials, traditions, history, and culture. Cookie-cutter variations of building "styles" (e.g. International Style, Post Modern Style, Green Architecture, etc.) will be seen as formulaic compositions intended to limit good regional and vernacular design.

The myth of one internationally famous designer making buildings all over the world will be replaced with the reality of local "heroes". Regional designers will certainly collaborate and share design ideas, but good design will require a consummate knowledge of the place. This is impossible to acquire when a designer is only in town for one or two projects.

For design to express profound truths and effect social change in the 21st century, it must speak in a dialect the locals will understand.

4. Residential and Vernacular Architecture must be studied, understood, and practiced as an independent design profession.

This is important for two reasons. First: homes are rarely an appropriate vehicle for pronouncing broad social ideas. Homes should be designed to express the personality, lifestyle, and intentions of the occupant, not the designer. Second: if architects hope to effect social change with the buildings they design, their audience must be able to easily comprehend the "language" being used. As homeowners learn to understand the meanings expressed in the architecture of their own homes, they will also start to comprehend the larger meaning expressed in non-residential architecture.

There needs to be a separate profession — Residential Design/Builder — with a separate training sequence from traditional architects. While much of the design training will be similar, the relationship to the client and the building will

WIO Riverhouse Model © J. Connell

necessarily be different Residential Design/Builders will facilitate the client making their own place on their own terms. As an analogy, if the Architect is a doctor, the professional Residential Design/Builder might be seen as a midwife. In addition to design and structures, they will receive training in sociology, psychology, family planning, and conflict resolution!

They will also be experienced (i.e. hands-on) in construction. The traditional three way argument between the Client, the Architect, and the Builder will be replaced with a working arrangement between the Client and the Residential Design/Builder.

This particular suggestion is so overdue that we cannot wait for the 21st century. It should be implemented immediately!

5. Occupant and user needs must be given higher priority and explored as design resources rather than problematic complications.

In its constant play for press and media coverage, the architectural profession has established a tradition of making good looking buildings that are inhuman and don't work. Although I assume every professional designer reading these pages is quietly excepting themselves from this generalization, the record is clear. Current architectural training gives the same cursory consideration to user needs as it does to codes, budget, and materials.

In the future, user needs must become a fundamental point of departure for good design. This may require an ongoing professional relationship with the building (see #7). In a limited resource world, buildings that don't work will be understood as unethical and badly designed. They should not be featured in the design press no matter how "sweet"their visual statement. Because user profiles must evolve and

358

change, this part of the new design curriculum will likely focus on adaptability and flexibility. For good design to comment on the human condition it must first accommodate the human condition[1].

6. Architectural training must incorporate a <u>hands-on training</u> in craftsmanship and materiality (see #2).

    The hands-on study of materials and methods must be returned to our design curriculae. Abstract notions of materiality currently presented in the support courses at most design schools utterly fail to get at the essential nature of materials.

    Designers must learn to build, assemble, and prototype. Wood, stone, glass, clay, plastics, composites, metals — each family of materials implies a whole history of tools and assembly technologies. These traditions are still very much alive and evolving even today. Without hands-on experience, designers cannot take part in this critical process. The materiality of designed products necessarily limits any designer not intimately familiar with the tools and technologies required to implement his design ideas. Innovation requires an understanding of the making, not just the made.

    Additionally, there is something unique but ephemeral in every material. Call it the essence or the spirit; Louis Kahn referred to it as "what the material wants". In any event, historically this aspect of materials has always marked great design. In the future, as all materials are understood to be limited and therefore sacred, the eloquent expression of the ephemeral quality of materials will become a minimum condition for good design

7. Design must be studied as an enduring process. Design professionals (especially architects) must take responsibility for their designs for the lifetime of the designed object or building.

    There is probably no more significant reason for the marginalization of the architecture profession than its fail-

[1] One need only look at the Industrial Design profession to see the dividends of closely considering user needs. This field of design, having addressed ergonomics and lifestyle so successfully, is enjoying a popular vitality equal to the confusion and disdain currently being felt by the architecture profession.

359

ure to take ongoing responsibility for its effects. Buildings that don't work or consume an inordinate amount of resources would be rare if the designer was required to redress these shortcomings for the life of the building.

Interestingly, this would result in a more viable profession as well as better building designs. When designers consider the entire life of the building it makes more sense to incorporate sustainable materials and appropriate methodologies. It also reduces the temptation to design something simply for the press. On the other hand, no design is perfect forever.

Yestermorrow School Professional Course
© J. Connell

Who better to modify the design than the original architect? This additional work should be negotiated in the original design contract including some additional fee. This will provide a disincentive for short sighted design solutions while rewarding architects who design long lived, efficient, and useful structures. Finally, it would allow clients to review past performance instead of glossy photos when hiring an architect.

If we are to survive as a species we must value long term solutions. In the future, good design must seek solutions that will be worthy of media attention only after they have been around for a couple of decades.

8. Preservation and Adaptive Re-Use should be seen as the first design solution whenever there is a pre-existing structure on a site.

The built legacy of earlier designs is not without value. It is our peoples' history and wisdom. It also represents the majority of our refined resources and materials as well as a huge repository of embodied energy. The casual removal of older structures as a knee jerk first step in providing a contemporary design solution can not be valued in the 21st century.

Good design will be marked by innovative use and reuse of the buildings — designed or not — from our past. These will become the best opportunities to express new sustainable design values in contrast to our past decisions for the built environment.

CONCLUSION: YESTERMORROW

If we go back in time, many of the principles enumerated above were standard procedure. Most of them have only fallen into decline since the end of the Second World War. As we look into the future, these principles are still our best hope for a meaningfully designed world. Of course they will need some updating, but basically these principles are timeless. These principles constitute the educational philosophy of the Yestermorrow Design/Build School.

Currently, as we play out the last inning of this century, the school's focus is on residential vernacular architecture — owner/builders. These are the people who are making the biggest difference in our built environment[1]. These are the people eager to re-establish meaning in their homes and houses. These are the people who will understand all architecture meaning once it reemerges from its elite inner sanctum.

At Yestermorrow we are also training the first generation of Residential Design/Builders (the new profession described in #4 above). Increasing numbers of architecture students are seeing more promise for their design skills and more consistency with their values in this mode of professional practice.

If we do our job right, by the dawn of the 21st century there should be a generation of designers capable of making buildings that reflect a shared set of sustainable values. There will also be a general public that will "understand" the architectural language used to express these values.

Yestermorrow Design/Build School 1984 © J. Connell

[1]The amount of square footage of residential space built each year exceeds all other categories by a factor of two. Professional architects are involved in the design of less than 2% of this space.

362

ESSAY: Anthony Walmsley

ECOLOGICAL

DESIGNS:

MAKING

NATURE

VISIBLE

Ecological designs are those compositions or constructions that reveal to others something about nature– the way the world works. Van der Ryn and Cowan (1996) call this "making nature visible"– an essential step towards restoring nature to the forefront of peoples' awareness and, consequently, influencing their values priorities and actions. Thayer (1994) describes it as "expressing the unseen" and proposes "Visual Ecology" to help de-natured people– whether actual users or outside observers— "see into and understand the inner workings of a landscape."

Through two centuries of industrialization and urbanization, many people have become divorced from their natural surroundings; and increasing numbers of them are impacting the human habitat in ways that are damaging and detrimental. Yet, these profound changes seem to have little discussion in our cacophonous world— dominated by the powerful socio-economic forces of mass-production and consumption, pleasure-seeking and material success. They are left to the pioneer outlaws of this book's title to question.

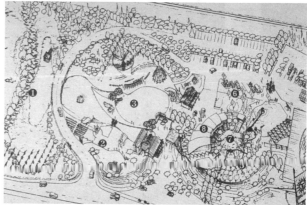

/

These pioneers admit that, although we understand many of the pieces in the puzzle, we are far from developing integrated design solutions. Even the Ecological Design Institute's model of sustainability at The Real Goods Trading Company's Solar Living Center in Hopland, CA (1) appears as a potpourri of disparate elements. Ecological processes are complex and inter-connected, and we are only just beginning to realize how separate and individual actions can be aggregated into sequences. "We are trying to get the pieces right," says

Van der Ryn; now, we must put them together in whole designs. Just as ecological processes are holistic, ecological designs should show connectivity.

What, then, should designers be doing and teaching in response to the challenges of our time? Surely, they should be promoting and communicating the ecological themes of our common yet distinctive humanity and our earthly heritage. They should be celebrating place and people, through appropriate technology and relevant art. These four lenses or prisms— environmental fitness, social cohesiveness, technical aptness and artistic wholeness— can be thought of as tool for evaluating designs' ecological content. Not all four need be equally present; there will be variations with different emphases. But the measure of success is the degree to which each is integrated into a whole composition that is greater than the sum of the parts.

To produce a generation of ecological designers, we need to make re-connections between history, science, philosophy and art. Some would say it is a religious quest; it is certainly a moral one— what we ought to do. Here is a four-part 21st century agenda:

I. INVENTING A MODERN VERNACULAR.

All occupied landscapes can be read as "narratives" and many designers have turned for inspiration to craft traditions and pre-industrial patterns of building for fresh answers to the perennial question of how to build in harmony with nature. Take early modernists, such as Eric Asmussen at Jarna, Sweden; Hassan Fathy at New Gourna, Egypt; and, inspired by Fathy, a whole generation of younger designers in Third World countries.

Jarna (2), an anthropomorphic community founded on the ideas of Rudolf Steiner in 1935, has irregular and incremental ranges of buildings, with pitched roofs and strong colors that express and stim-

3

ulate human activity, creating through art Goethe's "manifestation of the secret laws of nature, which without it would remain for ever hidden". The community practices sustainability: it operates organic farms, and treats it own wastes through connected ponds and a unique system of sculptured water channels— modern water chains called Flow Forms that aerate and purify flows as they cascade in figure-of-eight motions.

At New Gourna outside Luxor (3), Fathy demonstrated an alternative model of urban planning for hot, arid lands— traditional villages designed around the life styles and needs of the rural poor, and built in a hybrid vernacular of mud-brick and age-old Nubian arch construction. The system was endlessly adaptable to different sites, programs and budgets; it allowed individuality and community; it was infinitely rich in aesthetic possibilities; and it was cheap and affordable.

Indigenous culture is a rich mine of ideas to be explored: with current sensibilities, technical knowledge and artistic vision, a new vernacular can be invented which is traditional and modern at the same time. Consider, for example, Geoffery Bawa in Sri Lanka, Glenn Murcutt in Australia, Ralph Erskine in Sweden and Peter Forbes in New England: all are post-war architects that in various ways have rejected canonical modernism for a "critical regionalism" that is a personal response to the universal human needs of shelter and territory, for

4

specific sites and particular climates, with a long history of successful adaptations to learn from and respectfully improve upon.

Bawa says, "Although the past gives lessons it does not give the whole answer to what must be done now." His projects in Sri Lanka and Southeast Asia meld elements from many sources, compressing layers of understanding, history and experience. Some are traditional: calm, cool, peaceful and welcoming rooms with pitched and tiled roofs, around couyrtyards with brimful pools and abundant plants. Others have flat roofs, can-

tilevers, steel and glass— as at the Kandalama Hotel at Dambulla (4)— but the thrust of each design is a constant "search for an appropriate image of dwelling place, in perfect sympathy with the environment."

5

Murcutt has adapted the Australian tradition of agricultural and industrial "tin sheds" to the minimalism of international modern. "Less is more" became "doing the most with the least"— a gradual paring down to the truly essential, which also accorded with native Aboriginal lessons of "building lightly on the land." The continuous wing-shaped roof of the Magney House at Bingi Point, New South Wales, 1982–84 (5) responds to the different angles of sun penetration, prevailing winds and ventilation, while collecting precious rainwater in a giant trough. Just as in D'Arcy Thompson's seminal work on Growth and Form, the configuration of the built object and its siting in the landscape can be read as a "force-field" revealing the play of elemental powers that, as in nature, condition the growth of an organism in its environment such that it, too, must accomplish the maximum performance from minimum materials if it is to survive.

Erskine came to similar conclusions when planning new settlements for northern latitudes, and building in the harsh Baltic winters of his adopted Sweden: designs must come out of site and climate, the special needs of isolated, close-knit communities and the limited building techniques available. In the 1950s and 60s, he conceptualized

6

Arctic towns on south-facing slopes, closed on the east, west and north sides by continuous facetted "wall" buildings, in the protected sun-traps of which were smaller buildings and outdoor areas that could be enjoyed during the brief, hot summers. Climate and community— any climate and any community— were and remain the principal determinants. He has worked for the Innuits of northern Canade and poor black South Africans. More usual, he has planned and designed many inner-city neighborhoods throughout Scandinavia and England

7

(6)— where shelter from winter winds off the Baltic or North Sea and the needs of ordinary people to have a "feeling of identification, protection and togetherness" has resulted in user-friendly, easily legible urban environments telling of the importance of the individual in community, and nature manipulated for human benefit and delight.

Forbes' houses grow out of the rigorous New England landscapes of rocky shores and northern forests. Each, in its formal development and placing in the landscape intensifies the drama of establishing a human presence in the wild, and reflects the special interests of fastidious clients. For the house on Mount Desert island, ME (7), the owner wanted the fullest experience of the near and distant landscape, but was allergic to a myriad of substances— both natural and manufactured. Conventional materials— plywood, gypsum wallboard, plaster and most paints— were out. Instead, the house became an open framework of steel tubes with glass and aluminum window walls on two long sides, rising forty feet in the trees. The only partitions for bathrooms and closets are of cedar with a water-based stain finish. Floors are open platforms within the steel grid, from which the immediacy and power of nature can be consciously felt and experienced.

2. EXPLORING "BLUE/GREEN" IDEAS.

Blue/green is more than a Yin-Yang symbol for the hydrological

8

cycle. It says that water and terrestrial ecosystems must be considered together and their renewable needs seamlessly woven together into whole sustainable designs. My offices and I have spent thirty years on various aspects of this ongoing effort.

One approach is the use of native species in ecologically correct associations— "the right thing in the right place" (Caparn, 1929). Plant combinations that look and work well are like plant "indicators" discriminating one habitat from another. Years ago, I proposed this for the show gardens of an ecological arboretum. Later, for the large-scale planting programs of Pakistan's new capital, Islamabad, we tried to match a full spectrum of canopy, understorey, shrub and ground layer species to the different micro-habitats of the foothills, old fields, plains and ravines to reveal the "structure" of the landscape. The first results were achieved in the ravines, where steep erodable banks were graded to stable slopes and the sides and bottoms reinforced with mats of round stones (8), producing designs that were grounded in the ecological, social and technical realities of

9

the place. On moving to New York City and engaged on the first landscape restoration projects in Brooklyn's Prospect Park, we worked with the park's Director of Landscape Management on a similar strategy, documented as "An Ecosystem Approach to Woodland Management". My partner, J. Toby Tourbier, brought to the firm the problem of a large regional high school, actually being built on filled wetlands. Instead of the usual manicured school grounds, we proposed that the 40-acre site be thought of as a nature education park with the centerpiece being three acres of new wetlands showing how urban runoff from roofs and paved areas could be stored and cleansed by natural processes (9). (It was estimated that the basins could trap 80–100% of suspended sediments, 60–80% of trace metals, 60–70% of total phosphorus and 40–60% of total

368

nitrogen.) Students through their formative years, as they parked their cars or waited for the bus, or moved between classroom and sports-field, would see water storing and cleansing processes in action.

Later the same year, my partner and I led a team to compete for an International Garden Festival (Internationale Gartenbau–ausstellung, IGA), 2003, for the German City of Dresden. Here there was an opportunity to reorient the usual emphasis of European garden shows on horticulture, gardening and spec-

10

tacular floral displays in a strongly ecological direction. A blue/green metamorphosis concept was proposed for the 495-acre IGA site in a bend of the Elbe, in the form of a disintegrating grid pattern (10): as the

visitor moves west from the tightly bounded architectural exhibit spaces of a former meat-packing plant, the grid unravels into a more organic pattern of ribbon-like walks in a "labrynth of gardens," ending in the broad, natural landscapes of the river. Blue/green demonstration environments are integral with this metamorphic design: in the IGA grounds are forty runoff cleansing, detention and

11

infiltration gardens (11); the Elbe floodway and floodplain become large-scale artworks, showcasing water conservation and cleansing functions. "The grid describes Dresden's classic origins and the sense of measure and proportion needed to create a stable and productive society. The blue/green technology shows how expediently and productively our usually high-tech obsessed culture can convert its relation to earth into poetic, responsible and innovative interventions with nature."

3. MAKING NATURE VISIBLE.

Recent projects, built and unbuilt, attest that designers from both the artistic and technical sides are grappling with the ecological aesthetic. Peter S. Hau (1996), winner of an ideas competition for the reuse of Governors Island in New York Harbor, proposed an environmental park on the theme of "Open Narratives: Reconfiguring the Air, Land and Waters." He pointed out that New York City's urban success story as an international center of trade, culture and political exchange had a downside in its massive problems of industrial and municipal waste, water contamination and air pollution. Why not, within sight of the peerless symbols of freedom and opportunity (Liberty and Ellis Islands) promote "a strategy to purify, cleanse and refresh the city?" He suggested ten gardens: "Descending River Cleanser— a salt water marsh as a simple water purification system; Rain Grabber— collects, stores and reuses storm water runoff; Heavy Metal Filter— sifts and disposes heavy metals; Organic Air Freshener— plantings that absorb atmospheric toxins; Atmospheric Guages— monitors air pollutants and suspended particulates; Breezy Turbines— windmills that harness wind into usable energy; Solar Alchemy— converts sunshine into a useable power source; Cogeneration Machine— reclaims, converts and reuses recyclable refuse; Strata Cliff— exposes history of the island; Geotransformer— cultivating the growth potential of the organic." Hau's literary agenda is our ecological crisis: he set up ideas with exciting dramatic possibilities for the island's open space that, if pursued, could be a revolutionary expression of a Declaration of Interdependence within

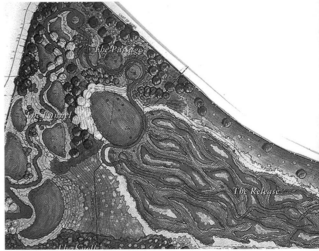

12

sight of the icons of the Declaration of Independence.

For a fully functioning ecological design that "conveys a story about the filtering power of plants to cleanse water" there is Lorna Jordan's and Jones & Jones' Waterworks Gardens in Renton, near

Seattle, WA (1996). Jordan tells it in five garden "rooms" (12). The first is the Knoll, an elevated entry plaza below which 2,000 gallons per minute of untreated runoff are seen to be entering the first of seven leaf-shaped settling ponds— the next room, the Funnel. A snake-like path takes visitors to the Grotto, an assemblage of leaning concave walls and writhing benches, reminiscent of Gaudi's Parque Guell, built up out of waste materials from demolition projects, formed into fantastic shapes and faced with broken marble-tile mosaics depicting a seed pod of spreading vines. Next is the Passage with four more settling basins, leading to the fifth and final room, the Release (13), a constructed wetland of braided streamlets and narrow strips of land, which will create a flame pattern when the native plantings have matured. The design is driven by the artists's vision; its engineering has been scrupulously learnt and applied; landscape architects have researched and specified the materials (both "hard" and "soft") to

13

ensure sound construction; and public interest has been elevated and challenged.

14

Not all ecological designs need stress the romantic and the picturesque. The most environmentally sensuous design tradition— that of the oasis garden in Persia and throughout the Islamic world— employed a straight-line ground pattern of axes and cross-axes. It is reinterpreted in three representative designs from the American Southwest.

At the entrance to the degraded Papago Desert Park, on the boundary of Phoenix and Scottsdale, AR, artist Jody Pinto and landscape architect Steve Martino searched for forms that would "say" regeneration, as well as start the process of re-vegetation of the lost, indigenous desert flora. They chose a "Tree of Life" (14): it became the primary design motif for celebrating the ancient rainwater-harvesting practices that had sustained seven principal Indian civilizations, of

371

which the Hohokoms were famous for their extensive irrigation canals over an area 800 miles across. The tree stem is a water channel that fills up after rains; the branches are seven agricultural terraces to which water is distributed from the stem. There are seven stone markers recognizing in their alignments the Summer Solstice, the longest farming day of the year. Papago

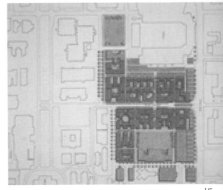

15

Park evokes universal human lessons of living with nature, harvesting the desert and discovering through solar movements our relationships to the earth.

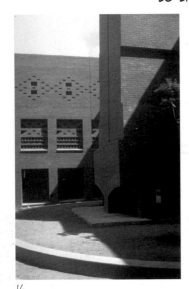

16

The central element of Carnegie-Armory Park Retrofit Design Plan for the University of Arizona's Arts and Theater District in Tuscon, AR, is an outdoor performance area adjoining a senior-citizens' center (15). The designers (artists Douglas Hollis and Anna Valentina Murch, landscape architects George Hargreaves and Mary Margaret Jones, and engineer Martin Yoklic) consulted the community and learnt "about the special qualities of the desert environment and how living in the desert might be expressed in our work." The resulting design for the amphitheater incorporates evaporative cooling, water harvesting, sun control, photovoltaic lighting, misting systems and native landscape materials.

The plan for a New Campus District and the first two Residential Halls at the same university by architects/urbanists Moule & Polyzoides and landscape architect Michael van Valkenberg, 1989-96, also recognizes the indigenous urban tradition of small "self-shading" courtyards, encouraging the movement of air but keeping the sun out during most of the day (16). Massive masonry

17

walls neutralize the extreme temperature swings between hot days and cool nights. 50' high, 6' diameter passive cooling towers and wind catchers cause a temperature drop in the court of about 20°F (17). Courtyards, shady passages and open-air iwan study rooms (an Arabic term) allow groups of students to live both inside and out. The

project shows how far ecological designs can go when the principles of environmental fit (site and climate), social cohesiveness (community-making) and apt technology (regionally validated materials and construction) are integrated through art into whole compositions blending architecture, urbanism and landscape.

4. FURTHERING THE ECOLOGICAL REVOLUTION.

There is a danger of superficially accepting the necessity of a blue/green approach without undertaking the hard thought necessary for real progress. "Green labeling" of products often raises more questions than answers. Life-cycle costing of materials to determine a product's total environmental "burden" is still a very inexact science. "Obviously, least is best. But least of what is best?" said Tim

Ream, heading up the EPA's working group on life cycle methodology. It behooves us all as designers "to make as many blue/green moves as we can" at each and every opportunity, and to express them in a strong aesthetic language. Sym Van der Ryn likens it to an "Ecological Revolution

18

19

every bit as profound as the preceding Industrial Revolution. The pieces are well understood, from energy efficiency and sustainable agriculture, to ecological waste-water treatment and bioregional design." In this quest, we may expect to see ecological designs from cities to dwellings that stretch our imagination, surprise and possibly disturb us by their frontal assault on established ways and mind-sets.

New "working" landscapes for waste-water treatment linked to food production are both possible and practicable, such as Viet Ngo's vast Lemna lagoons that have been proposed for Boulder City, Nevada (18). These are surface water plants of the Lemnaceae family controlled by a network of floating barriers that can take the form of a grid over vast land acreages and naturally process urban wastes and reuse the residue to raise fish and grow produce. Utilizing the

sun's energy for harvesting the plants year-round, a new vision of the desert oasis is presented.

Energy conservation will figure prominently. The technology will increasingly shape building and site configurations, whether an isolated structure in the wilderness or an urban-density development in the city. A solar-powered ski lodge at Sun

20

Valley, ID adopts an ground-hugging profile that, like Erskine's earth-bound buildings, reduces wind turbulence and snow drifting, and opens its southern face to the sun (19). In the foreground, landscape architect Robert Murase has planted a meadow of native grasses and flowers within indigenous sagebrush ground cover.

In the city, sun access will lead to new zoning formulations based on the "solar envelope" which constrains development on a given site to ensure future rights of sun access to adjoining sites. Far from restricting choice, Ralph Knowles and his students at the University of Southern California have shown that, even at densities exceeding 100 dwelling units/acre, a rich diversity is possible when designing within the solar envelope (20). Knowles writes, "it is a concept that can help [the designer] uncover unique, significant and beautiful form."

21

Erosion control and habitat creation will become essential parts of "ecology gardens" in future parks. Patricia Johanson's Fair Park Lagoon in Dallas, TX, though modified during construction, is a notable example of the meshing of natural phenomena with an artists's aesthetic ideas (21). Johanson's first thoughts were to create a functioning ecosystem, control bank erosion, restore water quality, introduce living exhibits and provide ways over the water so people could become immersed in the life of the lagoon. Eventually, two Texas plants were chosen as models for her sculpture— the delta duck potato, Saggitaria platyphylla, and an indigenous fern, Pteris multifida— which became five-foot paths rising and falling as twisted roots, with spaces in between for micro-habitats of shallow-water plants, fish, turtles and birds.

We should expect more new formulations for consolidating urban growth around existing centers, or establishing new centers where existing infrastructure is in place. Compact new towns around transit stops (Transit oriented developments, TODs) will be seen as attractive alternatives to suburban sprawl as housing costs escalate, highway construction slows, and pressures to save rural lands increase. Not least will be developers' and customers' growing awareness that a sense of community-belonging is a vital component of the quality-of-life equation which sells homes. Winning competition proposals such as St. Vincents Station outside San Rafael, CA for a new town of 7,000 people on 1,200 acres around a transit stop will become common (22). It has

22

a compact town-form at higher densities to encourage walking, centered on the transit stop, regular street blocks and narrow tree-lined streets with parking on and off-street, and a range of housing and support facilities (predominantly walk-up apartments and row houses with some affordable units). The plan also emphasizes the protection of natural resources— a balance of conservation/ development that should be a constant for all future planning.

23

There will always be idiosyncratic gardens reflecting the special fads of their owners, such as Christopher Jencks' and Maggie Keswick's extraordinary estate at Dumfriesshire, Scotland (23). They decided that their 300-acre estate could be "molded and shaped to manifest some of their theories and interests"— Keswick's in feng-shui (the ancient Chinese form of geomancy) and Jencks' in chaos theory and fractals. Both involve currents of energy— the Taoist concept of earth forces, ch'i, that can be tapped into and determine the correct placing of structures in their surroundings and the "new sciences of complexity that posit the universe is … cosomogenic, meaning that it jumps all of the time to new levels of organization," characterized by continuously changing patterns of folds and waves. The climax in the landscape is the twisted and folded double-wave earthworks and curved ponds fed by a nearby river— sound ecology in that flows are detained and reinfiltrated through the ponds, valleys and hollows of the grassy landforms. The only feature missing is, perhaps, sheep.

How to make the dream come true

Jean-Paul Poliniere & Catherine Simon

"For millennia men have had a spontaneous understanding of themselves, which has been dependent upon the culture of their era; now, for the first time, this popular vision of the mind has entered into contact with science and is transformed by it."
Varela, 1989. Biologist.

Allowing new "living" designs to be heard and implemented

Strangely enough, active interest in the Earth's needs is rarely observed in most of us, whereas some of us believe that we do have such an interest. Today, there are efficient solutions for acquiring the ability to hear and put into action proven information foreign to one's habits.

Opening ourselves to the advances in ecological*[1] design

They result from the cross-fertilization of recent discoveries concerning:
• how we function here and now (genetics, and cognitive* science),
• what our place is in the environmental space (ecology),
• where we come from in time (evolutionary and historical scences).

Notice to the reader
➥ *If you want to get something practical out of these pages, memorizing what is in italics is a quick way to do it.*
➥ *Please do not concentrate on the statistics and words, but on the main trends.*

Why does ecological design meet with such resistance?

In a study made between 1994 and 2000, 403 Western decision-makers self-measured their approach to the biosphere*. Result: fewer than 9 percent were actively conscious of the biosphere's existence. Given this finding, one can easily understand why so few of the resolutions adopted by 178 nations at the Earth Summit in Rio de Janeiro (1992) have been implemented. Vital but disturbing information has simply been ignored or rejected.

«*The difficulty lies, not in the new ideas, but in escaping the old ones, which ramify, for those brought up as most of us have been, into every corner of our minds*». Keynes

Try springing a novel idea on someone, it's surprising how often it turns out being a waste of time. What we thought would inspire interest ends up falling flat or even provoking hostility. But then, we're the same: if an idea doesn't fit our experience or way of thinking, we reject it and take that as proof of maturity or knowledge.

---

1. The first time a word appears that is used with a specific, technical meaning, you will find an asterisk referring you to the glossary at the end of this essay.
2. In alphabetical order.

Surveys made on thousands of people in North America and Western Europe show that over 98 percent of people do not properly control information they have stored (or that they receive). Among others, two main errors: a) welcoming ideas that strengthen beliefs they've acquired through family and society even if these ideas are not proven, b) ignoring or rejecting ideas that are foreign to their experience even if these ideas are proven. An example of the former: the fervent anti-hunting activist who unquestionably believes that hunting is bound to be wrong (even though it is proven that controlled hunting may be useful in some circumstances). An example of the latter: the hunter who simply cannot understand why a government is imposing new restrictions on his activity (even though he is aware that over-hunting may ultimately deprive him of his game).

Paradoxically, more than 94 percent of those surveyed believe that they control the information they receive (Simon 1992)[1] ; so instead of knowing we are blinkered, we believe we are open-minded. One of the authors of this essay had a startling experience when he discovered that he, too, suffered from this inability to accept ideas foreign to his experience; even though he had spent most of a lifetime in foreign countries, living with local people. He was working for the United Nations, looking for tools that can measure our ability to change. When asked what he thought was his capacity to change, he responded 80 on a scale of 100. Then he sat a marks-out-of-a-hundred test to show openness to change. Result: he rated 7. The thousands of Westerners who tested themselves in the surveys cited above did not fare any better.

Self-deception is at the center of these findings, ranging from more or less consciously refusing reality to actually lying to oneself. Not only do we lack the ability to sort vital from toxic information but we also "pretend" to have that ability; and most of us do not allow our "pretending" opinions to be questioned.

"Self-deception is the process or fact of misleading ourselves to accept as true or valid what is false or invalid. Self-deception, in short, is a way we justify false beliefs to ourselves".
Caroll

The phenomenon of rejecting information foreign to one's vision of the world is particularly strong when it comes to ecological innovations; that, by definition, respect life and the environment. Rifkin (1991) talks about the "little-known but decisive political phenomenon in the history of Western culture: the 500-year journey to enclose the vast reaches of the global commons æ the land masses, oceans, atmosphere, electromagnetic spectrum, and gene pool." He argues that since Francis Bacon, man has undertaken the massive task of turning nature into his personal property, to exploit and play with as his fancy strikes him. In other words, ecological design questions our constant need for power over other living organisms. Such fundamental challenges to our way of doing things lead to strong resistance from the average person.

1. See details on references at the end of this essay.

We are therefore facing a very logical super-resistance. Since ecological design contradicts two basic values of our 500-year-old culture. First, that information foreign to our ways of thinking, traditions and beliefs is absurd at best and heretical at worst. Second, that nature is only a cheap resource to be used, not something to be conserved and replenished.

There is a third explanation for our indifference and even outright opposition to the ecological disaster in the making. It is that we have no pressure to respect other living organisms on Earth. After all, whales, dolphins, oceans and trees cannot argue in the halls of Congress, sit on Boards of Directors, or protest against our use of polluting cars...

Examples of our usual responses to ecological needs and design

When faced with ecological accidents, most of us have one or several of the following reactions.
• A calm or jovial indifference, of the type expressed by the Mexican truck driver. He had shot one of the last two imperial woodpeckers. His comment: "It was a great piece of meat" (Wilson, 1992). Or doubt the existence of the problem, its dimension or its urgency.
• Getting oneself out of the picture completely, an/or putting others down: "It's up to governments to take responsibility", "The rich only care about profit," "Poor people have too many children".
• Intellectualizing, as in this testimony: "I've read a lot on the subject. That gives me the feeling I'm doing something. And I keep on gathering more and more information. I sound pretty much like I know what I'm talking about."
• Feeling powerless, or making it commonplace: "It's too big a problem for the man on the street", "You have to take your car to go to work, a plane to go on vacation", "It's a normal evolution, and we've always pulled through. "
• And many others that you have probably identified. Always wondering with the amusement of discovery: do any one of these examples look like me or the people I love?

When presented with person reacts favorably. However, the idea is often met with indifference and even solutions such as the barge that uses fish to clean rivers æ an example cited in this book æ the average outright opposition from numerous politicians and other decision-makers; as it may go against established interests, whether these be social, political, or economic.
We have learned these reactions probably since the invention of language and the power it gives. For thousands of years, humanity has been working almost exclusively on how it expresses itself for power (whether seduction of defense). Very little work has been

"Convictions are more dangerous enemies than lies."
Nietzsche

379

done on how we can hear and listen in order to solve life problems harmoniously. From the rhetoric of Aristotle to present-day advertising campaigns, the arts of persuasion, speaking and writing, have multiplied; while how we listen or read actively has been almost entirely ignored. As an example, in a large Western book- shop, the ratio of books sold in 1993 on "How to listen and read" compared with those on "How to emit and write" was that of 1 to 12.

A consequence of this dysfunction is our frequent inability to avoid repeating the same errors. We find it almost impossible to change the ingrained habits that we consider part of our personality. We say, with either resignation or pride: "I'm a pretty angry kind of person," or "I can't keep still". We believe in the unalterable character of our genetic and cultural roots.

Unfortunately, this manifestation of our self-deception is not commonly considered as a dysfunction but as fate. Sometimes we look at it as a blessing, sometimes as a curse, but almost invariably we believe it remains irreversible.

From what we have seen so far, we can put two facts in perspective:
- very logically, our resistance to ecological design is much stronger than we imagine;
- our traditional reactions and solutions fall most often between inefficiency and counter-productivity.

*"The worst thing today is that we are interested superficially in subjects outside ourselves, instead of taking care or ourselves seriously".
Anonyme*

Fortunately, the breakthroughs in our knowledge since the 1970s hold an enormous potential for restoration. By enabling us to better identify the causes of our difficulties, research opens up for us new approaches for treatment.

A revolution in our knowledge of our world (including ourselves)

Today, scientific discoveries and studies provide us with information on why our self-deception is so strong. More than that, these advances enable us to do something about it. This is mostly thanks to work done in the field of the sciences of change: how we think (genetics and cognitive* science); our place among all other living beings (ecology); and where we come from (evolutionary and historical sciences). We will now look more closely at some major attainments in each one of these three fields.

*"Other animals fight for their food; but, uniquely in animal kingdom, human beings fight for their beliefs".
Crichton*

1st attainment. The information of our genes and of our culture plays the major role in our functioning. Our dysfunctions are not, therefore, a fatality (genetics and cognitive science)

Scientific discoveries, starting from the 1940s and building since the 1970s, have ended in a revolution: for the first time in history, we are beginning to understand how we function as human beings. This is recognized in scientific circles, not by the general public. Yet these discoveries have broad implications, particularly for people in the ecological field, as we shall see later.

Up till the 1940s, the study of the human mind was mostly intuitive and philosophical. Through scholars like McCulloch (1943), Wiener (1948) and others, the cybernetic movement established the bases of a true science of mind. As Fourastié said in 1947: "Psychological science should be rebuilt upon the notion of information." In 1956, Chomsky, Newell, Simon and others initiated the cognitive revolution. Through the cross-fertilization of epistemology, neuroscience, cognitive* psychology, linguistics, anthropology and artificial intelligence, the "mind's new science" was born (Gardner 1987).

At the end of the 1950s, Ellis showed that our functioning is not a product of mysterious desires or impulses inherent to our nature, but quite simply the product of deeply-rooted information that we acquired at an early age: that is to say, our beliefs, our dispositions and more generally, our visions of the world and of the self. Ellis concluded that we can discover and treat that deep-rooted information.

Beck demonstrated in the 1970s that the information we have received can lead to depression (by information, we mean here the beliefs inculcated into us from a very early age, including the need to receive approval from others, the necessity of being socially accepted, the belief that only results count, etc.). It has also been discovered that this condition can be cured at any age. In the case of moderate depressions, results with cognitive* therapy can be better than with anti-depressants, and without any relapse. Studies also show that other dysfunctions, such as destructive hatred and paralyzing guilt can be treated similarly. Simultaneously, Lafferty (1980) showed that to a very large extent inadequate information (in the sense discussed above) is at the base of most people's functioning. We suffer from a large variety of information dysfunctions, the existence of which we do not suspect, for the most part, in ourselves. One of the origins of our functioning was bluntly summed up on the back cover of Dawkins' book (1989): "Our genes made us. We animals exist for their preservation and are nothing more than their throwaway survival machines. The world of the selfish gene is one of savage competition, ruthless exploitation, and deceit."

From the 1980s to today, Gee (1992) and others have shown the importance of well-defined means for evaluating information as an antidote to the degradation of our critical abilities.

We discover therefore there are no genius nor imbeciles, no good nor bad guys. But just more or less well-provided "informationally". And who can

381

therefore "heal" themselves in most cases.

2nd attainment. Our dysfunctions are hurting the Earth (ecology)

Studies done mainly since the 1970s demonstrate that man is not the only victim of his information dysfunctions. Wilson (1992) and others have shown that human activity has dramatically increased the normal extinction rate of living species. In the world's rain forests, for example, extinction rates have increased by some 1,000 times because of logging, hunting, burning and road building. We are threatening the very basis of life.

But our information dysfunctions have wider repercussions still, as Vaneighen has made clear. "Nothing that oppresses life can be tolerated," he wrote. This includes murder, rape, pollution, the mistreatment of children or torture. If life needs our laws to defend itself, it is obvious that we have never attempted to actively understand the law of life, a law aptly recalled by Quinn (1992) and respected by all animals with the exception of man. This law of life forbids hunting down and killing competitors, destroying a competitor's food supply to make room for one's own or denying him access to food.

3rd attainment. Consciousness is learned (evolutionary and historical sciences)

Since the 1970s, studies of transformations through time, whether of the universe, biological species, or human societies, have shed new light on the understanding of reality. Laszlo (1987) has shown that understanding the general structures of change can help us to identify the processes that decide the future of societies and of ourselves.

The work and hypotheses of Jaynes (1976) allow us to better understand why we can't see where we're going wrong. Jaynes shows that up to the second millennium B.C., we had very little consciousness, and that we took our internal voices as being the voices of kings, king-gods, or gods. Consciousness appears to pre-exist as a "structure," but its development is not inherent only to our nature. Among other influences, it is the product of language and particularly, of metaphors. In other words, consciousness is something that can be learned, like the aptitude for change. Today, this learning is only in its infancy.
Synthesis

An international team of consolidators has been at work on these results since the late 1980s. Information consolidation* is an information technology. It evalueates and it compresses, making it possible to reduce the volume of information from more than 100 pages to 1 without losing any substance; and, with considerable increase of reliability.

Following these studies and other (see bibliography), the consoli-

"The sun, the moon, and the stars would have disappeared long ago, had they happened to be within reach of predatory human being."
Ellis

dating team came up with four principles.

1. There is a need for tools that allow people to discover the state of their generalized* information; that is the information, common to all of us, that we need to live with ourselves, with others, and with the environment (like criticizing ourselves, educating our children, etc.). It basically has to do with how we function, and how we can correct our dysfunctions ourselves. As opposed to specialized information (like building a bridge), this information is of a political nature (in the sense of the general interest). It concerns our place in relation to all living beings.

2. There is a need to reconsider our way of living and our learning systems in the new framework of the threats that exist against life on Earth. Particularly in the light of a double discovery: a) what it means genetically to be an animal ("ruthless selfishness", as Dawkins describes); b) what it implies as far as endangering life on Earth to be an animal with unbridled power.

3. There is a need for tools that can help us greatly increase our consciousness; and our potential to search for reality.

4. These features can only be put together effectively within the structure of a true system of generalized information (Laborit 1973).

Till the 1800s, our "collective nest" was strong enough to allow the healthy testing of natural selection. Unfortunately, we have gotten so powerful that our collective nest is being destroyed. There is a way out of seeing the branches of our nest collapse: to choose cooperation, which occurs when people search for reality together. And to let go of the four million-year-old natural selection game of power struggles (though it was healthy initially).

At the gateway of this system, there is a tool that enables the user to be able to appreciate and comfortably use the consolidated generalized information within the system.

The name of this tool is "mastering information". It has some connections with critical thinking and critical literacy. Mastering information can be easily measured. It is the ability to reject non useful-proven information (even if familiar to one's system), and to absorb useful-proven information (even foreign to one's system).

Solutions for restoration are now available

We have seen in preceding chapters to what extent our reactions can harm life. And how much acquiring information of quality can settle important problems easily.

A system of consolidated generalized information is currently being developed in several countries. In the same way that specialized information systems have been developed internationally like Agris, Medlars, and many others.

Special care has been given to developing tools needed for acquiring mastery* of information, the gateway into the system. Since the 1990s, these tools are used both in the US and Northern Europe.

The discoveries concerning the human mind explored earlier have provided us with the knowledge we need for getting to the root of the problem. We now know that our low-level ability to master information (less than 5 percent) is due to the poor state of the system that controls how we receive and evaluate information. This system is essentially made up of our motivations, our priorities and our procedures for evaluating reality. By analogy with the DOS in computers, this is our operating system.

The "motivations" part of our operating system is of particular importance. A given stimulus usually leads us off down the same cognitive* chain. At the source of our motivations, our basic beliefs (visions of the world and of self) condition our emotions, our behavior and, consequently our results. Once our motivations and priorities have been treated, it becomes relatively easy to acquire the procedures for evaluating reality; we can, for example, start thinking more scientifically.

The treatment of our operating system guarantees our multiplying by at least nine times our level of mastering information. Upstream, mastering of information enables us to understand the bases of our own functioning and to question them. Downstream, it enables us to avoid implementing "more of the same thing" which would be inadequate, and to implement "some other thing" which would be relevant; therefore to change in the direction of life.

The mastery of information controls our ability to search for reality together, and to adapt ourselves to it. Its deficiency leads to the worst kind of submission and/or violence.

How to learn mastering information

Self-development tools are is the best route for this type of learning for two reasons. The first is that it enables us to avoid the confusion and loss of control that arise from having to deal with another human being (e.g. his desire to impress, your desire to please). The second is that it's important to realize that we're responsible for our own evolution. The development of expert-systems (i.e. interactive software that does the work of human experts) ensures reliability, neutrality, confidentiality and continuous updating.

The user self-measures the state of his motivations and priorities

"Progress is impossible without change, and those who cannot change their minds cannot change anything."
Shaw

that govern his reception of information. He also measures the procedures for evaluating reality that control his critical ability. He then receives in-depth reports on the how and why of his informational functioning. He is given exercises that allow him to strengthen his productive tendencies and diminish or eliminate those that are counter-productive.

Example of results

Once the mastery of information has been acquired, people can use any consolidated information system. This means users will be able to recognize useful-reliable information and to respond to new ideas at least nine times faster than today. This will bring down barriers to ecological innovation, allowing ecological designers to move more confidently towards a sustainable society.

What do you do when you're face to face with a congressman or CEO who can't or won't hear what you are saying? Once you begin to understand how you function and to master your own information, you'll find new channels to navigate down. You will be alert, first of all, to those automatic reflexes that you have when communicating with others that tend to get in the way, and you will learn how to replace them. You will have a better idea how to create cooperative situations so that each person can express his ideas and be heard. Since your goal is now clearly to accomplish your "mission," you'll be better able to handle tendencies towards power playing or submission.

If you need more information on mastering information:
- in the U.S., contact Chantal Krey, e-mail: zelov@geniusloci.com
- in Europe, contact Catherine Simon, e-mail: igsmi@wanadoo.fr

© Igs Paris 2000

Bibliography

- Alexander, R.D. 1987. The biology of moral systems. New York: Adeline de Gruyter.
- Beck, A. 1979. Cognitive therapy and emotional disorders. New York: New American Library.
- Dawkins, R. 1989. The selfish gene. New York: Oxford University Press.
- Ellis, A. 1957. Outcome of employing three techniques of psychotherapy. Journal of clinical psychology 14.
- Fourastié, J. 1974. Comment mon cerveau s'informe. Journal d'une recherche/1947-1974. (How my brain gets its information. Journal of a research 1947-1974). Paris: Robert Laffont.
- Gardner, H. 1987. The mind's new science. A history of the cognitive revolution. New York: Basic Books.
- Gee, J.P. 1992. The social mind. New York: Bergin & Garvey.
- Hamilton, W.D. 1964. The genetical evolution of social behaviour (I and II). Journal of theoretical biology 7, 1-16; 17-52.
- Jaynes, J. 1976. The origin of consciousness in the breakdown of the bicameral mind. Boston: Houghton Mifflin Company.
- Laborit, H. 1973. La société informationnelle (Informational society.). Paris: Les Éditions du Cerf.
- Lafferty, J.C. et alii. 1980. Item frequency and distribution - Level 1: life styles inventory. Plymouth: Human Synergistics.
- Laszlo, E. 1987. Evolution. The grand synthesis. Boston: New Science Library.
- McCulloch, W. and Pitts, W. 1943. A logical calculus to the ideas immanent in nervous activities. Bulletin of mathematical biophysics 5: 115-133.
- MacLean, P.D. 1964. Man and his animal brains. Modern Medicine.
- Milgram, S. 1974. Obedience to authority and experimental view. New York: Harper and Row.
- Polinière, J.P. et alii. Évoluer ou disparaître. Mais peut-on changer? (Evolve or disappear. But can we change?) L'enjeu humain de l'entreprise, vol 2.
- Quinn, D. 1992. Ishmael. An adventure of the mind and spirit. New York: Bantam/Turner Books.
- Rifkin, J. 1991. Biosphere politics. San Francisco: Harper.
- Simon, C. et alii. 1992. L'ergothérapie et le changement : une synergie pour l'autonomie (Ergotherapy and change: synergy for autonomy). In M.H. Izard et alii eds., Expériences en ergothérapie. Paris: Masson.
- Unesco. 1976. Consolidating information for development. Paris: Unesco.
- Vaneighen, R. In Mamou-Mani, A. 1995. Au delà du profit (Beyond profit). Paris: Albin Michel.
- Varela, F.J. 1989. Connaître les sciences cognitives. Tendances et perspectives (Knowing the cognitive sciences. Trends and perspectives). Paris: Le Seuil.
- Wiener, N. 1948. Cybernetics, or control and communication in the animal and the machine. Cambridge: MIT Press.
- Wilson, E. 1992. The diversity of life. New York: W.N. Norton & Company.

Glossary

Biosphere: Layer formed around the earth's crust by the whole of living beings.

Cognitive chain:The chain of reactions which, under the effect of a stimulus interacting with a belief, is triggered automatically in the order of belief-thought-emotion-behavior.

Cognitive distortion:An illusion that results from unconscious automatic errors of language and/or reasoning. Through our repeated use of these illusions in our ways of thinking, we interpret reality in an unreal way.

Cognitive psychology: A general and scientific approach of psychology, which joins behaviorism in its attention to observable facts of behavior with the experimental method, but goes beyond it by taking into account internal mental processes.

Cognitive science: A system of disciplines that study the human mind. It includes: epistemology, neurosciences, cognitive psychology, linguistics, anthropology and artificial intelligence.

Cognitive therapy: Psychotherapy based on the notion that the way in which an individual structures and interprets his experiences determines mood and subsequent behavior.

Consolidation of information: An information technology, involving evaluating and compressing, and making it possible to reduce the volume of information from an average of 400 to 1, without losing any substance.

Ecological design: Synergy with nature, technology, and humanity. Regenerative design. Intention to give back more than to take.

Generalized information: Information concerning us personally in our relations with ourselves and with others, and with life as a whole (criticizing ourselves, educating our children, etc.).

Mastery of information: An ability to accept useful-proven information (even if foreign to one's system), and to reject non useful-proven information (even if familiar to one's system). It involves two operations: (1) receiving information and (2) evaluating the accuracy of the information with adequate technologies (as in using external, proven references) This newly-defined ability is for observing, listening and reading It is an important operation in the field of critical literacy.

Procedures for evaluating reality: Procedures calling for methods that are proven, and accepted international by the scientific community. For example: the systemic approach, the experimental method, turning to models and simulation methods, etc.

387

Epilogue

INTRODUCTION   By Brian Danitz

BROOKLYN IN THE AMAZON

It is early morning in the Amazonian village of Ituwassu. I am here, with Chris and Phil, to film the traditional thatched homes of the Waiapi people for the opening of "Ecological Design: Inventing the Future"; a film which we have been making now for nearly five years. The mist is on the treetops, the buzzing song of the rain forest is beginning, family groups around the small morning fires do chores, and as the camera motor whirs I realize that there is no way that these frames will capture the spirit of this place and time. That is, the spirit which is the living fabric woven of the intimate ties between a people and a place. Here is an overwhelming sense of continuity and appropriateness between a people's way of life, architecture, culture, and their local ecosystem. Five years into the making of this project, it is here and now that the many inter-complimentary concerns and considerations of ecological design are finally coming together for me as a coherent and sensible whole.

With my ear close, the camera motor sounds like any motor: perhaps like the motor of the boat which brought us up river, or like the engine of the prop planes which bring the illegal gold miners who spread disease and poison the river with mercury, or perhaps like the distant sound of chainsaws "harvesting" hardwoods or the earthmovers clearing the forest. They are coming. Fifty years ago there were 3000 Waiapi living their traditional lives, today there are 300.

The "image rights" price of this trip up river was $750 U.S. worth of shotgun shells and .22 caliber bullets: gifts to the chiefs to help them fend off the illegal incursions of the gold miners who wish to pan their river. As we negotiated these terms in the small office of the local FUNAI administrator Antonio Pereira Neto, (of the Brazilian Department of Indian Affairs) who controls a region the size of Texas, he told us that "Once you meet the Waiapi you will never be the same. They are a beautiful people." He was right. I am changed.

The contrast between Brooklyn, my hometown, and Ituwassu could not be greater and yet I identify with the Waiapi; with their battle to maintain their continuity against the onslaught of machines, urban industrial culture, and homogeneity. Is this the same battle being waged for a life of quality, a life safe from cancer and decay, in our neighborhoods? Or is this the battle our culture has already waged and lost? While the genetic diversity surrounding Ituwassu, burns like the libraries of Alexandria, robbing us of life's long legacy of balance and good medicine— how many volumes of traditional wisdom are lost In the cultures who inhabit and cultivate these places? This wisdom is the spirit of this place. It is a climax culture finely adapted to a climax ecosystem.

Chief Matapi Waiapi of the village of Taitetuwa' is walking swiftly and barefoot on the footpath— a muddy and partial clearing less than 10 inches wide running along the river and intersected by huge tree buttresses and low hanging liana vines. I am trying to follow in my "Technica" boots, carrying the camera. I am trying to step as he steps. Matapi turns to our Funai guide, Edmar Mata, who translates. "He says you don't know where you're stepping. You don't even know how to walk."

I had asked Chief Matapi to show us a part of the local forest which he considers especially beautiful. We stop at a spot to my eye no more or less spectacular than the rest of this dark, expanse of towering green. Matapi tells us that this is a special spot. He points to some spent shafts of arrows which had successfully found their targets here. While I film, he speaks of trees. "Is it true that there are no trees where you come from? Without trees there would be no Waiapi. The sun would burn us up."

Like our culture of machines and cities, the rain forest succors only those with the matching biological or cultural code. I have heard that forest dwellers seeing mountains for the first time will reach out to touch them, unable to decode the distance to the huge range. I suppose part of the rain forest code reads "Learn how to walk. Love trees." If I stayed here long enough I believe that my children would know this code completely, but it has been three days and my visit is over. I am returning to the city and its concrete and machines where I know the code and I know that part of it reads "Homogenize. Simplify. Expand."

391

TEACH WHAT YOU NEED TO LEARN

*"If I had my way ecological design would become central to
the curriculum at every single level of education: kindergarten,
lower school, upper school, college, and university."*
— Ian McHarg
Landscape Architect

When, in his interview, Ian McHarg remarked that ecological design should become the centerpiece of education, it seemed at the time to be hyperbole at best. But with time, I have become convinced that ecological design, a field which did not appear in my (1970's) high school courses or (1980's) college courses, has an essential and central role to play in organizing educational curricula.

For centuries European education was organized through the conceptual frame of Religion and Philosophy. Within its broad scope the various fields of mathematics, astronomy, chemistry, biology, physics and the "humanities" found common ground for interpretation and interpolation. During Europe's Age of Discovery and Exploration (sometimes called the Age of Exploitation), which lasted from the 15th through the 19th centuries, humanity's range of exploration was extended into the heavens with the telescope, into the microcosm with the microscope and throughout the world through the improved art of celestial navigation. As our knowledge base of natural phenomena increased, the conceptual frame of Religion and Philosophy was increasingly seen as inadequate to the task of integrating these new diverse experiences and was eventually discarded in favor of a new conceptual frame: Science.

Science did indeed "put in order the facts of our experience" (Alfred N. Whitehead's definition of science). Natural Selection and Evolution for example, revolutionized our view of life on Earth, elegantly accounting for life's diversity and distribution. But between themselves, the various sciences could offer no more unifying concept than the Scientific Method. The ties which integrate diverse disciplines and which guide our application of knowledge had been lost.

Today our sciences and school curricula are in disarray: a hodge podge of too often unrelated fields and specializations whose only relevance to the human experience is the job market. R. Buckminster Fuller once stated that "Children are born planetarium goers, they are naturally attracted to the largest questions." I am convinced that most of us would like to know how a particular lesson fits in with the "big picture". Why is math important? How does geology or biology effect my life? How does physics relate to Los Angeles or to Kansas City?

The field of Ecological Design has the potential to become a central and unifying conceptual frame. It is active and exploratory, inviting the participant to join in the adventure of designing our collective future. It is interdisciplinary and integrative in a way which is tolerant of local differences and expertise. It is fundamentally pragmatic in its intention, as it attempts to understand the various systems which operate in our world and to design human systems which will increase the wealth of the natural world as well as the wealth of humanity as a whole. It fosters social responsibility and proactive conflict resolution.

In presenting the film "Ecological Design: Inventing the Future" to educators throughout America, we have found a range of responses ranging from unabashed enthusiasm to deep pessimism. On the subject of Design Outlaws one teacher remarked "These kids are criminals not design outlaws." Others have lamented that an ecological design curricula would be calling for creative thinking rather than learning, and "Isn't that a bit much to ask, when these kids are barely learning 'the three R's'." But it is the opinion of this interloper, this product of the New York public education system, that curricula needs to be relevant, integrative and creative. All Learning is creative learning. Today's successful learners have either somehow managed to develop their own framework for integration and creative application or they have benefited from the truly heroic efforts of their teachers. In either case, these successes are in spite of the way the current curriculum is organized.

Buckminster Fuller's statement that "All children are born geniuses" but they get de-geniused through misguidance, and his life-long call for the field of "Comprehensive Anticipatory Design Science" to become the basis of our sciences, businesses, and education has never rung more true to me. Neither has his conviction that humanity is not doomed to be a failure, and that we should get conscious and busy making 100% of us a success on planet earth. If education is to be relevant, it must involve our children and communities in the designing of our collective future.

If today "The planet is teaching us directly," as systems theorist Hazel Henderson states in the film, it is so because we have developed the means for listening to the planet's feedback on a very fine and still global scale. All conceptual revolutions have been closely associated with such quantum leaps in information which challenge accepted world views with contradictory data and paradoxes. Today, the planetary feedback is pointing to seemingly intractable conflicts between: nature and technology, science and the sacred, wealth and well-being, conservation and development, north and south, and human beings and the rest of nature. The successful resolution of these conflicts may very well depend on our ability to re-frame our world-view.

Sigmund Freud once stated that the most important scientific revolutions have, as their only common feature, the de-thronement of human arrogance about our cosmic importance. Copernicus removed us from the center of the solar system. Darwin removed us from the center of all life. Freud removed even the illusion of control over our own thoughts and actions. Ecological design and the Gaian perspective continues this pattern, offering us a more accurate and revitalized view of life on earth, along with our slice of humble pie.

The making of the film Ecological Design: Inventing the Future and this book has been an ongoing learning process in a field whose practitioners are impresarios of experiment. If human history is becoming, as H.G. Wells characterized, "more and more a race between education and catastrophe" then education can ill afford to ignore the work of these designers. They have pioneered entire fields of work and study, and seen, as if with new eyes, a world of possibilities which we can now dimly discern on the horizon.

Book/Article Index

Title:
Design Concept, The

Author:
Hurlburt, Allen

Date: 1981

Publication:

Page No. 1

Publisher:
Watson-Guptill
New York

General Topic:
graphic design

Notes:

Book/Article Index

Title:
Way of the Animal
Powers

Author:
Campbell, Joseph

Date: 1988

Publication:
Myths of Great Hunt

Page No. 2

Publisher:
Harper & Row
New York

General Topic:
Mythology

Notes:

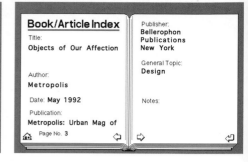

Book/Article Index

Title:
Objects of Our Affection

Author:
Metropolis

Date: May 1992

Publication:
Metropolis: Urban Mag of

Page No. 3

Publisher:
Bellerophon
Publications
New York

General Topic:
Design

Notes:

Book/Article Index

Title:
Structure in Nature is a
Strategy for Design

Author:
Pearce, Peter

Date: 1990

Publication:

Page No. 4

Publisher:
MIT Press
Cambridge

General Topic:
Design

Notes:

Book/Article Index

Title:
Shelter

Author:
Kahn, Lloyd-Ed.

Date: 1973/1990

Publication:

Page No. 5

Publisher:
Shelter Publications
Bolinas CA

General Topic:
Architecture

Notes:

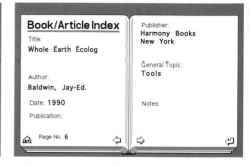

Book/Article Index

Title:
Whole Earth Ecolog

Author:
Baldwin, Jay-Ed.

Date: 1990

Publication:

Page No. 6

Publisher:
Harmony Books
New York

General Topic:
Tools

Notes:

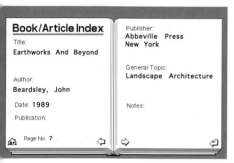

Book/Article Index

Title:
Earthworks And Beyond

Author:
Beardsley, John

Date: 1989

Publication:

Page No. 7

Publisher:
Abbeville Press
New York

General Topic:
Landscape Architecture

Notes:

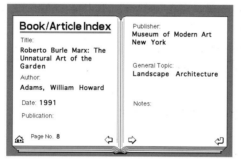

Book/Article Index

Title:
Roberto Burle Marx: The
Unnatural Art of the
Garden

Author:
Adams, William Howard

Date: 1991

Publication:

Page No. 8

Publisher:
Museum of Modern Art
New York

General Topic:
Landscape Architecture

Notes:

Book/Article Index

Title:
Architecture of Exile,
The

Author:
Tigerman, Stanley

Date: 1988

Publication:

Page No. 9

Publisher:
Rizzoli International
New York

General Topic:
Architecture

Notes:

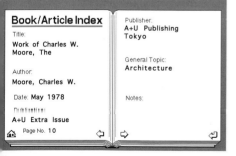

Book/Article Index

Title:
Work of Charles W.
Moore, The

Author:
Moore, Charles W.

Date: May 1978

Publication:
A+U Extra Issue

Page No. 10

Publisher:
A+U Publishing
Tokyo

General Topic:
Architecture

Notes:

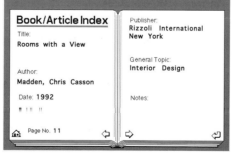

Book/Article Index

Title:
Rooms with a View

Author:
Madden, Chris Casson

Date: 1992

Publication:

Page No. 11

Publisher:
Rizzoli International
New York

General Topic:
Interior Design

Notes:

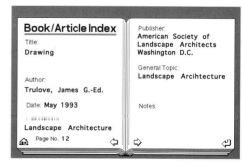

Book/Article Index

Title:
Drawing

Author:
Trulove, James G.-Ed.

Date: May 1993

Publication:
Landscape Architecture

Page No. 12

Publisher:
American Society of
Landscape Architects
Washington D.C.

General Topic:
Landscape Arcihtecture

Notes:

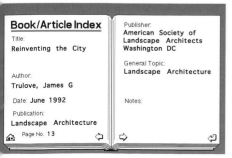

Book/Article Index

Title:
Reinventing the City

Author:
Trulove, James G

Date: June 1992

Publication:
Landscape Architecture

Page No. 13

Publisher:
American Society of
Landscape Architects
Washington DC

General Topic:
Landscape Architecture

Notes:

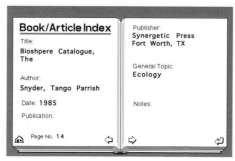

Book/Article Index

Title:
Bioshpere Catalogue,
The

Author:
Snyder, Tango Parrish

Date: 1985

Publication:

Page No. 14

Publisher:
Synergetic Press
Fort Worth, TX

General Topic:
Ecology

Notes:

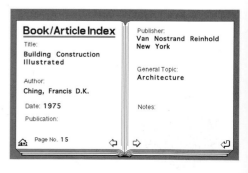

Book/Article Index

Title:
Building Construction
Illustrated

Author:
Ching, Francis D.K.

Date: 1975

Publication:

Page No. 15

Publisher:
Van Nostrand Reinhold
New York

General Topic:
Architecture

Notes:

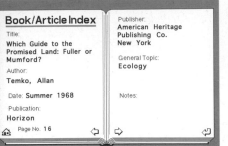

Book/Article Index

Title: Which Guide to the Promised Land: Fuller or Mumford?

Author: Temko, Allan

Date: Summer 1968

Publication: Horizon

Publisher: American Heritage Publishing Co. New York

General Topic: Ecology

Notes:

Page No. 16

Book/Article Index

Title: Bauhaus, The

Author: Wingler, Hans M.

Date: 1986

Publication:

Publisher: MIT Press Cambridge

General Topic: Design

Notes:

Page No. 17

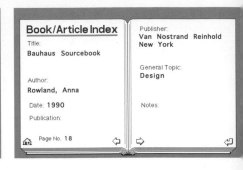

Book/Article Index

Title: Bauhaus Sourcebook

Author: Rowland, Anna

Date: 1990

Publication:

Publisher: Van Nostrand Reinhold New York

General Topic: Design

Notes:

Page No. 18

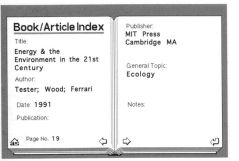

Book/Article Index

Title: Energy & the Environment in the 21st Century

Author: Tester; Wood; Ferrari

Date: 1991

Publication:

Publisher: MIT Press Cambridge MA

General Topic: Ecology

Notes:

Page No. 19

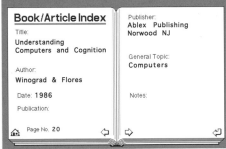

Book/Article Index

Title: Understanding Computers and Cognition

Author: Winograd & Flores

Date: 1986

Publication:

Publisher: Ablex Publishing Norwood NJ

General Topic: Computers

Notes:

Page No. 20

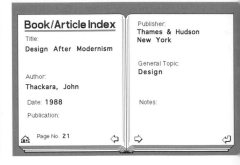

Book/Article Index

Title: Design After Modernism

Author: Thackara, John

Date: 1988

Publication:

Publisher: Thames & Hudson New York

General Topic: Design

Notes:

Page No. 21

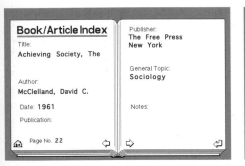

Book/Article Index

Title: Achieving Society, The

Author: McClelland, David C.

Date: 1961

Publication:

Publisher: The Free Press New York

General Topic: Sociology

Notes:

Page No. 22

Book/Article Index

Title: Many Dimensional Man

Author: Ogilvy, James

Date: 1977

Publication:

Publisher: Harper & Row New York

General Topic: Sociology

Notes:

Page No. 23

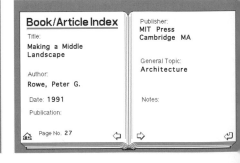

Book/Article Index

Title: Synchronocity: The Bridge Between Matter & Mind

Author: Peat, F. David

Date: 1987

Publication:

Publisher: Bantam Books New York

General Topic: Psychology

Notes:

Page No. 24

Book/Article Index

Title: High Tech Architecture

Author: Davies, Colin

Date: 1988

Publication:

Publisher: Rizzolli International New York

General Topic: Architecture

Notes:

Page No. 25

Book/Article Index

Title: Site Planning 3rd Ed.

Author: Lynch & Hack

Date: 1984/1993

Publication:

Publisher: MIT Press Cambridge MA

General Topic: Architecture

Notes:

Page No. 26

Book/Article Index

Title: Making a Middle Landscape

Author: Rowe, Peter G.

Date: 1991

Publication:

Publisher: MIT Press Cambridge MA

General Topic: Architecture

Notes:

Page No. 27

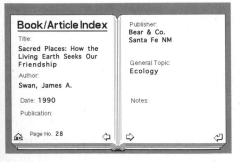

Book/Article Index

Title: Sacred Places: How the Living Earth Seeks Our Friendship

Author: Swan, James A.

Date: 1990

Publication:

Publisher: Bear & Co. Santa Fe NM

General Topic: Ecology

Notes:

Page No. 28

Book/Article Index

Title: Tomorrow is Our Permanent Address

Author: Todd, John & Nancy Jack

Date: 1980

Publication:

Publisher: Harper & Row New York

General Topic: Design

Notes:

Page No. 29

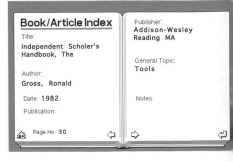

Book/Article Index

Title: Independent Scholer's Handbook, The

Author: Gross, Ronald

Date: 1982

Publication:

Publisher: Addison-Wesley Reading MA

General Topic: Tools

Notes:

Page No. 30

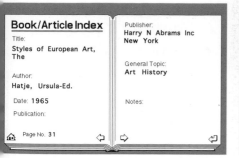

Book/Article Index

Title:
Styles of European Art, The

Author:
Hatje, Ursula-Ed.

Date: 1965

Publication:

Page No. 31

Publisher:
Harry N Abrams Inc
New York

General Topic:
Art History

Notes:

Book/Article Index

Title:
Designing for Human Behavior

Author:
Lang; Burnette et al.

Date: 1974

Publication:

Page No. 32

Publisher:
Dowden, Hutchinson &
Ross Inc
Stroudsburg PA

General Topic:
Architecture

Notes:

Book/Article Index

Title:
TED3: Technology,
Entertainment, Design

Author:
Wurman, Richard Saul

Date: August 1992

Publication:
Design World

Page No. 33

Publisher:
Design Editorial Pty Ltd
Victoria Australia

General Topic:
Design

Notes:

Book/Article Index

Title:
Product Development
Management

Author:
Rothschild F F

Date: 1987

Publication:

Page No. 34

Publisher:
T. Wilson Publishing Co.
South Yarra Australia

General Topic:
Design

Notes:

Book/Article Index

Title:
Natural Energy &
Vernacular Architecture

Author:
Fathy, Hassan

Date: 1986

Publication:

Page No. 35

Publisher:
University of Chicago
Press
Chicago IL

General Topic:
Architecture

Notes:

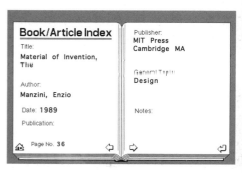

Book/Article Index

Title:
Material of Invention,
The

Author:
Manzini, Enzio

Date: 1989

Publication:

Page No. 36

Publisher:
MIT Press
Cambridge MA

General Topic:
Design

Notes:

Book/Article Index

Title:
Design Simulation

Author:
Burden, Ernst

Date: 1988

Publication:

Page No. 37

Publisher:
Whitney Library of
Design
New York

General Topic:
Design

Notes:

Book/Article Index

Title:
Design Strategies in
Architecture

Author:
Baker, Geoffrey H.

Date: 1989

Publication:

Page No. 38

Publisher:
Van Nostrand Reinhold
International
London

General Topic:
Architecture

Notes:

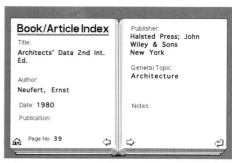

Book/Article Index

Title:
Architects' Data 2nd Int.
Ed.

Author:
Neufert, Ernst

Date: 1980

Publication:

Page No. 39

Publisher:
Halsted Press; John
Wiley & Sons
New York

General Topic:
Architecture

Notes:

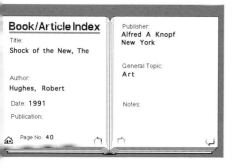

Book/Article Index

Title:
Shock of the New, The

Author:
Hughes, Robert

Date: 1991

Publication:

Page No. 40

Publisher:
Alfred A Knopf
New York

General Topic:
Art

Notes:

Book/Article Index

Title:
Magnificent Builders &
Their Dream Houses, The

Author:
Thorndike, Joseph J. Jr.

Date: 1978

Publication:

Page No. 41

Publisher:
American Heritage
New York

General Topic:
Architecture

Notes:

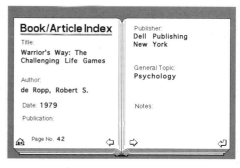

Book/Article Index

Title:
Warrior's Way: The
Challenging Life Games

Author:
de Ropp, Robert S.

Date: 1979

Publication:

Page No. 42

Publisher:
Dell Publishing
New York

General Topic:
Psychology

Notes:

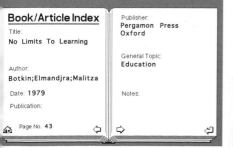

Book/Article Index

Title:
No Limits To Learning

Author:
Botkin;Elmandjra;Malitza

Date: 1979

Publication:

Page No. 43

Publisher:
Pergamon Press
Oxford

General Topic:
Education

Notes:

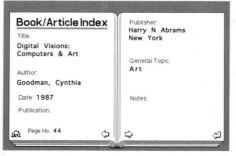

Book/Article Index

Title:
Digital Visions:
Computers & Art

Author:
Goodman, Cynthia

Date: 1987

Publication:

Page No. 44

Publisher:
Harry N Abrams
New York

General Topic:
Art

Notes:

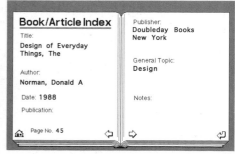

Book/Article Index

Title:
Design of Everyday
Things, The

Author:
Norman, Donald A

Date: 1988

Publication:

Page No. 45

Publisher:
Doubleday Books
New York

General Topic:
Design

Notes:

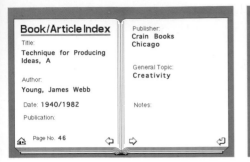

Book/Article Index
Title: Technique for Producing Ideas, A
Author: Young, James Webb
Date: 1940/1982
Publication:
Publisher: Crain Books Chicago
General Topic: Creativity
Notes:
Page No. 46

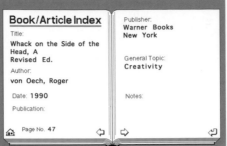

Book/Article Index
Title: Whack on the Side of the Head, A Revised Ed.
Author: von Oech, Roger
Date: 1990
Publication:
Publisher: Warner Books New York
General Topic: Creativity
Notes:
Page No. 47

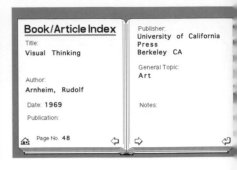

Book/Article Index
Title: Visual Thinking
Author: Arnheim, Rudolf
Date: 1969
Publication:
Publisher: University of California Press Berkeley CA
General Topic: Art
Notes:
Page No. 48

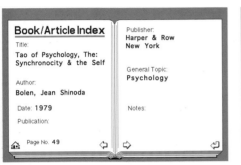

Book/Article Index
Title: Tao of Psychology, The: Synchronocity & the Self
Author: Bolen, Jean Shinoda
Date: 1979
Publication:
Publisher: Harper & Row New York
General Topic: Psychology
Notes:
Page No. 49

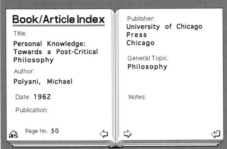

Book/Article Index
Title: Personal Knowledge: Towards a Post-Critical Philosophy
Author: Polyani, Michael
Date: 1962
Publication:
Publisher: University of Chicago Press Chicago
General Topic: Philosophy
Notes:
Page No. 50

Book/Article Index
Title: Today's Architectural Mirror: Interiors, Buildings & Solar Design
Author: Heyne, Pamela
Date: 1982
Publication:
Publisher: Van Nostrand Reinhold New York
General Topic: Architecture
Notes:
Page No. 51

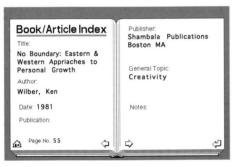

Book/Article Index
Title: Philadelphia Architecture
Author: Foundation for Arch.
Date: 1984
Publication:
Publisher: MIT Press Cambridge MA
General Topic: Architecture
Notes:
Page No. 52

Book/Article Index
Title: Form, Function & Design
Author: Grillo, Paul Jaques
Date: 1960
Publication:
Publisher: Dover Publications New York
General Topic: Design
Notes:
Page No. 53

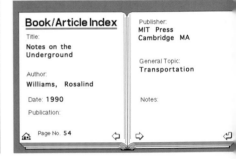

Book/Article Index
Title: Notes on the Underground
Author: Williams, Rosalind
Date: 1990
Publication:
Publisher: MIT Press Cambridge MA
General Topic: Transportation
Notes:
Page No. 54

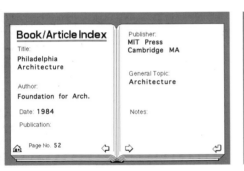

Book/Article Index
Title: No Boundary: Eastern & Western Appriaches to Personal Growth
Author: Wilber, Ken
Date: 1981
Publication:
Publisher: Shambala Publications Boston MA
General Topic: Creativity
Notes:
Page No. 55

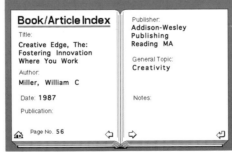

Book/Article Index
Title: Creative Edge, The: Fostering Innovation Where You Work
Author: Miller, William C
Date: 1987
Publication:
Publisher: Addison-Wesley Publishing Reading MA
General Topic: Creativity
Notes:
Page No. 56

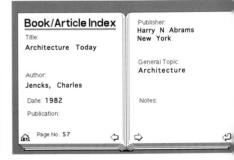

Book/Article Index
Title: Architecture Today
Author: Jencks, Charles
Date: 1982
Publication:
Publisher: Harry N Abrams New York
General Topic: Architecture
Notes:
Page No. 57

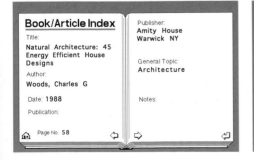

Book/Article Index
Title: Natural Architecture: 45 Energy Efficient House Designs
Author: Woods, Charles G
Date: 1988
Publication:
Publisher: Amity House Warwick NY
General Topic: Architecture
Notes:
Page No. 58

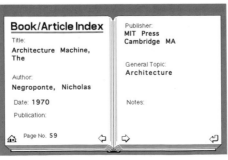

Book/Article Index
Title: Architecture Machine, The
Author: Negroponte, Nicholas
Date: 1970
Publication:
Publisher: MIT Press Cambridge MA
General Topic: Architecture
Notes:
Page No. 59

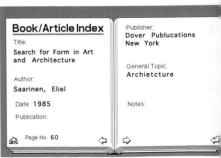

Book/Article Index
Title: Search for Form in Art and Architecture
Author: Saarinen, Eliel
Date: 1985
Publication:
Publisher: Dover Publucations New York
General Topic: Architetcture
Notes:
Page No. 60

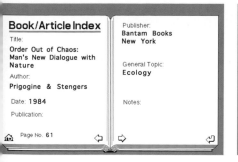

Book/Article Index

Title:
Order Out of Chaos: Man's New Dialogue with Nature

Author:
Prigogine & Stengers

Date: 1984

Publication:

Publisher:
Bantam Books
New York

General Topic:
Ecology

Notes:

Page No. 61

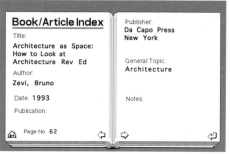

Book/Article Index

Title:
Architecture as Space: How to Look at Architecture Rev Ed

Author:
Zevi, Bruno

Date: 1993

Publication:

Publisher:
Da Capo Press
New York

General Topic:
Architecture

Notes:

Page No. 62

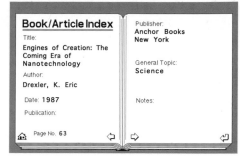

Book/Article Index

Title:
Engines of Creation: The Coming Era of Nanotechnology

Author:
Drexler, K. Eric

Date: 1987

Publication:

Publisher:
Anchor Books
New York

General Topic:
Science

Notes:

Page No. 63

Book/Article Index

Title:
Cosmic Conciousness: A Study in the Evolution of the Human Mind

Author:
Bucke, Richard Maurice

Date: 1977

Publication:

Publisher:
Citadel Press
Seacaucus NJ

General Topic:
Mysticism

Notes:

Page No. 64

Book/Article Index

Title:
Gentle Architecture

Author:
Wells, Malcolm

Date: 1981

Publication:

Publisher:
McGraw Hill
New York

General Topic:
Architecture

Notes:

Page No. 65

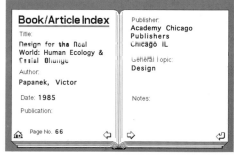

Book/Article Index

Title:
Design for the Real World: Human Ecology & Social Change

Author:
Papanek, Victor

Date: 1985

Publication:

Publisher:
Academy Chicago Publishers
Chicago IL

General Topic:
Design

Notes:

Page No. 66

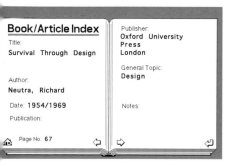

Book/Article Index

Title:
Survival Through Design

Author:
Neutra, Richard

Date: 1954/1969

Publication:

Publisher:
Oxford University Press
London

General Topic:
Design

Notes:

Page No. 67

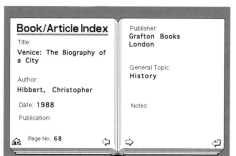

Book/Article Index

Title:
Venice: The Biography of a City

Author:
Hibbert, Christopher

Date: 1988

Publication:

Publisher:
Grafton Books
London

General Topic:
History

Notes:

Page No. 68

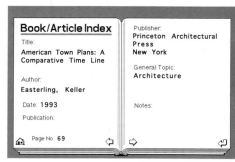

Book/Article Index

Title:
American Town Plans: A Comparative Time Line

Author:
Easterling, Keller

Date: 1993

Publication:

Publisher:
Princeton Architectural Press
New York

General Topic:
Architecture

Notes:

Page No. 69

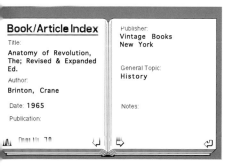

Book/Article Index

Title:
Anatomy of Revolution, The; Revised & Expanded Ed.

Author:
Brinton, Crane

Date: 1965

Publication:

Publisher:
Vintage Books
New York

General Topic:
History

Notes:

Page No. 70

Book/Article Index

Title:
Perspective Drawing

Author:
Way, Mark

Date: 1989

Publication:

Publisher:
Outline Press
London

General Topic:
Design

Notes:

Page No. 71

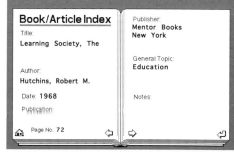

Book/Article Index

Title:
Learning Society, The

Author:
Hutchins, Robert M.

Date: 1968

Publication:

Publisher:
Mentor Books
New York

General Topic:
Education

Notes:

Page No. 72

Book/Article Index

Title:
Perennial Philosophy, The

Author:
Huxley, Aldous

Date: 1945/1985

Publication:

Publisher:
Triad Grafton
London

General Topic:
Mysticism

Notes:

Page No. 73

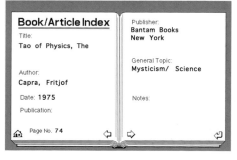

Book/Article Index

Title:
Tao of Physics, The

Author:
Capra, Fritjof

Date: 1975

Publication:

Publisher:
Bantam Books
New York

General Topic:
Mysticism/ Science

Notes:

Page No. 74

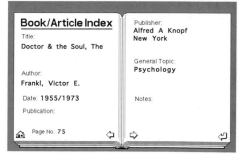

Book/Article Index

Title:
Doctor & the Soul, The

Author:
Frankl, Victor E.

Date: 1955/1973

Publication:

Publisher:
Alfred A Knopf
New York

General Topic:
Psychology

Notes:

Page No. 75

Book/Article Index

Title:
Plastics/ Design &
Materials

Author:
Katz, Sylvia

Date: 1978

Publication:

Publisher:
Studio Vista
London

General Topic:
Design

Notes:

Page No. 76

Book/Article Index

Title:
Complexity &
Contradiction in
Architecture 2nd Ed
Author:
Venturi, Robert

Date: 1988

Publication:

Publisher:
Museum of Modern Art
New York

General Topic:
Architecture

Notes:

Page No. 77

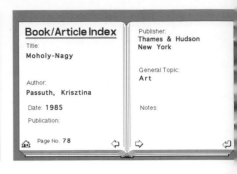

Book/Article Index

Title:
Moholy-Nagy

Author:
Passuth, Krisztina

Date: 1985

Publication:

Publisher:
Thames & Hudson
New York

General Topic:
Art

Notes:

Page No. 78

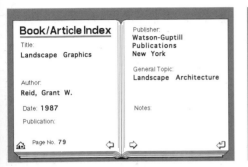

Book/Article Index

Title:
Landscape Graphics

Author:
Reid, Grant W.

Date: 1987

Publication:

Publisher:
Watson-Guptill
Publications
New York

General Topic:
Landscape Architecture

Notes:

Page No. 79

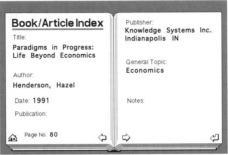

Book/Article Index

Title:
Paradigms in Progress:
Life Beyond Economics

Author:
Henderson, Hazel

Date: 1991

Publication:

Publisher:
Knowledge Systems Inc.
Indianapolis IN

General Topic:
Economics

Notes:

Page No. 80

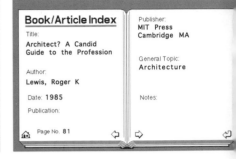

Book/Article Index

Title:
Architect? A Candid
Guide to the Profession

Author:
Lewis, Roger K

Date: 1985

Publication:

Publisher:
MIT Press
Cambridge MA

General Topic:
Architecture

Notes:

Page No. 81

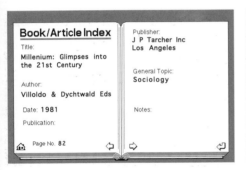

Book/Article Index

Title:
Millenium: Glimpses into
the 21st Century

Author:
Villoldo & Dychtwald Eds

Date: 1981

Publication:

Publisher:
J P Tarcher Inc
Los Angeles

General Topic:
Sociology

Notes:

Page No. 82

Book/Article Index

Title:
Design Thinking

Author:
Rowe, Peter G

Date: 1987

Publication:

Publisher:
MIT Press
Cambridge MA

General Topic:
Design

Notes:

Page No. 83

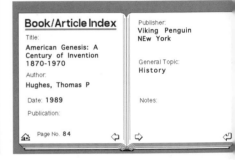

Book/Article Index

Title:
American Genesis: A
Century of Invention
1870-1970
Author:
Hughes, Thomas P

Date: 1989

Publication:

Publisher:
Viking Penguin
NEw York

General Topic:
History

Notes:

Page No. 84

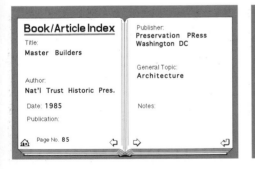

Book/Article Index

Title:
Master Builders

Author:
Nat'l Trust Historic Pres.

Date: 1985

Publication:

Publisher:
Preservation PRess
Washington DC

General Topic:
Architecture

Notes:

Page No. 85

Book/Article Index

Title:
De-Architecture

Author:
Wines, James

Date: 1987

Publication:

Publisher:
Rizzoli International
New York

General Topic:
Architecture

Notes:

Page No. 86

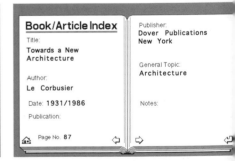

Book/Article Index

Title:
Towards a New
Architecture

Author:
Le Corbusier

Date: 1931/1986

Publication:

Publisher:
Dover Publications
New York

General Topic:
Architecture

Notes:

Page No. 87

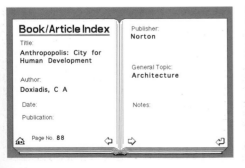

Book/Article Index

Title:
Anthropopolis: City for
Human Development

Author:
Doxiadis, C A

Date:

Publication:

Publisher:
Norton

General Topic:
Architecture

Notes:

Page No. 88

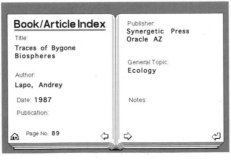

Book/Article Index

Title:
Traces of Bygone
Biospheres

Author:
Lapo, Andrey

Date: 1987

Publication:

Publisher:
Synergetic Press
Oracle AZ

General Topic:
Ecology

Notes:

Page No. 89

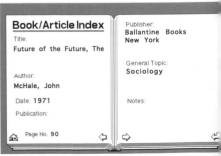

Book/Article Index

Title:
Future of the Future, The

Author:
McHale, John

Date: 1971

Publication:

Publisher:
Ballantine Books
New York

General Topic:
Sociology

Notes:

Page No. 90

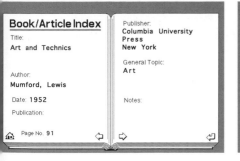

Book/Article Index

Title:
Art and Technics

Author:
Mumford, Lewis

Date: 1952

Publication:

Publisher:
Columbia University Press
New York

General Topic:
Art

Notes:

Page No. 91

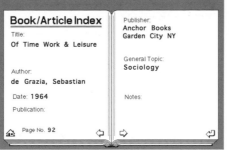

Book/Article Index

Title:
Of Time Work & Leisure

Author:
de Grazia, Sebastian

Date: 1964

Publication:

Publisher:
Anchor Books
Garden City NY

General Topic:
Sociology

Notes:

Page No. 92

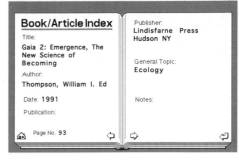

Book/Article Index

Title:
Gaia 2: Emergence, The New Science of Becoming

Author:
Thompson, William I. Ed

Date: 1991

Publication:

Publisher:
Lindisfarne Press
Hudson NY

General Topic:
Ecology

Notes:

Page No. 93

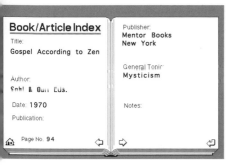

Book/Article Index

Title:
Gospel According to Zen

Author:
Sohl & Carr Eds.

Date: 1970

Publication:

Publisher:
Mentor Books
New York

General Topic:
Mysticism

Notes:

Page No. 94

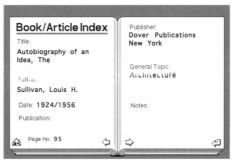

Book/Article Index

Title:
Autobiography of an Idea, The

Author:
Sullivan, Louis H.

Date: 1924/1956

Publication:

Publisher:
Dover Publications
New York

General Topic:
Architecture

Notes:

Page No. 95

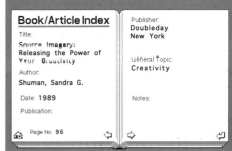

Book/Article Index

Title:
Source Imagery: Releasing the Power of Your Creativity

Author:
Shuman, Sandra G.

Date: 1989

Publication:

Publisher:
Doubleday
New York

General Topic:
Creativity

Notes:

Page No. 96

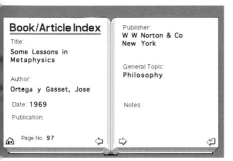

Book/Article Index

Title:
Some Lessons in Metaphysics

Author:
Ortega y Gasset, Jose

Date: 1969

Publication:

Publisher:
W W Norton & Co
New York

General Topic:
Philosophy

Notes:

Page No. 97

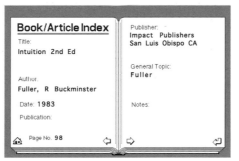

Book/Article Index

Title:
Intuition 2nd Ed

Author:
Fuller, R Buckminster

Date: 1983

Publication:

Publisher:
Impact Publishers
San Luis Obispo CA

General Topic:
Fuller

Notes:

Page No. 98

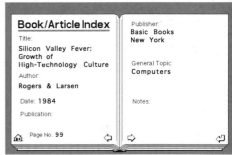

Book/Article Index

Title:
Silicon Valley Fever: Growth of High-Technology Culture

Author:
Rogers & Larsen

Date: 1984

Publication:

Publisher:
Basic Books
New York

General Topic:
Computers

Notes:

Page No. 99

Book/Article Index

Title:
Sphere & the Labyrinth: Avante-Gardes & Architecture

Author:
Tafuri, Manfredo

Date: 1990

Publication:

Publisher:
MIT Press
Cambridge MA

General Topic:
Architecture

Notes:

Page No. 100

Book/Article Index

Title:
History of the Future

Author:
Lorie & Murray-Clark

Date: 1989

Publication:

Publisher:
Doubleday
New York

General Topic:
Future

Notes:

Page No. 101

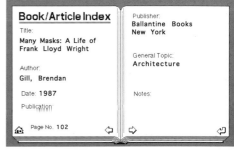

Book/Article Index

Title:
Many Masks: A Life of Frank Lloyd Wright

Author:
Gill, Brendan

Date: 1987

Publication:

Publisher:
Ballantine Books
New York

General Topic:
Architecture

Notes:

Page No. 102

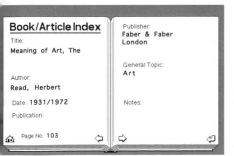

Book/Article Index

Title:
Meaning of Art, The

Author:
Read, Herbert

Date: 1931/1972

Publication:

Publisher:
Faber & Faber
London

General Topic:
Art

Notes:

Page No. 103

Book/Article Index

Title:
Progress Without Loss of Soul

Author:
Abt, Theodor

Date: 1989

Publication:

Publisher:
Chiron Publications
Wilmette IL

General Topic:
Urban Planning

Notes:

Page No. 104

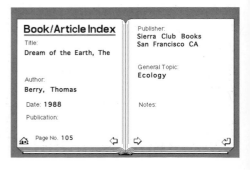

Book/Article Index

Title:
Dream of the Earth, The

Author:
Berry, Thomas

Date: 1988

Publication:

Publisher:
Sierra Club Books
San Francisco CA

General Topic:
Ecology

Notes:

Page No. 105

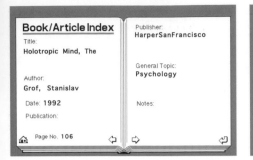

Book/Article Index

Title:
Holotropic Mind, The

Author:
Grof, Stanislav

Date: 1992

Publication:

Publisher:
HarperSanFrancisco

General Topic:
Psychology

Notes:

Page No. 106

Book/Article Index

Title:
Design Talks!

Author:
Gorb, Peter Ed.

Date: 1988

Publication:

Publisher:
The Design Council
London

General Topic:
Design

Notes:

Page No. 107

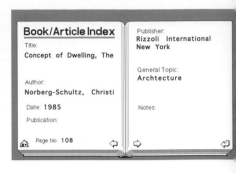

Book/Article Index

Title:
Concept of Dwelling, The

Author:
Norberg-Schultz, Christi

Date: 1985

Publication:

Publisher:
Rizzoli International
New York

General Topic:
Archtecture

Notes:

Page No. 108

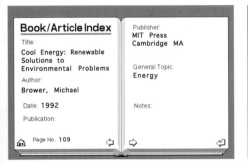

Book/Article Index

Title:
Cool Energy: Renewable
Solutions to
Environmental Problems
Author:
Brower, Michael

Date: 1992

Publication:

Publisher:
MIT Press
Cambridge MA

General Topic:
Energy

Notes:

Page No. 109

Book/Article Index

Title:
Nine Chains to the Moon

Author:
Fuller, R Buckminster

Date: 1971

Publication:

Publisher:
Anchor Books
New York

General Topic:
Fuller

Notes:

Page No. 110

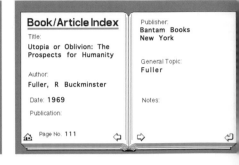

Book/Article Index

Title:
Utopia or Oblivion: The
Prospects for Humanity

Author:
Fuller, R Buckminster

Date: 1969

Publication:

Publisher:
Bantam Books
New York

General Topic:
Fuller

Notes:

Page No. 111

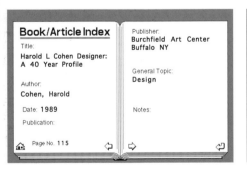

Book/Article Index

Title:
I Seem To Be A Verb

Author:
Fuller, R Buckminster

Date: 1970

Publication:

Publisher:
Bantam Books
New York

General Topic:
Fuller

Notes:

Page No. 112

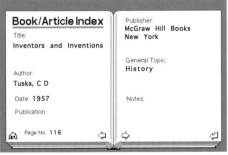

Book/Article Index

Title:
Sketchbook

Author:
Fuller, R Buckminster

Date: 1981

Publication:

Publisher:
University Science
Center
Philadelphia

General Topic:
Fuller

Notes:

Page No. 113

Book/Article Index

Title:
No More Secondhand God
& Other Writings

Author:
Fuller, R Buckminster

Date: 1963

Publication:

Publisher:
Southern Illinois
University Press
Carbondale & Edwardsville

General Topic:
Fuller

Notes:

Page No. 114

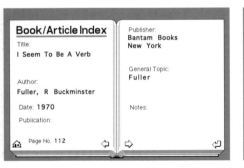

Book/Article Index

Title:
Harold L Cohen Designer:
A 40 Year Profile

Author:
Cohen, Harold

Date: 1989

Publication:

Publisher:
Burchfield Art Center
Buffalo NY

General Topic:
Design

Notes:

Page No. 115

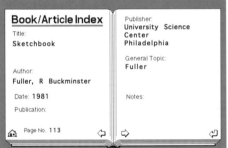

Book/Article Index

Title:
Inventors and Inventions

Author:
Tuska, C D

Date: 1957

Publication:

Publisher:
McGraw Hill Books
New York

General Topic:
History

Notes:

Page No. 116

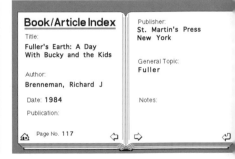

Book/Article Index

Title:
Fuller's Earth: A Day
With Bucky and the Kids

Author:
Brenneman, Richard J

Date: 1984

Publication:

Publisher:
St. Martin's Press
New York

General Topic:
Fuller

Notes:

Page No. 117

Book/Article Index

Title:
Ideas & Integrities: A
Spontaneous
Autobiographical Disclo
Author:
Fuller, R Buckminster

Date: 1963

Publication:

Publisher:
Prentice Hall Press
Englewood Cliffs NJ

General Topic:
Fuller

Notes:

Page No. 118

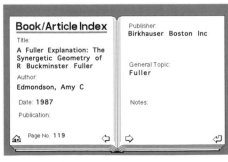

Book/Article Index

Title:
A Fuller Explanation: The
Synergetic Geometry of
R Buckminster Fuller
Author:
Edmondson, Amy C

Date: 1987

Publication:

Publisher:
Birkhauser Boston Inc

General Topic:
Fuller

Notes:

Page No. 119

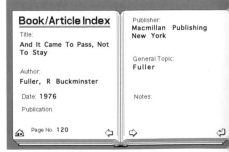

Book/Article Index

Title:
And It Came To Pass, Not
To Stay

Author:
Fuller, R Buckminster

Date: 1976

Publication:

Publisher:
Macmillan Publishing
New York

General Topic:
Fuller

Notes:

Page No. 120

Book/Article Index

Title:
An Open Life

Author:
Campbell, Joseph

Date: 1988

Publication:

Publisher:
Larson Publications
Burdett NY

General Topic:
Mythology

Notes:

Page No. 121

Book/Article Index

Title:
Synergetic Stew

Author:
Fuller, R Buckminster

Date: 1982

Publication:

Publisher:
Buckminster Fuller
Institute
Philadelphia

General Topic:
Fuller

Notes:

Page No. 122

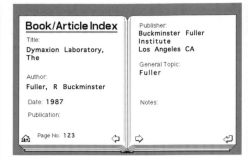

Book/Article Index

Title:
Dymaxion Laboratory,
The

Author:
Fuller, R Buckminster

Date: 1987

Publication:

Publisher:
Buckminster Fuller
Institute
Los Angeles CA

General Topic:
Fuller

Notes:

Page No. 123

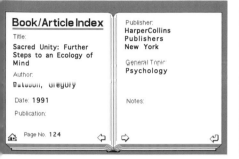

Book/Article Index

Title:
Sacred Unity: Further
Steps to an Ecology of
Mind

Author:
Bateson, Gregory

Date: 1991

Publication:

Publisher:
HarperCollins
Publishers
New York

General Topic:
Psychology

Notes:

Page No. 124

Book/Article Index

Title:
Operating Manual for
Spaceship Earth

Author:
Fuller, R Buckminster

Date: 1963/1971

Publication:

Publisher:
E P Dutton
New York

General Topic:
Fuller

Notes:

Page No. 125

Book/Article Index

Title:
Buckminster Fuller's
Universe: An
Appreciation

Author:
Sieden, Lloyd Steven

Date: 1989

Publication:

Publisher:
Plenum Press
New York

General Topic:
Fuller

Notes:

Page No. 126

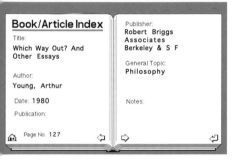

Book/Article Index

Title:
Which Way Out? And
Other Essays

Author:
Young, Arthur

Date: 1980

Publication:

Publisher:
Robert Briggs
Associates
Berkeley & S F

General Topic:
Philosophy

Notes:

Page No. 127

Book/Article Index

Title:
Cosmography

Author:
Fuller, R Buckminster

Date: 1992

Publication:

Publisher:
Macmillan Publishing Co.

New York

General Topic:
Fuller

Notes:

Page No. 128

Book/Article Index

Title:
Synergetics

Author:
Fuller, R Buckminster

Date: 1975

Publication:

Publisher:
Macmillan Publishing
New York

General Topic:
Fuller

Notes:

Page No. 129

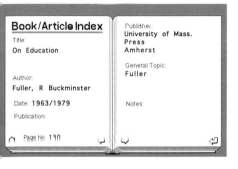

Book/Article Index

Title:
On Education

Author:
Fuller, R Buckminster

Date: 1963/1979

Publication:

Publisher:
University of Mass.
Press
Amherst

General Topic:
Fuller

Notes:

Page No. 130

Book/Article Index

Title:
50 Years of the Design
Science Revolution &
the World Game

Author:
Fuller, R Buckminster

Date: 1969

Publication:

Publisher:
Buckminster Fuller
Institute
Los Angeles

General Topic:
Fuller

Notes:

Page No. 131

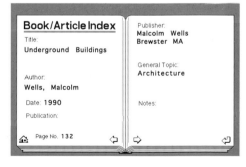

Book/Article Index

Title:
Underground Buildings

Author:
Wells, Malcolm

Date: 1990

Publication:

Publisher:
Malcolm Wells
Brewster MA

General Topic:
Architecture

Notes:

Page No. 132

In the process of making the film it became necessary to crystallize the mazeway of R. Buckminster Fuller's pantheon of fertile ideas. Here is the hyper card generated list that was used to navigate in the filmmaking process. Please feel free to cut and paste in your own magic theater of the imagination.

C.Z.

Mistake Mythology

Making Man a 100% Success
in Universe

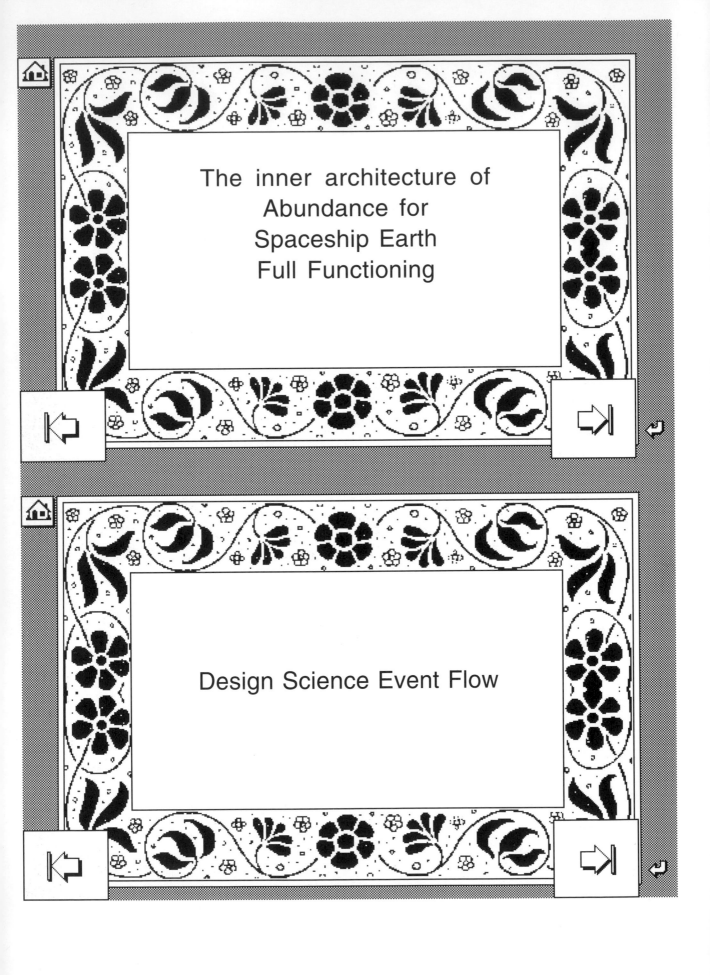

The inner architecture of
Abundance for
Spaceship Earth
Full Functioning

Design Science Event Flow

Scenario
Universe

E=MC2
and
Mrs. Murphy

Know-How based wealth
vs.
Real Estate based wealth

The Eternally Regenerative
Universe

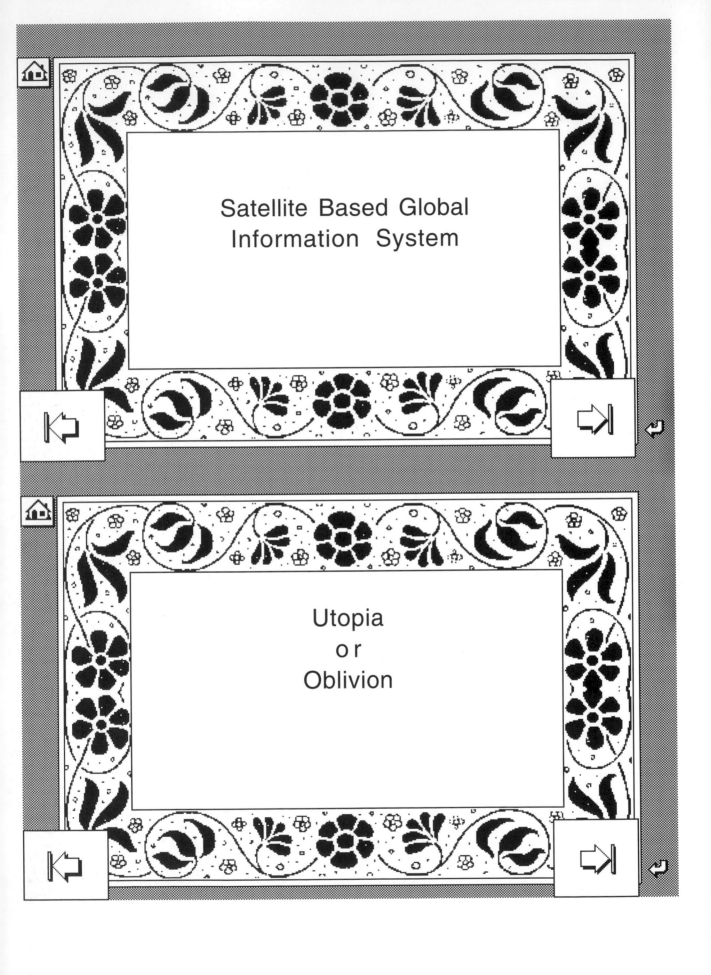

Satellite Based Global
Information System

Utopia
o r
Oblivion

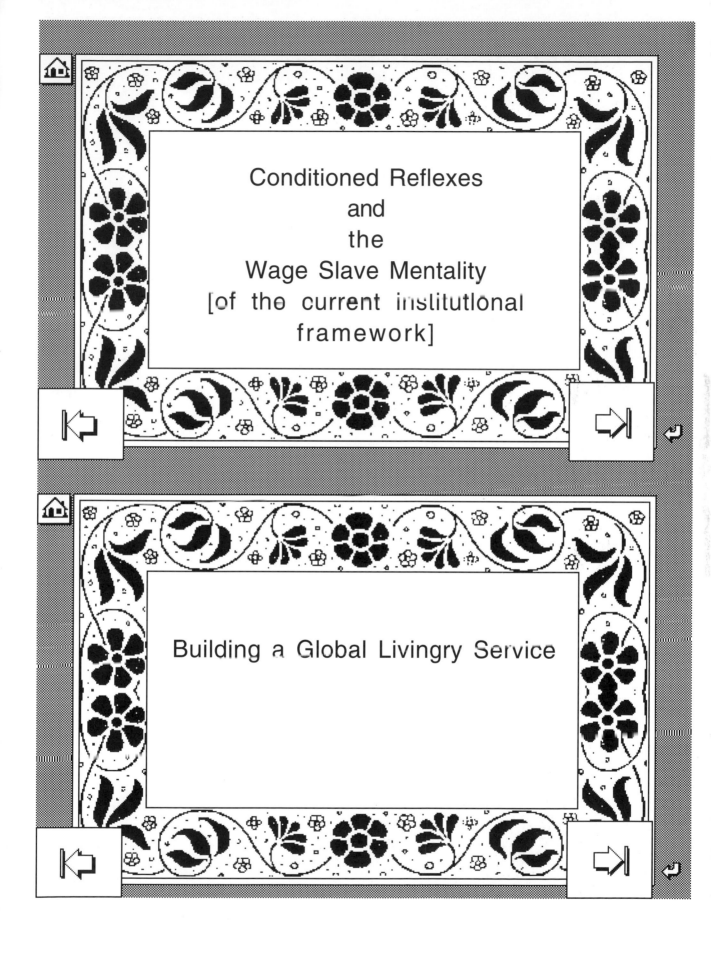

Conditioned Reflexes
and
the
Wage Slave Mentality
[of the current institutional
framework]

Building a Global Livingry Service

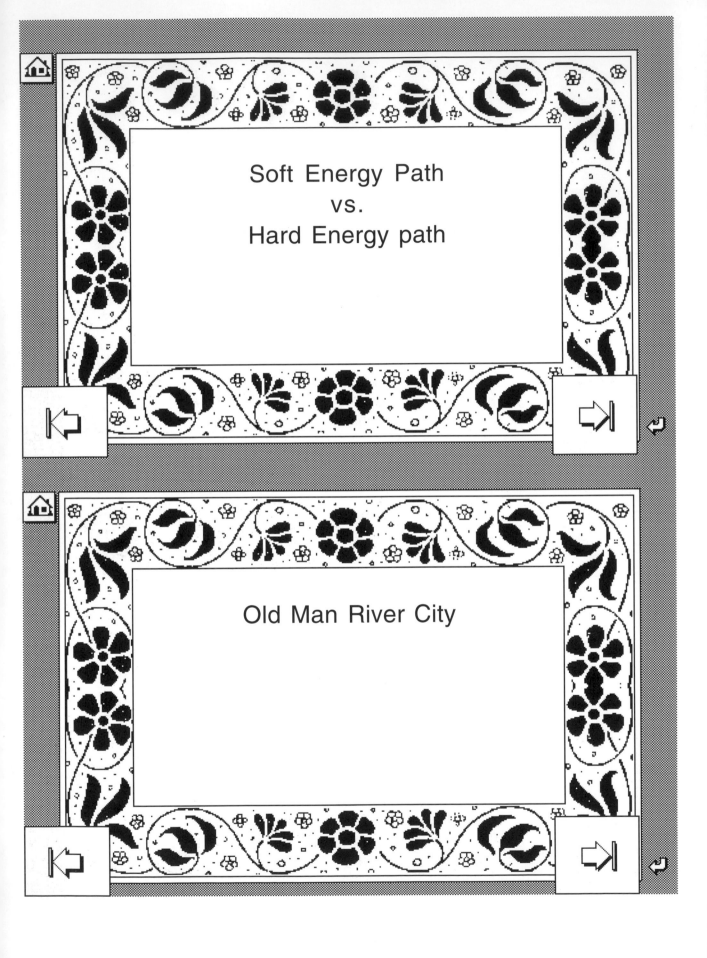

Soft Energy Path
vs.
Hard Energy path

Old Man River City

The Shadow Captain

SPACESHIP EARTH

Living Off Our Energy Income
vs.
Living Off Our Storage Account

The Dymaxion Map

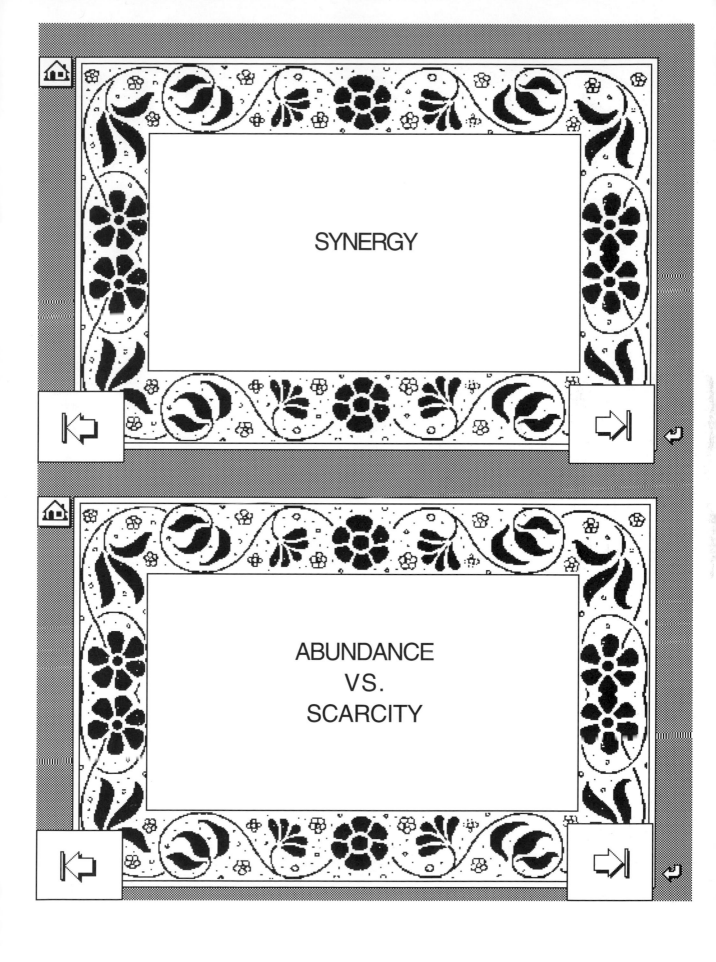

SYNERGY

ABUNDANCE
VS.
SCARCITY

EMERGENCE
THROUGH
EMERGENCY

EPHEMERALIZATION

ONE WORLD
ELECTRICAL
GRID

INDIVIDUAL
INITIATIVE

PERSONAL CHRONOFILE

Earth as a place where energy is being collected

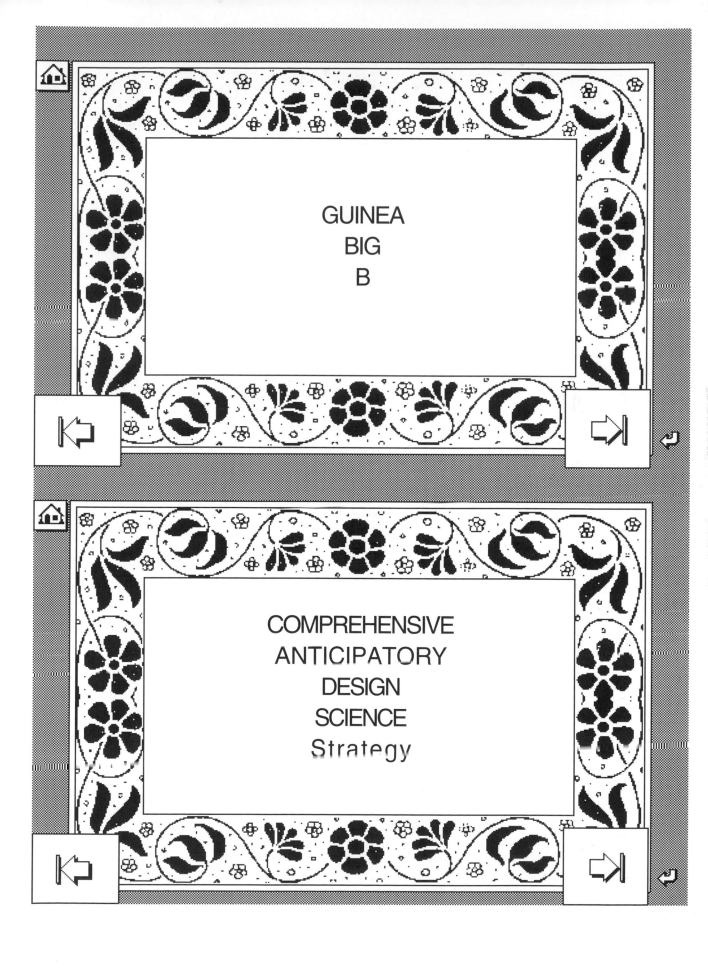

GUINEA
BIG
B

COMPREHENSIVE
ANTICIPATORY
DESIGN
SCIENCE
Strategy

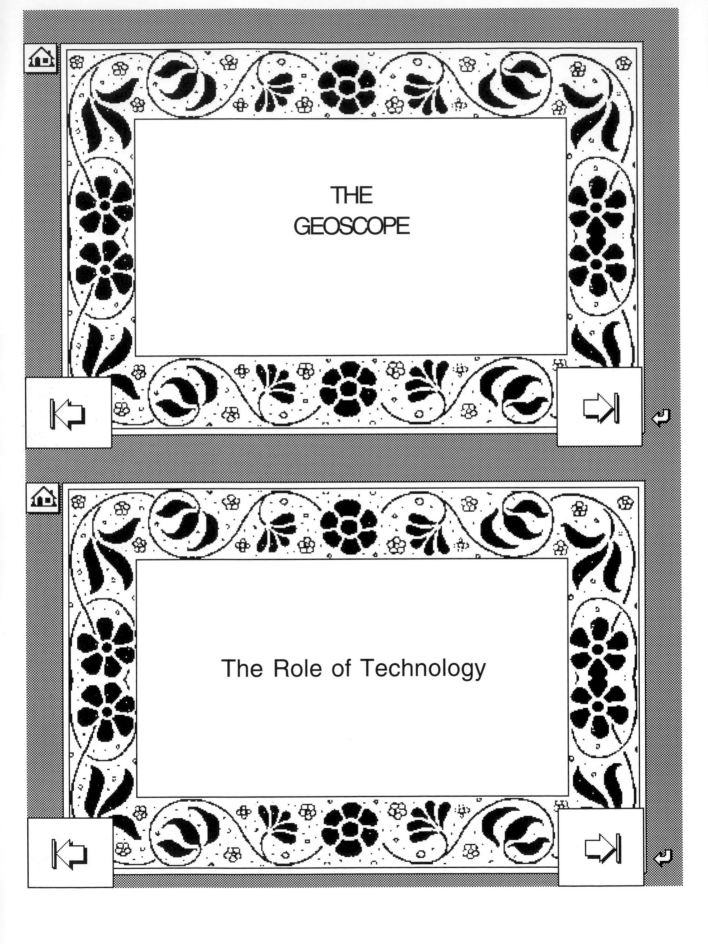

THE
GEOSCOPE

The Role of Technology

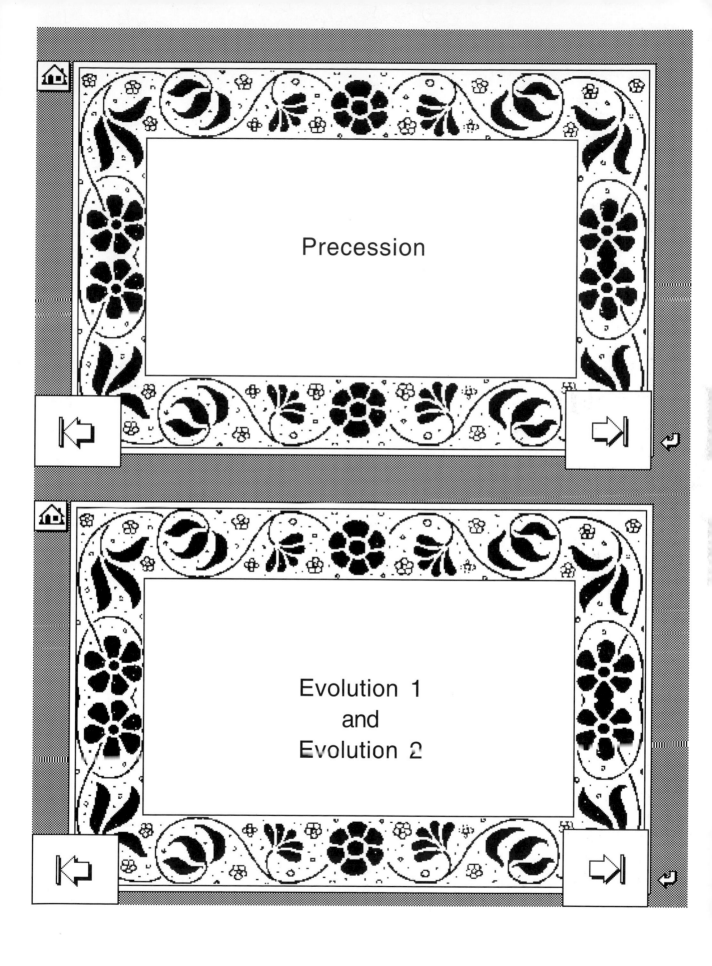

Precession

Evolution 1
and
Evolution 2

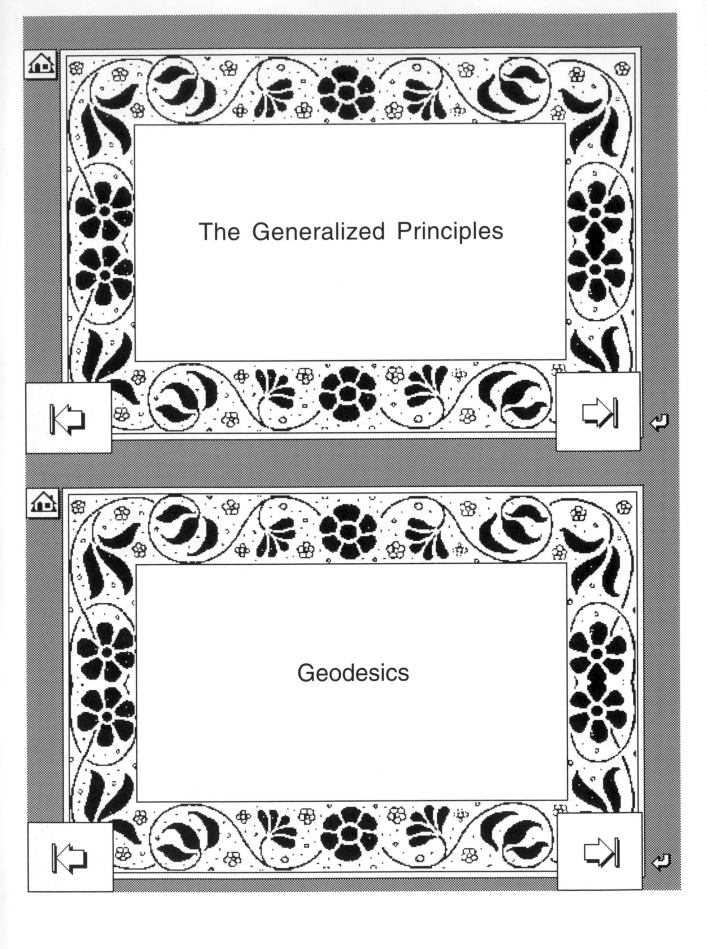

The Generalized Principles

Geodesics

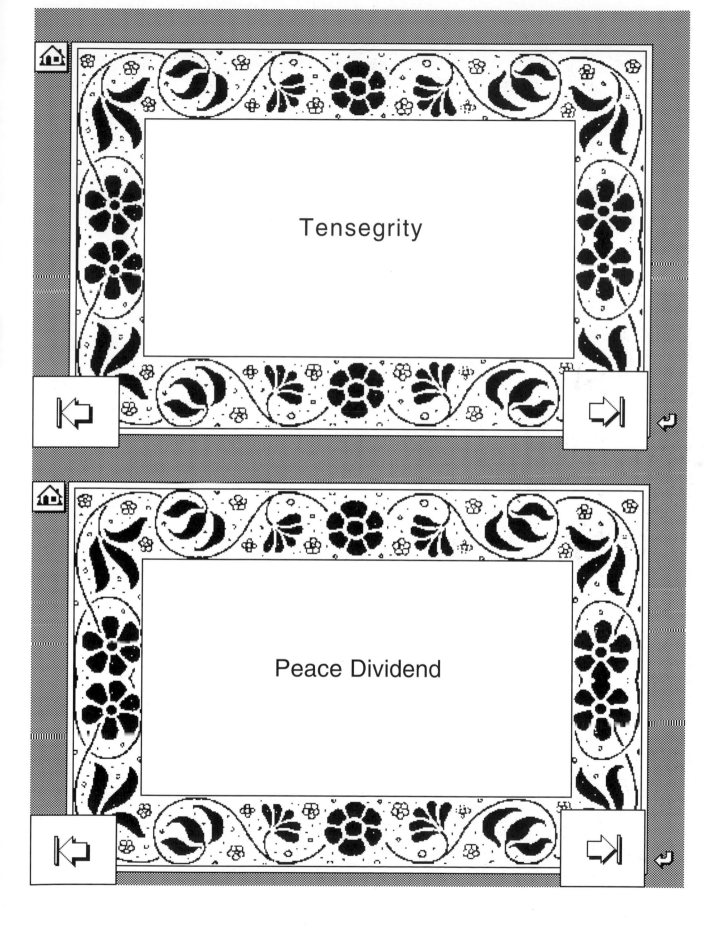

Tensegrity

Peace Dividend

The Definition of Wealth
[Energy directed by know-how]

The World Game

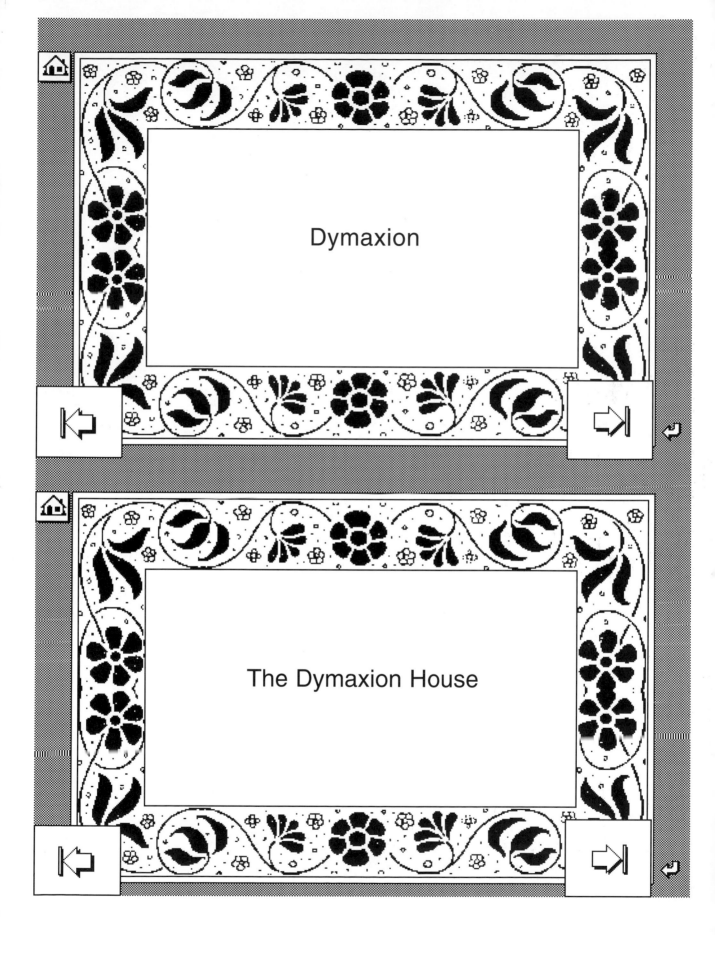

Dymaxion

The Dymaxion House

The Dymaxion Car

The Role of the Design Outlaw
Through Time

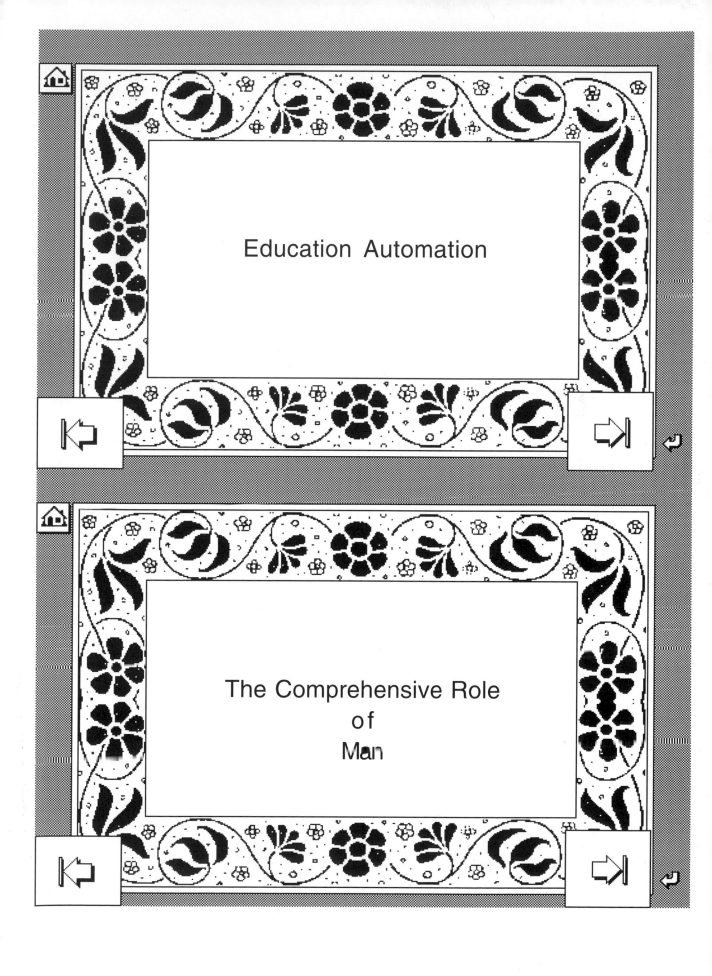

Education Automation

The Comprehensive Role
of
Man

Mind as Syntrophic in Nature

Index

Nelson, Ted, xvi, 299
neoconstructivism, 188
New Alchemy Institute, 115, 130, 172-75
New College, Oxford, 77
New Mexico, 68-69
New York (NY), 256, 258, 264, 268
nuclear energy, 83

O

obsolescence, cycle of, 46, 249, 250
"Odyssey of the Mind," 304-306
office buildings, 208, 258
oikos logos, 137
oikos poesis, 236
oil. See petroleum
"omega seed," 253
open spaces for invention, 6
open systems, systems theory and, 156
O'Reagan, Brendan, xiii, xv, 28, 152, 200

P

Papago Park (Arizona), 169
passive solar design, 262
petroleum, x, 83, 100-102, 107
Philadelphia (PA), 74, 211, 264
Phoenix (AZ), 251, 256
photovoltaics, 108
Politics of the Solar Age: Alternatives to Economics (book), 127
pollution, 260, 265
Portland (OR), 121
Post Petroleum City (book), 73
Power of Ten, The (film), 153
Power Shift (book), 232
problem solving, invention and, 7

Q

Quakers, 73-74

R

radical vs. conservative invention, 12
renewable energy supplies/technology, 98, 100-108
Rocky Mountain Institute, 110-115
Roots and Branches (book), xiv
Rotunda Dome, Ford Motor Co., 44
Ruskin, John, 15
Russell, Bertrand, 151
Russian Constructivists, 188

Wright, Frank Lloyd, xiv, 188, 193, 296, 301, 321, 335

Contributors:

Douglas Adams—is a writer based in London, and is the author of several books including: <u>The Hitchhikers Guide to the Galaxy, The Restaurant at the End of the Universe, Thanks for all the Fish.</u>

John Allen—is the Vice-President of Research and Development for Space Biospheres Ventures and a practicing playwright and Futurist.

Christopher Alexander—is the author of <u>A Pattern Language,</u> and a Professor of Architecture at the University of California at Berkeley.

Edmund Bacon—is the former city planner of Philadelphia and the author of <u>The Design Of Cities.</u>

Jay Baldwin — is the inventor of the pillow-dome, a compelling design teacher, and the recent author of <u>Bucky Works.</u>

Mary Catherine Bateson—is a Professor at Old Dominion University and the author of numerous books including: <u>Composing a Life</u>

Stewart Brand— is an author, editor, publisher and designer of cultural artifacts. He is best known for founding, editing, and publishing the Whole Earth Catalog (1968-1985; National Book Award, 1972) and the Co-Evolutionary Quarterly (now called the Whole Earth Review). He has also had a long-standing involvement in computers and the media arts He is the originator of the WELL (Whole Earth 'Lectric Link) and author of the books <u>The Media Lab: Inventing the Future at M.I.T.</u> and <u>How Buildings Learn.</u>

Peter Calthorpe—is a practicing Architect with an office based in Berkeley, California. He is the recent author of <u>The Next American Metropolis.</u>

Tom Casey—is a Green Entrepreneur based in the New York City bioregion.

Mike Corbett—is the former mayor of Davis, California and is the developer/architect of Village Homes.

Harold Cohen— worked with Buckminster Fuller at Southern Illinois University and is a Professor of Design at Suny Buffalo.

John Connell— is an architect, educator, author and artist. He taught at the Yale School of Architecture for five years. He has written and illustrated numerous articles including his comprehensive book on green residential design and construction: HOMING INSTINCT. He is best known for founding the Yestermorrow Design/Build School in 1980. Yestermorrow is a school that teaches homeowners how to design and build their own homes as well as teaching architecture students how to design and build sustainable architecture.

Duane Elgin—is an author and futurist based in Northern California. His recent books include: Voluntary Simplicity, Earth Awakening.

Pliny Fisk & Gail Vittori— Co-director and co-founder of the Center for Maximum Potential Building Systems. They are leaders in the worlds of sustainable design and building practices and prime consultants to the City of Austin, Texas "Green Builder Program". They have been involved in planning, architectural design and appropriate technology building projects including a commercial integrated mushroom farm in East Texas, industrialized building systems using low energy materials and total resource self-sufficiency, including sustainable, water, waste, building and landscaping systems; a passive solar school, passive solar homes and commercial buildings' technical design and engineering.

The 15th Year Distinguished Appropriate Technology Award, recognizing significant work in the field of environmental protection was awarded to Max's Pot in 1991 by the National Center for Appropriate Technology. In that same year his firm was chosen as one of five national design firms by the American Panning Association representing the future of the ecological planning work begun by Ian McHarg.

Hazel Henderson—is an independent futurist, author, lecturer, television producer/moderator, syndicated columnist, international consultant on alternative development, activist and founder of many public service groups. She has authored over two hundred articles and three books, including: Creating Alternative Futures, Politics of Solar Age, and Paradigms in Progress.

Thomas Hughes—holds the Mellon Professor of the History and Sociology of Science at the University of Pennsylvania, along with Torten Althin Chair at the Royal Institute of Technology, Stockholm. His books include: Networks of Power, Electricification in Western Society (1880-1930), Elmer Sperry: Inventor and Engineer, and American Genesis: A Century of Invention and Technological Enthusiasm

Tony Gwilliam—worked with Buckminster Fuller on the Design Science Decade Documents, is the President of Tensegrity International and a practicing inventor/architect.

Jaime Lerner— is an architect and urban planner. In 1988 he elected mayor of Curitiba, Brazil. He received the United Nations Environment Program 1990 Award and the International Institute for Energy Conservation award in 1990. He is an Honorary Fellow of the Royal Institute of Canada and the America Institute of Architects.

Amory Lovins— is a consultant physicist and 1993 MacArthur Fellow. He has been active in energy and environmental policy in more than 25 countries, and in 1984 was elected a fellow of the American Association for the Advancement of Science for his book, <u>Soft Energy Paths.</u> Together with his wife and colleague, Hunter Lovins, a lawyer, sociologist and political scientist who cofounded California's leading urban-forest group, the Loven's shared a 1982 Mitchell Prize and a 1993 Right Livelihood Award, often called the 'alternative Nobel Prize". In 1982 they cofounded the Rocky Mountain Institute.

Paul MacCready—is an inventor whose unique vehicles have pushed the envelope of the possible. He has received four honorary degrees, as well as the Engineer of Century Gold Award on 1980, the Lindbergh Award in 1982, and the Inventor of the year Award in 1981 from the Association for the Advancement of Invention and Innovation.

Ian Mcharg-founded the department of Landscape Architecture at the University of Pennsylvania in 1954 and has become identified as founder of ecological planning and design. He has written numerous articles and professional reports, but is best known for the classic <u>Design with Nature,</u> a finalist for the National Book Award in 1969. He was awarded the National Medal of Art from President Bush in 1992.

William McDonough—is an architect noted for his environmental sensitivity and celebrated for his creative designs. In preparation for the World's fair 2000 in Hannover, Germany, he was commissioned to author, <u>The Hannover Principles: Designs fro Sustainability.</u> He was recently named Dean of Architecture at the University of Virginia.

Ted Nelson—is a Software designer and inventor based in Northern California.

Brendon O'Reagan— worked with Buckminster Fuller, and was the research director for the Institute of Noetic Sciences

Jean-Paul Poliniere & Catherine Simon-are active information design scientists based in Paris, France.

John Todd—is the author of over one hundred technical and popular articles on biology and planetary stewardship, a series of books, including The Village as Solar Ecology, Tommorrow is our Permanent Address, Bioshelters, Ocean Arks, City Farming: Ecology as the Basis for Design. He has received a myriad of recognition for his ground breaking invention work, including The Threshold Award, the Chico Mendes Environmental Merit Award, and the Teddy Roosevelt Conservation Award.

James Wines is the co-founder and current President of S.I.T.E, a non-profit architectural organization founded in 1970 for the purpose of exploring a more social and contextual way of approaching the design of buildings. S.I.T.E. has become identified internationally with innovative ideas in architecture and public space; a number of the firm's early projects anticipated the current interest in Narrative, Deconstructivist and Green Architecture. In 1982 he won the National Endowment for the Arts:Distinguished Designer Award", and the American Society of Landscape Architects "Bradford Williams Medal" (1990)

Carol Franklin & Lesley Sauer-are the co-founders of the leading edge eco-design firm ANDROPOGON ASSOCIATES.They have pioneered the development of an ecological aesthetic where the primary patterns of design are drawn from those of the native landscape in order to sustain the natural processes of each site. Andropogon translates this vision into action by developing an ecological design process that builds consensus among the many disparate individuals and agencies that impact the landscape. Andropogon has been awarded the Environmental Enhancement Award (1992) and the Award in Master Planning and Landscape Design (1991) by the American Society of Landscape Architects.

Paolo Soleri—received his doctoral in architecture from the Turin Polytechnical Institute, apprenticed with Frank Lloyd Wright, and in 1979 founded Arcosanti in Paradise Valley, Arizona, a unique center for the arts, urban planning and design.

Virginia Thigpen—is a practicing Architect based in Davis, California

Acknowledgments

The filmmakers would like to express their gratitude to those people who have shared their inspiration, wisdom, knowledge in the creation of this book: J. Baldwin, who proved to be a hidden tour guide; John Todd, for the beauty of his inventions and the gift of his exploratory powers; Malcolm Wells, for his gentle architecture; Tom Casey, for embodying the soul of mentor ship; Ian McHarg, for his leadership, and Anthony Lawlor, for his work on sacred architecture.

We would also like to thank Brian Danitz, for his steadfast adherence to the Cinematic Vision; Patricia Streeten, for her gentle and compassionate spirit; and David Darling, for his trickster soul and his soul-stirring cello music.

To all those at Chelsea Green Publishers we would like to express our thanks for their faith in this project, especially Jim Schley and Stephen Morris; Rachel Cohen, for her fastidious copy editing; and to John Raatz, for his Visioneering skills.

Special thanks to Sean Gannon and Teo Camporeale for their unique contributions to the graphic design of the book; Byte a Tree productions for their 11th hour multimedia skills, Enrique Kopke, for his sound work, friendship, and interpretation skills while we were filming in the Brazilian Rain forest; Thomas S., for the Shakespearean drama that only he can produce; Anne Hayes for her lynx-eyed copy editing; Lynne Dal Pogetto for her wide-ranging illustration research; and Barbara Hagerty for her patient indexing, and to all those who read this manuscript and gave their suggestions.

This book would not have been completed without the occasional "library angels," those spirits who gave us comfort and direction, including Jean-Paul Pollinaire and Catherine Simon, for their friendship and encouragement, Brian Swimme and Theodore Rozak, for their understanding of the implications of socially conscious design, and to all those at Cafe Kairos in Philadelphia for their participation in the creation of an alternative space to re-imagine the world, and Mario's Bohemian Cigar store Cafe in San Francisco for the atmosphere in which to guide the manuscript into a book.

Finally, warm appreciation to Yolanda Alegre and Jo Beaton for their sage advice and gentle love, which gave us the courage of our convictions to see this project through to publication.

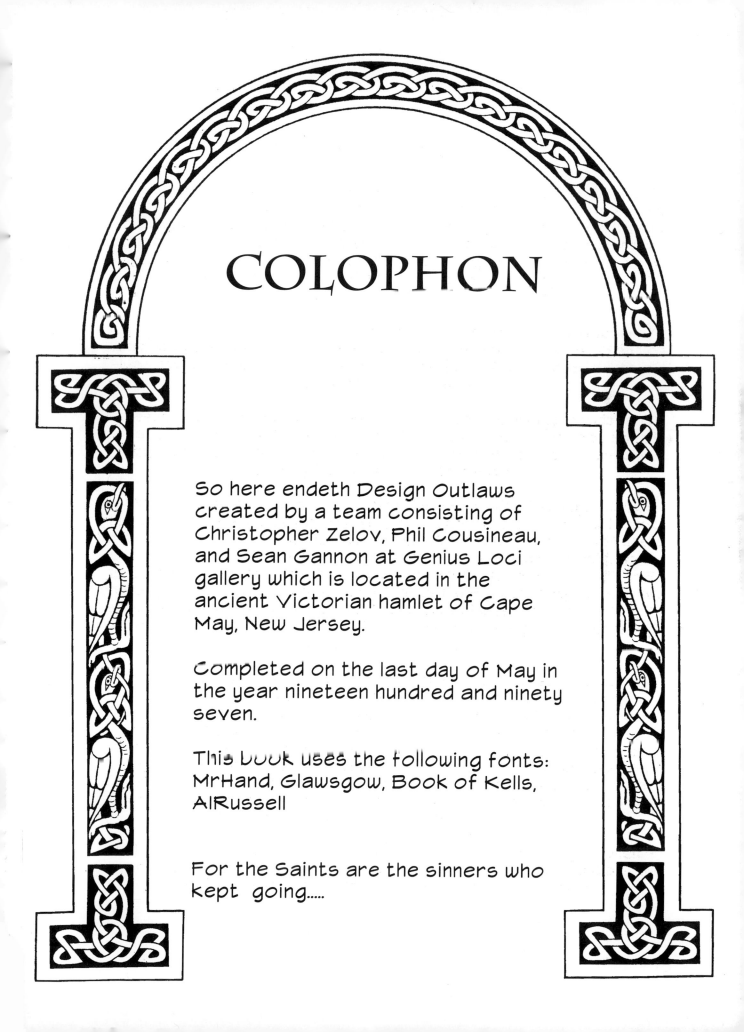

COLOPHON

So here endeth Design Outlaws created by a team consisting of Christopher Zelov, Phil Cousineau, and Sean Gannon at Genius Loci gallery which is located in the ancient Victorian hamlet of Cape May, New Jersey.

Completed on the last day of May in the year nineteen hundred and ninety seven.

This book uses the following fonts: MrHand, Glawsgow, Book of Kells, AlRussell

For the Saints are the sinners who kept going......

INVENTING THE FUTURE

NATURE

TECHNOLOGY

HUMANITY